THE Queens' ENGLISH

THE Queens' ENGLISH

CHLOE O. DAVIS

SIMON & SCHUSTER BOOKS FOR YOUNG READERS

New York London Toronto Sydney New Delhi

SIMON & SCHUSTER BOOKS FOR YOUNG READERS

An imprint of Simon & Schuster Children's Publishing Division

1230 Avenue of the Americas, New York, New York 10020

Text and crown illustration © 2021 by Chloe O. Davis

This young readers edition is adapted from *The Queens' English* by Chloe O.

Davis, published by Clarkson Potter in 2021

Book design by Laura Eckes © 2024 by Simon & Schuster, LLC

SIMON & SCHUSTER BOOKS FOR YOUNG READERS

and related marks are trademarks of Simon & Schuster, LLC.

Simon & Schuster: Celebrating 100 Years of Publishing in 2024

For information about special discounts for bulk purchases, please contact

Simon & Schuster Special Sales at 1-866-506-1949

or business@simonandschuster.com.

The Simon & Schuster Speakers Bureau can bring authors to your live event.

For more information or to book an event, contact the Simon & Schuster

Speakers Bureau at 1-866-248-3049 or visit our website at

www.simonspeakers.com.

The text for this book was set in TT Norms Pro.

Manufactured in China

0124 SCP

First Edition

10 9 8 7 6 5 4 3 2 1

CIP data for this book is available from the Library of Congress.

ISBN 9781665926867

ISBN 9781665926881 (ebook)

This dictionary is dedicated to all the LGBTQIA+ youth who take the courageous path each day to completely be yourselves.

You encourage us all to love our inner beauty and ideas, even when faced with the challenges of not being embraced by others. I write to affirm and remind you that you are exceptional and more than enough. I absolutely see your greatness! Together, we will build a safe, respectful, empowering, and loving environment for you to thrive. Always know there is a hug, high five, fist bump, or kind word ready for you whenever you need it.

CHLOE

INTRODUCTION

I AM LGBTQIA+! I am a part of a diverse community that represents the spectrum of human identities—amazing lesbians, courageous gays, pure-hearted bisexuals, extraordinary transgender people, revolutionary queers, dynamic questioning people, sensational intersex people, incredible agender people, beautiful asexuals, vibrant genderqueer people, fabulous nonbinary people, inclusive pansexuals, zestful polygender people, devoted same-gender-loving people, compassionate two-spirit people, excellent no label people, and the list can go on and on!

WE ARE LGBTQIA+! WE ARE RESILIENT! WE ARE HERE!

Our identities are unique and the core part of our makeup. How we label ourselves, or choose not to label ourselves, gives us confidence in that uniqueness.

Language has power! We use it to help us articulate who we are and our sense of belonging to the world. The language used within the LGBTQIA+ community is vast and dynamic. We use words, phrases, expressions, idioms, and pronouns to communicate not just our identity, but our beliefs, values, traditions, cultures, and histories.

Queer language was primarily used as a means of safety when many anti-LGBTQIA+ laws were set in place hindering queer people from being themselves in public. LGBTQIA+ people used coded words and expressions only known by those in the community to speak to one another. This provided protection, as well as a sense of pride in knowing a community existed where LGBTQIA+ experiences and people were visible. Now queer language is evolving and changing to honor cultural inclusion, diversity, and intersectionality. Words and phrases can even propel social justice movements and advocate for equality. The ability to claim language that expresses the pride in who you are is empowering!

I remember first learning the word "demisexual" and saying to myself, "Wow, that's me! There is a word that pinpoints my attraction to others. So I'm not alone?!" There are many other people who identity as demisexual and need a strong emotional connection to seal the romantic bond, just like me! And maybe just like you? Demisexuality is part of the asexuality spectrum, also known as ace. I also felt a wave of excitement when I researched the word "bi-curious." As a bisexual woman, this word helped me understand the evolution of my attraction. My "bi-curiosity" was the period when I first felt curious about exploring same-sex relationships. Learning new words like "demi," "bi," and even "flexible" gave me labels that identified the fluidity of my attraction to others.

Our identity is not just our attraction, but everything that encompasses who we are and what we are made of—sexual anatomy, gender, gender expression, sexual orientation, romantic orientation, platonic attraction, race, native language, culture, religion, spirituality, traditions, communities, and histories. Whew! Identity is surely a mouthful! Yes, our understanding of self is both beautiful and complex.

Words can help us articulate who we are to other people, and more importantly, words provide us with the ability to personally label ourselves in a way that feels right. Only you have the power to label yourself, no one else. And you always have permission to explore, question, and change those labels! The way we identify is constantly evolving. We can feel one way about ourselves and a day, a month, or a year later feel completely different. That is okay! Throughout the course of my life, I've identified as heteroflexible, bi-curious, and at a time, struggled with being a semi-closeted bisexual because I feared my family and friends would reject me. Now I'm a proud and openly biromantic, demisexual bisexual who continues to explore my gender expression as femme and/or androgynous. These words helped articulate my developing expression as I grew to understand myself, and writing *The Queens' English* gave me the courage to express my truth and become an advocate for understanding the spectrum of identity and sexuality.

WHAT IS *THE QUEENS' ENGLISH*?

The Queens' English is a dictionary that celebrates the etymological diversity of over eight hundred terms used to describe our collective gay and queer experience. It is an epic journey of understanding identity, sexuality, gender, equality, humor, community, and pride.

"Etymological" means the origin or history of a word. Terms can evolve and their meanings can expand or change over time. Throughout the decades, words often change based on how a community decides to define them, as words have the ability to clarify our ideas, principles, values, and needs. As you read through the dictionary, some terms will have more information about the etymology of a word in the Usage Notes sections or the Did You Know sections. Check it out to learn more!

A vibrant and rich history has been captured by the unique language created by and for the lesbian, gay, bisexual, transgender, two-spirit, queer, questioning, intersex, asexual, agender, nonbinary, fluid, gender nonconforming, and nonheteronormative—commonly abbreviated as LGBTQIA+—community. This dictionary is a resource for terminology and expressions with modern definitions, real-life usage examples, synonyms, important usage notes, and supporting background information to further enhance the understanding of each term. Reference summaries, how-to guides, and history lessons about trailblazing people, places, and events that have impacted language within the LGBTQIA+ community are included throughout.

ON THE WORD "QUEER"

"Queer" was once a derogatory slur for homosexuality. By the 1980s, HIV/AIDS activists were determined to reclaim the term as a badge of honor for the LGBTQIA+ community. Since the eighties, the younger LGBTQIA+

generation have adopted "queer" as an umbrella term for anyone who identifies as lesbian, gay, bisexual, trans, two-spirit, queer, questioning, intersex, asexual, nonbinary, genderfluid, or otherwise nonheteronormative.

There are many identities within the LGBTQIA+ community, and each person's label preference and interpretation of that identity should be respected. Only use the term(s) with which a person identifies. If you don't know, just ask!

PLEASE NOTE:

The term "queer" is used throughout this dictionary as a catchall for people who identify as anything other than heterosexual and/or cisgender. But! Please be aware that not all members of the LGBTQIA+ community feel comfortable using the word "queer" in this way. While it has largely been reclaimed as an inclusive term for those of us who have been marginalized due to sexuality, gender identity, and/or gender expression, the term still holds negative connotations for some.

Much of my research came from the cultural heartbeat of our queer community, consisting of personal interviews and group discussions with people who identify as LGBTQIA+. I filled in the gaps using digital and print references and content from queer and mainstream media outlets, taking sensitive measures to define every term appropriately and inclusively, while respecting (and encouraging!) the flexibility of other interpretations. I also was committed to highlighting the diversity of language that lives within our community—from ace, boi, butch, ChapStick lesbian, cub, drag queen, enby, femme queen, feminine-presenting, lipstick lesbian, masc-of-center, otter, queen, and zaddy, to ally, bicon, BIPOC, BlaQueer, cis-het, chosen family, dykon, fairy, gay father, house mother, icon, LATINX, theyby, Q/TAAPI, zucchini, and everything else in between. LGBTQIA+ language is explosive!

However, my research only captures a sliver of the sub-communities that make up LGBTQIA+ culture. *The Queens' English* is merely a starting point for the important conversations around inclusivity, sexuality, gender expression and identity, gay slang that's been co-opted by mainstream culture, and queer American terminology that's been around for decades.

WHY DO WE NEED LABELS?

Many years ago, a close friend asked how I wanted to be perceived. He knew I had been attracted to more than one gender and he was secretly testing me. "Chloe, what are you going to say when people ask your sexuality?" I told him I was open to identifying however I saw fit and asked him, "Why do I need a label?" He replied, "You don't need a label, I just recommend you live in your truth." His words prompted me to challenge myself and reflect on my journey.

I did not meet anyone who openly identified as bisexual until I was well into my twenties! Whoa, right? For a long time, I did not have the support or guidance to unpack my identity. I felt confused and even ashamed at times to speak my truth; completely uncomfortable telling my family and my friends because I feared they would speak negatively about me. Unconsciously, I believed they would not understand me because I was "different."

The Queens' English is a resource that reflects the diverse ways people experience identity because I believe representation is important. I am passionate about celebrating all queer identities and uplifting the myriad of LGBTQIA+ stories and experiences throughout our generations. It is my goal to change the narrative of LGBTQIA+ people feeling invisible, unrepresented, and uninformed, especially our queer youth. I advocate for creating more affirming resources, books, and educational materials, and engaging in open-minded conversations around the spectrum of identity. You deserve to feel empowered to be your most authentic selves; to stand proud and bold in your identity and ignite the curiosity to explore deeper within yourselves to unfold even more of your uniqueness. Every part of your identity—labels or no labels—is distinctive, valid, and extraordinary.

Research for *The Queens' English* has provided me with a new understanding of human identity, and as a result, I feel empowered by who I am. I believe that outward expression and feelings of attraction are two inherent components of every human—gay, straight, cis, trans, and beyond. These two ideas of **expression** and **attraction** show the dynamic and layered depth of each person's existence.

While our unique expression and attraction—our labels— are used by society to categorize or even divide people, how we express our identity to the world and the spectrum of attraction we feel for others actually unites us. Our differences should be celebrated. Our similarities *and* our differences unite us, and as a result, labels unite us, too. *The Queens' English* celebrates the diversity, intersectionality, and beautiful complexity of human identity. This expansive world of almost eight billion humans represents a multitude of identities and they all should be celebrated and respected.

You are unique, you are loved! You are enough!

BUT IS IT APPROPRIATION?

Queer lingo carries with it a vast history. It is important to understand that much of the language you see in this book has been adopted from specific subcommunities of LGBTQIA+ culture. Some terms originated in Harlem's Black gay scene in the 1920s or white working-class lesbian bars in the 1940s, while others came from New York City's drag scene or gay male social settings and have since been appropriated by the LGBTQIA+ community at large, or, in some cases, by mainstream culture, too.

Many of the terms in this book come from a community of Black and Latinx gay and trans people who faced systematic attacks for being queer and people of color. This language was created to supplement a marginalized community's self-worth and ideas.

Mainstream culture views queer language as cool, hip, fresh. Today, words like "shade," "fierce," "slay," and "yaaaas!" are all used freely by the masses without acknowledging the generations of Black and Latinx queers who created this language as a form of survival. Buzzwords are printed on clothing, used candidly in media, and have been adopted by non-queer celebrities and predominantly white social groups. Regardless of how cool or popular something is, appropriation—taking ownership of something without permission or proper acknowledgment—is concerning and problematic within the LGBTQIA+ community.

When our language is ruled over by mainstream culture, its value is minimized—especially if terms are not used correctly and respectfully. I created *The Queens' English* to give proper documentation to queer vernacular and to appropriately credit the LGBTQIA+ subcommunities for their contribution, while acknowledging the creation and re-creation of jargon is an ongoing process.

You hold something very valuable in your hands. Even if you are not part of the LGBTQIA+ community, this is an opportunity to gain insight into our culture. With access to our language comes a responsibility to be sensitive and respectful to the community it belongs to, a community that persisted in the face of hate. Before RuPaul graced us with "Shantay, you stay" and Madonna's hit dance song "Vogue" beamed light on New York's underground ballroom scene, living as a lesbian, gay, bi, trans, or queer person in America meant living in fear and secrecy. This book is not permission to use this language flippantly; it is meant to be an educational tool, a conversation starter, and a celebration of the history of gay coded language, queer spaces, and the LGBTQIA+ experience.

ON USAGE NOTES

▶ Language is always evolving. There may be definitions that are not present in the dictionary that are still valid.

▶ Not all of this language is used by everyone in the LGBTQIA+ community.

▶ Many of the terms are not appropriate for members *not* in the LGBTQIA+ community to use, either.

While *The Queens' English* encourages all readers to engage with this vibrant language, usage notes have been attached to terms that need extra context. Several terms, while they are considered derogatory stereotypes or slurs, have been a part of gay language for decades. The intent of the dictionary is to document queer language in its entirety, not to censor it, which is why it's important for readers to take heed of the usage notes.

The saying "Speak, so you can speak again" (often credited to she-ro Zora Neale Hurston), holds great relevance today. In speaking now, *The Queens' English* will use the nuances of queer language to shed light on the lives of the people who define LGBTQIA+ culture. It shows the brilliance, strength, and power in queer people telling our unique stories and is a testament to the value of marginalized people's voices.

So come indulge in *The Queens' English*. This dictionary welcomes all readers. All of us have a gender identity, a way of expressing our gender, a sexual orientation, a romantic orientation, and a need to understand those who are different from us. Be PROUD of the lingo within our LGBTQIABCDEFGHIJKLMNOPQRSTUVWXYZ+ community because, yes, ladies and gentlemen and gender nonconforming queens alike, this lingo does slay!

TERM

HOW TO GET DOWN WITH

Lowercase words and phrases in quotes provide alternate ways you might hear a term used in everyday encounters.

Capitalized words and phrases are cross-references that can be found elsewhere in the dictionary by looking them up alphabetically.

Related terms provide alternate parts of speech to familiarize yourself with.

▼ *1st part of speech*

First definition. Often used in the phrase "abc xyz."

Second definition.

> SEE ALSO
> **TERM A, TERM B**

▼ *2nd part of speech*

Definition. The terms XYZ and ABC can also be used.

> RELATED
> **TERM C,** *part of speech*

❝ *Highlighting real-life examples of how to use the term in a sentence.*"

 WANT MORE INFO?
THINK: **HERE'S A QUICK SYNONYM FOR THE TERM.**

USAGE NOTE: For understanding the origin and appropriate usage of the term.

DID YOU KNOW Historical references and/or information that contribute to the understanding of the term or phrase.

Aa

AAPI

▼ *noun*

An acronym for "Asian American and Pacific Islander(s)." API (Asian/Pacific Islander), APIA (Asian and Pacific Islander American), and Asian American and Native Hawaiians/Pacific Islander (AANHPI) can also be used.

SEE ALSO
Q/T APA or Q/T AAPI

❝ *Today, the queer AAPI student body is speaking out on equality! We want our school to be more inclusive, supportive, and safer for ALL students, including students of color. Let's diversify our curriculum with all the many histories that make America so unique."*

 WANT MORE INFO?
THINK: **A PERSON OF ASIAN DESCENT.**

DID YOU KNOW Queer Asian organizations like the National Queer Asian Pacific Islander Alliance, Visibility Project, Asian Pride Project, Q-Wave, and the Desi LGBTQ+ Helpline for South Asians are working on cultivating support, visibility, coming-out resources, and safer spaces for the Asian LGBTQIA+ community. There are many AAPI queer youth who feel unsafe at school because of their Asian and queer identity.

They often experience racism and discrimination from their peers that hinders their educational experience. Empowering AAPI pride is important and activists like Cecilia Chung and Chella Man, drag performer Gia Gunn, supermodel Geena Rocero, actors Maulik Pancholy and BD Wong, comedians Awkwafina and Margaret Cho, and the first openly gay congressperson of color, Mark Takano, have all broken down barriers for Asian equality and have had a substantial impact upon the queer communities.

ABLEISM

▼ *noun*

Discrimination in favor of able-bodied people.

❝ *Stop ableism, include and empower all."* –**PARTNERS FOR YOUTH WITH DISABILITIES**

WANT MORE INFO?
THINK: **LACK OF CONSIDERATION FOR DISABLED PEOPLE.**

DID YOU KNOW Some students have physical or functional differences and may require extra assistance from the teacher to get through their daily activities, assignments, and other classroom work. These types of differences are often called disabilities. Having a disability is challenging, but it should never be looked at negatively or less than equal. Each person is unique and should be treated with respect and care. Many schools and organizations are actively implementing strategists to accommodate and provide greater access to youth with disabilities. Stop Ableism, Partners for Youth with Disabilities, Ramapo for Children, and Disability Justice and Youth are just a few organizations dedicated to promoting equal access for youth with disabilities and creating a world where all students have pride in their uniqueness.

ABOUT THIS LIFE

▼ *idiom*

To be completely interested and involved.

❝ *Yaassss, honey! Six Flags, here we come! I am about this life!"*

WANT MORE INFO?
THINK: **TO BE TOTALLY, WHOLLY ENTHRALLED.**

USAGE NOTE:
This term originated in Black American culture and is commonly used in the Black gay and queer community. It has been appropriated by mainstream culture.

ABSOLUTE CODE

▼ *idiom*

A pledge to not disclose someone's LGBTQIA+ identity without permission. The term GOLDEN RULE can also be used.

SEE ALSO
"Coming Out 101," *p. 38*

❝*Absolute code, dude! It's my choice when I want to come out, not yours!*❞

 WANT MORE INFO?
THINK: **AN UNSPOKEN AGREEMENT TO KEEP SOMEONE'S SEXUAL ORIENTATION OR GENDER IDENTITY PRIVATE.**

AC/DC

▼ *adjective*

Referring to a person who has an attraction toward males and females. This term often refers to the gender binary, girl or woman and boy or man.

❝*I mean, I kind of feel AC/DC. I can kiss a boy or a girl. I actually like both!*❞

 WANT MORE INFO?
THINK: **BISEXUAL.**

USAGE NOTE: The term was commonly used in Polari, a coded slang used by British gay men during the rise of anti-LGBT laws. It may carry a negative meaning because it limits bisexuality to the gender binary. It is inappropriate to use this label if a person has not self-identified as such.

DID YOU KNOW AC/DC is a commonly used electrical term that stands for Alternating Current/Direct Current, which are two different methods of delivering electricity. The queer community began to use this acronym to show how a bisexual person could receive power (or romantic energy) from people of different gender identities.

ACE

▼ *adjective*

An abbreviation of the word "asexual."

❝ *Today, Mrs. Ellis put up a black, gray, white, and purple pride flag for Ace Awareness Week. She said this is a special week she is using to teach us that love is on a spectrum.*❞

 WANT MORE INFO? THINK: THE MIGHTY (AND GROWING!) ASEXUAL POPULATION OF SEVENTY MILLION PEOPLE WORLDWIDE.

CHLOE O. DAVIS

DID YOU KNOW There are many different ways to show romantic love and attraction between people. Those who identify as ace may not want to kiss or physically show their love, but attraction can still be present (possibly through words). Queer Kid Stuff is an educational and entertaining LGBTQIA+ social justice media platform, created by Lindz Amer, to help both youth and their families understand queer identity. Lindz, and their amazing sidekick host, Teddy, teach about the *ABC*s of LGBTQ+, queer social justice, and empower young people to explore their identities.

ACEFLUX

▼ adjective

An identifier for people who experience a range of intensity within the asexual spectrum, from feeling a strong physical attraction to others to not feeling any physical attraction to others.

SEE ALSO
ACE

❝ *I know I'm attracted to any gender and I like identifying as panromantic.*

But sometimes I don't know how intensely I'm physically attracted to people. Sometimes I feel asexual and other times I don't. I want to explore identifying as aceflux and see if that fits me."

WANT MORE INFO? *THINK:* **A PERSON'S PHYSICAL ATTRACTION TO OTHERS MAY CHANGE OR FLUCTUATE OVER TIME.**

USAGE NOTE: This term is commonly used in the asexual community.

ACEPHOBIA

▼ noun

Aversion, fear, or hatred toward asexuality.

RELATED
ACEPHOBIC adjective
ACEPHOBE noun

SEE ALSO
BIPHOBIA, FEMMEPHOBIA, HOMOPHOBIA, LESBOPHOBIA, QUEERPHOBIA, TRANSPHOBIA

❝ *I read an article about all the harmful things people are saying about asexuality. My oldest sibling is asexual and there's nothing wrong with them not wanting to be physically romantic. Acephobia is so uncool!"*

WANT MORE INFO? *THINK:* **DISLIKE OF OR PREJUDICE AGAINST ASEXUAL PEOPLE.**

ACE QUEEN

▼ *noun*

A gay, bisexual, or queer male who grooms and styles himself in a traditionally feminine way.

SEE ALSO
QUEEN

❝*Honey, an ace queen will spray his mother's Chanel No. 5, paint his nails hot pink, and apply his Fenty makeup before watching every* Drag Race *episode.*"

 WANT MORE INFO? *THINK:* **A SUPER-FEMININE QUEER GUY.**

 USAGE NOTE: This term can be associated with males, boys, men, and masc people.

Ace Queen

Adorbs ▲

ADORBS

▼ *adjective*

An abbreviation of "adorable."

❝*O-M-G! Your rainbow 'This is Pride' T-shirt is adorbs!*"

 WANT MORE INFO? *THINK:* **DELIGHTFULLY SWEET.**

ADOPTION

▼ *noun*

The legal act—including the social, emotional, and financial process—of an adult caring and providing for a child as one's own when that adult is not the child's birth parent. Same-sex or queer parent adoption is when a LGBTQIA+ person or couple makes a choice to raise a child they did not birth as their own and provide that child with a nurturing and enriching life.

SEE ALSO

"Queer Parents and the Family Dynamic," *p. 330*

**" ** *Many same-sex couples use adoption agencies to grow their families. This allows loving and caring people to become parents to incredible kids who need homes. Families don't have to match; they just have to* be filled with joy, laughter, and love!"

 WANT MORE INFO?
THINK: **ADULTS AND CARETAKERS WHO ARE LEGALLY PARENTING A CHILD WHO IS NOT BIOLOGICALLY THEIRS.**

▲　　　　　　Adoption

AESTHETIC ATTRACTION

▼ *noun*

An admiration based solely on the way someone looks.

**" ** *I don't want to be her*

girlfriend, I just have an aesthetic attraction because she is beautiful."

WANT MORE INFO?
THINK: A NONROMANTIC AND NONPHYSICAL ATTRACTION.

USAGE NOTE: This term is commonly used in the asexual community.

AFAB

▼ *adjective*

An acronym for "assigned female at birth." This term is used by a range of people—including transgender, nonbinary, genderqueer, gender nonconforming, and/or intersex individuals—as a way to communicate to others the gender assigned to them at birth (based solely on their sexual anatomy). This term is usually used to describe different trans and gender nonconforming (TGNC) experiences, but

not solely considered a person's identity. The term "designated female at birth" or acronym "DFAB" can also be used.

SEE ALSO
AMAB

 Katie was AFAB but identifies as bigender."

WANT MORE INFO?
THINK: THE BOX LABELED "GIRL" WAS CHECKED IN THE DELIVERY ROOM.

USAGE NOTE: This term is commonly used in the intersex, transgender, nonbinary, and gender nonconforming communities. The use of this term relies on an individual's preference. Do not assume that an individual wants to be identified by this term. Please ask for and use a person's chosen name and pronouns.

AFFECTIONAL ORIENTATION

▼ *noun*

SEE **ROMANTIC ORIENTATION**

AG

▼ *adjective*

An abbreviation of "aggressive." When used in the Black lesbian community, it usually refers to a masculine girl or woman who has a dominant personality. The term "femme AG" can also be used to distinguish an AG girl or woman who identifies as femme.

SEE ALSO
STUD, SOFT STUD, "The **Lesbian Spectrum,"** *p. 255*

❝ *I like to be the one in charge in my relationship. I'm AG with it."*

 WANT MORE INFO? THINK: WANTS TO RUN IT ALL.

 USAGE NOTE: This term originated in the Black lesbian community. It has been appropriated by the larger lesbian community.

DID YOU KNOW Many Black lesbian communities in northeast American cities like Baltimore, Philadelphia, and New York use the term "AG" to identify a woman who has a dominant personality and/or is the dominant partner in a relationship. Black lesbians and bisexual women are often overlooked in the larger queer community, but organizations like Affinity, African Ancestral Lesbians United for Societal Change (AALUSC), bklyn boihood, and Zuna Institute–National Advocacy Organization for Black Lesbians center the diverse identities and relationship dynamics seen in the Black lesbian community.

AGENDER

▼ *adjective*

Not identified with any gender. The terms NONGENDER and GENDERLESS can also be used.

SEE ALSO
NEUTROIS, GENDERQUEER, NONBINARY

"All gender bathrooms are for everyone. Transgender, agender, bigender people, and those who identify within the gender binary. We can all pee together! Just don't forget to wash your hands afterward!"

 WANT MORE INFO? *THINK:* **NOT BOUND TO A SPECIFIC GENDER.**

AIDS

▼ *noun*

SEE **A-WORD, HIV/AIDS, "HISTORY LESSON: HIV/ AIDS,"** *p.213*

ALIAGENDER

▼ **adjective**

SEE **APORAGENDER**

A-LIST GAY

▼ *noun*

A queer person who is considered socially elite and has power, wealth, and privilege. The term "A-Gay" can also be used.

" *Who runs the world? Clearly the A-Gays like Zaya Wade, Hunter Schafer, Noah Schnapp, Demi Lovato, and Lil Nas X."*

 WANT MORE INFO? *THINK:* **AN INFLUENTIAL LGBTQIA+ PERSON.**

▼   **A-List Gay**

ALLOROMANTIC

▼ *adjective*

Experiencing romantic attraction. This attraction can exist with or without physical affection. Often shortened to "romantic."

▼ *noun*

An alloromantic person.

SEE ALSO
AROMANTIC

 "An alloromantic and an aromantic are like yin and yang—one has those mushy, romantic feelings; one doesn't."

 WANT MORE INFO? THINK: LOVE IS THE FAVORITE EMOTION.

USAGE NOTE: This term is commonly used in the asexual community.

ALLOSEXUAL

▼ *adjective*

Experiencing physical attraction. This attraction can exist with or without romantic affection. The term ZEDSEXUAL can also be used.

▼ *noun*

An allosexual person.

SEE ALSO
ASEXUAL

"

WINTER: *I like Melissa A LOT. I want to spend every waking moment with her!*

SETH: *I don't understand you alloromantics. Love letters, long walks after school, listening to each other's Spotify playlists? No, thank you! Let's just kiss and say goodbye. I am only allosexual.*

 WANT MORE INFO? THINK: WANT A KISS? YES!

USAGE NOTE: This term is commonly used in the aromantic and asexual communities. Please be aware that this term may be considered mature.

ALLY

▼ *noun*

An active supporter of the rights and causes of the LGBTQIA+ community. The term "super ally" can also be used.

RELATED
ALLYSHIP *noun*

❝ *I love when it's Pride Month! My parents and I always rank which companies get the super ally award! Drumroll please . . . the winners are Target, Google, and UGG!"*

 WANT MORE INFO?
THINK: A MEMBER OF THE QUEER FAN CLUB.

DID YOU KNOW This term often identifies someone who is cisgender and heterosexual; allies are not part of the inclusive identifying label of LGBTQIA+, but are often still acknowledged for their support. An ally can also refer to members of the LGBTQIA+ community who are in support

of a different member's values, ideas, and needs. For instance, the gay community can be allies to the TGNC community or the white queer community can be allies to the QTPOC or Q/T AAPI communities, supporting the fight for inclusion and equality.

▲ **Ally**

AMAB

▼ adjective

An acronym for "assigned male at birth." This term is used by a range of people—including transgender, nonbinary, genderqueer, gender nonconforming, and/or intersex individuals—as a way to communicate to others the gender assigned to them at birth (based solely on their sexual anatomy). This term is usually used to describe different trans and gender nonconforming (TGNC) experiences, but not solely considered a person's identity. The term "designated male at birth" or acronym "DMAB" can also be used.

SEE ALSO
AFAB

❝ *I'm proud to say that I'm the first AMAB genderqueer student to run for Jefferson Middle School Student Council. I pledge to listen to my fellow classmates and work hard to make the changes we want. Thank you for believing in me and seeing me as I am."*

 WANT MORE INFO? *THINK:* **THE BOX LABELED "BOY" WAS CHECKED IN THE DELIVERY ROOM.**

USAGE NOTE: This term is commonly used in the intersex, transgender, nonbinary, and gender nonconforming communities. The use of this term relies on an individual's preference. Do not assume that an individual wants to be identified by this term. Please ask for and use a person's chosen name and pronouns.

Androgyny ▼

ANDROGYNY

▼ *noun*

A display of both masculine and feminine qualities. The state of being androgynous. Can be abbreviated as "androj" or "andro."

A label used to define an androgynous gender identity.

RELATED
ANDROGYNOUS *adjective*
ANDROGYNE *noun*

❝ *Androgyny is not about trying to manage the relationship between the masculine and feminine opposites; it is about the freedom of flowing between them.*"

 WANT MORE INFO?
THINK: **AN AMBIGUOUS GENDER PRESENTATION.**

DID YOU KNOW Greek philosopher Plato writes about the idea of androgyny in his text *Symposium.* In this Platonic myth, Aristophanes delivers a speech explaining that "male-female" people came from the moon.

ANDROSEXUAL

▼ *adjective*

Experiencing attraction toward masculinity.

RELATED
ANDROSEXUALITY *noun*

SEE ALSO
GYNESEXUAL

▼ *noun*

An androsexual person. A label used to describe a sexual orientation where a person is attracted to masculinity.

❝ *If you identify as androsexual, you can have a crush on boys, bois, masc-of-center folx, or masc TGNC individuals, it's totally open.*"

 WANT MORE INFO?
THINK: **ATTRACTED TO MASC PEOPLE.**

THE QUEENS' ENGLISH

ANGEL FOOD

▼ *noun*

A gay pilot who serves in the United States Air Force.

❝ *From Leonard Matlovich to Kristin Goodwin, angel food activists and their heroism should be written about in our history books.*❞

 WANT MORE INFO? *THINK:* **AIRMAN, AIRWOMAN, OR AIRPERSON WITH THE RAINBOW BADGE OF HONOR.**

USAGE NOTE:	This term originated in the gay male community.

ANTI-LGBTQ

▼ *adjective*

Opposition and bias toward LGBTQIA+ identities, rights, and needs.

SEE ALSO
GAYBASHING, "Gaybashing Must Stop!" *p. 172*

❝ *Over 250 anti-LGBTQ bills were introduced across the United States over the last few years! Why is there still so much injustice!*❞

 WANT MORE INFO? *THINK:* **BANNING QUEER PEOPLE FROM PARTICIPATING IN SPORTS BECAUSE OF THEIR IDENTITY.**

DID YOU KNOW Anti-LGBTQ+ laws are ever-present, but in 2021, there were over thirty states that had passed policies and bills restricting certain access to LGBTQIA+ people. Some of these policies excluded queer people from receiving gender-affirming therapy and banned students from learning about LGBTQIA+ identity, culture, and history in schools. Other policies blocked transgender, nonbinary, and gender diverse youth from participating in sports or using restrooms that support their identities. Alabama, Oklahoma, Tennessee, and Arkansas were among the first states to prohibit transgender people at public and charter schools—prekindergarten to twelfth grade—from using restrooms and locker rooms that matched their gender identities. There is a deep concern that these anti-LGBTQ bills are negatively impacting our society and making it unsafe for LGBTQIA+ youth. Organizations like National Center for Transgender Equality, All Out, GLSEN, and Lambda Legal are working to fight these discriminations and demand queer youth receive equal rights.

ANTI-TRANS

▼ *adjective*

Opposition and bias toward non-cisgender identities, rights, and needs.

SEE ALSO

TRANSPHOBIA

❝ *Right now, there are hundreds of bills pending in state legislatures across the United States that target trans youth and aim to curb their rights. The impact of fighting these anti-trans bills and policies is felt all year by trans people, their families, and their loved ones.*❞

—ARIANA GRANDE

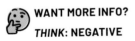 **WANT MORE INFO?**
THINK: NEGATIVE

ATTITUDES, BEHAVIOR, AND UNFAIR TREATMENT TO THE TRANSGENDER, NONBINARY, AND GENDER NONCONFORMING COMMUNITY.

DID YOU KNOW On September 27, 2022, thousands of Virginia students—from nearly one hundred middle and high schools—rallied together and organized a statewide school walkout to protest the anti-trans regulations proposed by the state governor, Glenn Youngkin. These policies ranged from requiring students to use restrooms that matched their assigned sex at birth to mandating parent permission if a student wanted to change their name and pronouns. Pride Liberation Project, a student-led coalition that advocates for queer students, assisted in organizing the youth walkout. Their mission was to make students more aware of the inequities transgender students were experiencing and stand up to adult authorities like politicians and other policy makers who dismiss LGBTQIA+ fundamental rights. The walkout had media coverage on a state, national, and international level, showing that when youth unite for the greater good, people will lean in and listen.

APORAGENDER

▼ adjective

A person who identifies with a gender that is separate from the binary male and female, or even a combination of both. Derived from the Greek word "apor" meaning "separate," this word is often used as an umbrella term for a person who identifies as nonbinary. The term ALIAGENDER can also be used.

❝Aporagender is a non-cisgender identity that is fluid and still has a sense of gender.❞

▲   Aporagender

SEE ALSO
NONBINARY, GENDER NONCONFORMING

 WANT MORE INFO? *THINK: SEPARATE* **GENDER.**

APPROPRIATE

▼ verb

To take ownership of something without permission or endorsement of those who created it.

RELATED
APPROPRIATION *noun*

SEE ALSO
CULTURAL APPROPRIATION, MISAPPROPRIATE, REAPPROPRIATE

❝Let's talk about pop culture's appropriation of Black gay lingo—child, yas, girl, fierce, shade, read! *Miss Honey! I mean, I can go on and on.*"

 WANT MORE INFO? *THINK*: **TO BORROW WITHOUT ASKING.**

AROFLUX

▼ *adjective*

An identifier for people who experience a range of intensity within the aromantic spectrum, from feeling a strong romantic attraction to others to not feeling any romantic attraction to others.

SEE ALSO
AROMANTIC

❝ *Sometimes you can be all the way alloromantic and then change and be all the way aromantic. The change is natural, so don't think anything is wrong with you. You are just aroflux.*"

 WANT MORE INFO? *THINK*: **A PERSON'S ROMANTIC ATTRACTION TO OTHERS MAY CHANGE OR FLUCTUATE OVER TIME.**

USAGE NOTE: This term is commonly used in the asexual community.

▲ **Aroflux**

AROMANTIC

▼ *adjective*

Lacking a romantic attraction toward someone. Physical attraction may still be present. Can be abbreviated as "aro."

▼ *noun*

An aromantic person. A label used to describe a romantic orientation that shows little to no romantic affection toward someone.

SEE ALSO
ALLOROMANTIC

❝ *Don't try to push aromantic people into doing 'romantic' things. Be mindful of how they identify."*

WANT MORE INFO?
THINK: MAY BE ASEXUAL, ALLOSEXUAL, OR SOMEWHERE IN BETWEEN, BUT DOES NOT EXPERIENCE ROMANCE.

USAGE NOTE: It is important to avoid the assumption that something is "wrong" with people in the aromantic community. It is common for aro people to engage in intimate connections through platonic relationships.

Aromantic

ASEXUAL

▼ *adjective*

Not experiencing physical attraction or desire. Can be abbreviated as ACE.

▼ *noun*

A person who is without physical yearnings. A label used to describe a sexual orientation where a person shows little to no physical affection to others.

RELATED
ASEXUALITY *noun*

SEE ALSO
ALLOSEXUAL

▲   **Asexual**

❝ *Unlike celibacy, which is a choice, asexuality is a sexual orientation."*

—ASEXUAL VISIBILITY AND EDUCATION NETWORK (AVEN)

 WANT MORE INFO? *THINK:* **MAY NOT EXPERIENCE PHYSICAL ATTRACTION BUT COULD EXPERIENCE ROMANTIC ATTRACTION.**

USAGE NOTE: It is important to avoid the assumption that something is "wrong" with people in the asexual community. It is common for ace people to engage in romantic relationships and desire to have families.

ASSISTED REPRODUCTION

▼ *noun*

A medical process used by same-sex, transgender, and/or queer parents that enhances fertility, allowing LGBTQIA+ adults to have children and start a family. This process may include sperm donation, egg donation, surrogacy, or using assisted reproduction technology (ART) like in vitro fertilization (IVF). The term DONOR-CONCEIVED PERSON can also be used.

> SEE ALSO
>
> **"Queer Parents and the Family Dynamic,"** *p. 330*

❝ *Some children of queer parents have a unique experience being born through assisted reproduction. A great youth book to read more about this is called Baking a Baby, by Lauren Knight.*❞

 WANT MORE INFO? *THINK:* **MEDICAL THERAPY USED TO BECOME FERTILE AND HAVE A BABY.**

ATTRACTION

▼ *noun*

Interest, connection, or desire toward someone.

❝ *There are many types of attraction. Romantic, physical, platonic, admirable, and others. Attraction differs for everyone and in every way.*❞

 WANT MORE INFO? *THINK:* **"I FEEL SOMETHING SPECIAL WHEN I AM AROUND YOU."**

AUNT(IE)

▼ *noun*

An endearing term used to identify a mature, often

effeminate, gay man. Alternate spelling includes "Aunty."

A respected transgender woman—often, a mentor.

❝ *You better behave at Pride or Auntie is gonna come get you. Do you hear me? Just kidding! Live your life, boo.*❞

 WANT MORE INFO? *THINK*: **AN EXPERIENCED, RESPECTED GAY MAN OR TRANS WOMAN.**

USAGE NOTE: This term originated in Black culture and is commonly used in the Black gay and trans community.

DID YOU KNOW "Auntie" is used in Black cultures as a way to identify a well-respected adult woman. During the nineteenth century, white Europeans and Americans used the term to belittle Black women, refusing to use Mrs. or Miss as a respectful honorific. The Black community reclaimed the term to dispel its negative connotation and empower Black women.

A-WORD

▼ *idiom*

A euphemism for AIDS.

SEE ALSO
HIV/AIDS, "History Lesson: HIV/AIDS," *p. 213*

❝ *The A-Word is not taboo. We want a world without AIDS! Let's speak out and together, we can make the change.*❞

 WANT MORE INFO? *THINK*: **ACQUIRED IMMUNE DEFICIENCY SYNDROME.**

DID YOU KNOW Human documentation of AIDS was found as early as the 1970s, and AIDS cases spread rapidly across North America, South America, Europe, Africa, and Australia. Today, the HIV/AIDS crisis is still one of the world's most serious public health challenges. More than 36 million people worldwide are currently living with HIV/AIDS.

Coming Out 101

ACCEPT the most AUTHENTIC you

IN THE LGBTQIA+ community, "coming out" is a phrase most commonly used in reference to a person sharing their sexual orientation, romantic orientation, gender expression, or gender identity with the world. It is part of a personal journey toward self-love, self-acceptance, and living authentically. Coming out can happen on your terms and at your own pace. It is never too early or too late to come out. Sometimes it's even better to think that you are not coming out, but coming into your most amazing self! Telling someone, especially your family or loved ones, you are LGBTQIA+ is a big step and can sometimes feel scary. For some encouragement, a few young friends share their best coming out (or coming into yourself!) advice:

> "Coming out is hard, but when you come out, you should surround yourself with people who love you no matter what. So, when you come out nothing should change, you should and they should love you/them no matter what."
>
> —LEXIE (she/her), fifth grader

"The most important thing is for you to come out when you feel ready."

"Gender expression is kind of like how you express yourself, like with your clothes, with your hair, or with your makeup and stuff. Your gender expression doesn't have to match your gender identity. And sometimes, your gender expression could be, maybe, giving off the vibe that you are masculine when you actually identify as a girl or the other way around. Just be you!"

—ATHENA (she/they/ze), fifth grader

"Sip out of a water bottle that says, 'I'm Gay!' I'm joking! But you could if you wanted! Whenever you are ready and feel comfortable, you can come out whenever you want. You are free to be whatever, it's your choice."

—DONTE (he/him), sixth grader

"There are a bunch of people that support you and you don't have to be scared to come out. Don't be afraid to be yourself because you are who you are and you can't really change that."

—DAISY (they/them), fourth grader

"Coming out can feel weird because you are sharing a special part about yourself and you are making yourself vulnerable. But remember, you are not alone. Millions of other people have done this, too. So it's not just you. Other people have tried to come out and felt the same awkward things you have been feeling. You are not alone."

—DANIEL (he/they), fourth grader

"Sometimes people will put you in a box and think of you as one gender based on how you look. They will think you are automatically a boy or a girl because of how you dress and look. Not everyone is going to understand that you are nonbinary. Still be yourself. Find people who can relate to you or know who you are, even who you want to be, and then they'll support you.

—EMERSON (she/they), fifth grader

"I'm not forcing you to do it right now, but don't ever be ashamed about it. If you don't really want to say it, you can give them hints or something. You can wear types of things that relate to you and your sexual orientation and what you identify as."

—MYA (she/her), seventh grader

ARE YOU INTERESTED in reading books about LGBTQIA+ youth experiences? Here is a list of books that you may enjoy and find helpful to assist you on your journey with exploring your gender identity and sexual orientation:

- All Boys Aren't Blue, by George M. Johnson
- Ana on the Edge, by A. J. Sass
- The Art of Being Normal: A Novel, by Lisa Williamson
- As the Crow Flies, by Melanie Gillman
- Bodies Are Cool, by Tyler Feder
- Beyond the Gender Binary, by Alok Vaid-Menon

- The Boy & the Bindi, by Vivek Shraya
- Cemetery Boys, by Aiden Thomas
- Ciel, by Sophie Labelle
- Continuum, by Chella Man
- Felix Ever After, by Kacen Callender
- Melissa (George), by Alex Gino
- If I Was Your Girl, by Meredith Russo

- It Feels Good to Be Yourself: A Book About Gender Identity, by Theresa Thorn
- Love Beyond Body, Space & Time, by Hope Nicholson, Erin Cossar, and Sam Beiko
- Love Frankie, by Jacqueline Wilson and illustrated by Nick Sharratt
- Middle School's a Drag, You Better Werk!, by Greg Howard
- My Rainbow, by Trinity and DeShanna Neal
- The Stars and the Blackness Between Them, by Junauda Petrus
- Things We Couldn't Say, by Jay Coles
- Trans Teen Survival Guide, by Owl and Fox Fisher
- When Aidan Became a Brother, by Kyle Lukoff
- Zenobia July, by Lisa Bunker

Bb

BABY BUTCH

▼ noun

A young, boyish lesbian, bisexual, or queer girl.

66 Look at that baby butch over there with all that swag. I see you, young one."

 WANT MORE INFO?
THINK: YOUNG LESBIAN TOMBOY.

USAGE NOTE: This term originated in the lesbian community.

BABY DYKE

▼ noun

A female who has newly revealed her sexuality as lesbian.

A young queer girl.

66

SPARROW: *If you like her, go talk to her! She looks nice and will probably like you back.*

HAILEE: *Uh . . . noooo . . . I can't! I'm scared. I'm just a baby dyke with no game. I'm not cool!*

SPARROW: *You are so cool! Stop being shy and say something to her during third period, okay?*

 WANT MORE INFO?
THINK: LESBIAN NEWCOMER OR YOUNG LESBIAN.

BABY
DYKE
CONT.

USAGE NOTE: This term originated in the lesbian community. The term "dyke" was once a derogatory slur for lesbians but has been reclaimed by some of the LGBTQIA+ community. It may still have negative connotations for some people. Please be aware that this term can be considered mature.

BACKBOOTS

▼ *exclamation*

SEE **BOOTS**

BALL

▼ *noun*

An event in ballroom culture where gay, transgender, and queer members of the ballroom scene gather and compete for awards in a series of categories based on self-expression. Free agents and competitors from different houses walk for awards based on appearance, attitude, dance, attire, and realness.

SEE ALSO

"History Lesson: The Ballroom Scene," *p. 308*

❝*I went to my first ball last night! It was so fiyah! House of Miyake-Mugler snatched wings and won all the categories."*

 WANT MORE INFO? *THINK:* COMPETITION IN THE HISTORIC FILM *PARIS IS BURNING.*

DID YOU KNOW In 1920s Harlem, gay balls were born out of racial tension. People of color were not allowed to participate in the lavish gay affairs of the white community, so the gay Black community created a social space to express their sexuality freely. Balls began as extravagant underground drag performances, but by the 1970s, the events had evolved to feature an array of themes to celebrate the performers' artistic expression, gender identities, sexual orientations, and ethnicities.

▼ noun

An unwarranted or poor excuse.

❝ You can stop singing your out-of-tune ballad now. I have I'm still telling Mom you skipped swimming practice to play Metroid Dread!"

 WANT MORE INFO? THINK: AN ATTEMPT TO JUSTIFY ONESELF.

BALL GOWN

▼ noun

A playful reference to a masculine pantsuit.

❝

Kierra: I'm going to look goooooood at my eighth-grade dance in this green velvet ball gown!

Makayla: Little sis, you always look good but tonight they gonna be taking so many pictures like you're on the cover of GQ magazine!

 WANT MORE INFO? THINK: EXQUISITE FORMAL ATTIRE.

BALLROOM SCENE OR **BALLROOM CULTURE**

▼ *noun*

A distinct social community comprised mostly of Black and Latinx gay and transgender members who use ballroom competitions as a safe place to express their gender, sexuality, and artistic spirit. The phrases "ball culture," "gay balls," and "drag ball" can also be used.

SEE ALSO

BALL, CATEGORY, HOUSE CULTURE, "History Lesson: The Ballroom Scene," **p. 308**

66 *The fairy godmother of the ballroom scene is New York City, honey! She has graced you with the houses of Ninja, Xtravaganza, Mizrahi, and LaBeija. All of the legendary walkers received their first real trophies in New York."*

WANT MORE INFO? *THINK:* THE SCENE PORTRAYED ON FX'S SHOW *POSE*—A SOCIAL AND ARTISTIC LIFESTYLE FOR QUEER AND TRANS PEOPLE OF COLOR.

DID YOU KNOW

The ballroom scene is centered around balls—competitions that champion self-expression. Competitors at a ball walk (much like a model on a runway) for titles and awards in themed categories. The best competitors are celebrated widely within the community's social house structure. Social houses are typically made up of a house mother and/or house father and their children, all of whom take the last name of their chosen family.

BANJI OR BANJEE

▼ *adjective*

Ill-mannered or unsightly.

▼ *noun*

A banji person, place, or thing.

TERRI: *Why are you slurping that tropical punch juice like that? And, you're spilling it on your desk. You are so banji! Didn't your mama teach you some manners?"*

CLASSROOM: *Oooooooohhh, dang!*

MRS. COLINS: *Class, please quiet down.*

WANT MORE INFO?
THINK: **NOT THE GOOD "RATCHET" LIKE MEGAN THEE STALLION, BUT A "RATCHET" DISASTER LIKE AN IPHONE SCREEN SHATTERED.**

USAGE NOTE: This term originated in ballroom culture. This term can be considered negative, but it has also been reclaimed by some as a positive self-identifier, similar to "ratchet," "fag," or "dyke."

BARBIE

▼ *noun*

A drag queen who is disorganized and lacking concentration.

 Please remove this Barbie from my presence and enroll her in charm school. She is a disaster."

 WANT MORE INFO?
THINK: **A DITZ.**

USAGE NOTE: This term is commonly used in the drag community.

Barbie ▼

BATTLE

▼ *noun*

In ballroom culture, this is a performance competition between opposing walkers.

SEE ALSO
"History Lesson: The Ballroom Scene," *p. 308*

❝ *The kids are about to gag! The battle for the grand prize is between House of Ebony and House of Balenciaga. LEGENDARY!!!!"*

 WANT MORE INFO? *THINK:* **A BALLROOM CONTEST TO WIN THE TITLE, THE TROPHY, THE PRIZE MONEY, AND THE GLORY.**

BEAR

▼ *noun*

A gay, bisexual, or queer man who has a large or stocky body with visible body hair, resembling a bear.

❝ *Black bears, brown bears, panda bears, polar bears, and grizzly bears all represent the diverse identities in the bear community."*

 WANT MORE INFO? *THINK:* **A STURDY, HAIRY GAY MAN.**

USAGE NOTE:	This term originated in the white gay male community.

BEAR COMMUNITY

▼ *noun*

A gay subcommunity that supports and celebrates the brotherhood of bears. This community also embraces other types of queer people who identify as a CUB, CHUB, OTTER, or URSULA.

SEE ALSO
"Help! What Type of Gay Am I?," *p. 203*

❝ *The Lazy Bear Fund is an organization created by the San Francisco bear*

community that actively provides generous support to local clinics, schools, and food banks."

 WANT MORE INFO?
THINK: THOSE WHO CELEBRATE THE *BEAR* NECESSITIES DURING P-TOWN BEAR WEEK.

USAGE NOTE: This term originated in the white gay male community.

DID YOU KNOW Many gay men categorize other gay men based on their body type and age. These playful labels are sometimes referred to as the "Animal Kingdom" or the "Gay Zoo." Bears—gay men who are large and hairy, resembling a bear—are a part of the Animal Kingdom, along with cubs, otters, wolves, bulls, giraffes, and many other gay identifiers.

BEARD

▼ *noun*

In binary terms, a partner of the opposite gender meant to cover up one's sexuality.

❝Harrison is just her beard. She dates him to make people think she's straight."

 WANT MORE INFO?
THINK: A FAKE PARTNER FOR A CLOSETED GAY OR QUEER PERSON.

USAGE NOTE: This term originated in the white gay male community.

BEARDED LADY

▼ *noun*

A woman dating or married to a gay man to help him pose as heterosexual.

❝I was gay in the sixties. So, yes, I had my bearded lady. The world wasn't always keen on me loving men."

 WANT MORE INFO?
THINK: A FAUX WIFE FOR A GAY MAN.

BEAT

▼ noun

Makeup or overall appearance. Often heard in the phrase "full beat."

▼ verb

To apply makeup extremely well. Often heard in the phrase "beat for the gods/gawds."

SEE ALSO
PAINTED

❝ *Every Thursday, I watch his YouTube channel on the best makeup pro tips. His makeup lessons are fun and he beats for the gawds!*"

 WANT MORE INFO? THINK: THE MAKEUP ARTISTS AT MAC OR SEPHORA, ON YOUTUBE OR INSTAGRAM, AT A DRAG SHOW OR BALL, WHEREVER A FIERCE FACE SHINES.

| **USAGE NOTE:** | This term originated in ballroom culture and is commonly |

used in the drag community. It has been appropriated by the larger LGBTQIA+ community and mainstream culture.

▲ Beat

BECHDEL TEST, THE

▼ noun

A test used to examine gender bias and female representation in fictional works—particularly film, television, and books. In order to pass the Bechdel Test, a work must feature two distinct female characters who talk about something other than a man.

SEE ALSO

**THE VITO RUSSO TEST,
RING OF KEYS**

66 *My parents only let me
watch movies that pass
the Bechdel Test. We are
definitely a proud feminist
household."*

 WANT MORE INFO?
THINK: **A FEMINIST
MEASURE OF
ACCOUNTABILITY FOR
ART.**

**DID
YOU
KNOW** Alison Bechdel,
the award-winning
lesbian cartoonist
who wrote *Fun Home*,
an autobiographical
"tragicomic" about her family, also
wrote a successful comic strip from
1983 to 2008. *Dykes to Watch
Out For* documented the lives of a
diverse group of fictional lesbians
alongside the cultural and political
landscape of their time, and it was
in the comic that the Bechdel Test
was introduced, forever changing
the way we look at gender bias in
the media.

BECKY

▼ *noun*

SEE **WENDY**

BEEFCAKE

▼ *noun*

A man or masc-identifying
person with a well-defined
muscular body.

66 *My dad said he thinks
Anderson Cooper is a
freakin' silver fox beefcake.
Whatever that means . . ."*

 WANT MORE INFO?
THINK: **GOOD LOOKING
MUSCLEMEN.**

**USAGE
NOTE:** This term is commonly
used in the gay male
community.

▲ **Beefcake**

BEEP

▼ *exclamation*

A sound used when confirming that someone is gay or queer.

SEE ALSO
GAYDAR

" *BEEP! BEEP! BEEP! My gaydar is going off facing northeast."*

 WANT MORE INFO?
THINK: ZEROING IN ON AN LGBTQIA+ PERSON.

BENT

▼ *adjective*

Not heterosexual.

" *If it ain't straight then it's bent."*

 WANT MORE INFO?
THINK: QUEER.

BETTY

▼ *noun*

SEE **MARY**

BICON

▼ *noun*

A bisexual icon.

SEE ALSO
DYKON, GAY ICON

" *Let's not forget our beautiful bicons, Shannon Purser, Keiynan Lonsdale, Auli'i Cravalho, Dove Cameron, and Willow Smith!"*

▼ **Bicon**

WANT MORE INFO? *THINK*: A BI TRAILBLAZER.

BI-CURIOUS OR BICURIOUS

▼ *noun*

Someone who identifies as heterosexual but is interested in exploring same-sex or queer relationships. This also can apply to a gay or lesbian person who is interested in experiencing a heterosexual relationship.

❝ Did you know Jasmine is bi-curious? She kissed Nicole in the projection room above the auditorium!❞

WANT MORE INFO? *THINK*: A PERSON EXPERIMENTING WITH BISEXUALITY.

BICYCLE OR BI-CYCLE

▼ *noun*

The changing of one's attraction between males and females. This term often refers to the gender binary, girl or woman and boy or man.

SEE ALSO
AC/DC, BISEXUAL

❝ I can be 70 percent gay one day and 15 percent gay the next. I think my bi-cycle is powered by two different wheels and I love it!❞

WANT MORE INFO? *THINK*: A BISEXUAL PLAY ON THE WORD "BICYCLE."

USAGE NOTE: This term may have negative connotations as it limits bisexuality to the gender binary. It is inappropriate to use this label if a person has not self-identified as such.

53

THE QUEENS' ENGLISH

BIGENDER

▼ adjective

A person who identifies as two genders (not limited to the gender binary)—a combination of male, female, and/or another gender identity.

SEE ALSO
POLYGENDER, PANGENDER, GENDERFLUID, GENDERFLUX, THIRD GENDER, NONBINARY

"

REID: *Brook is bigender, right?*

SAV: *Yeah, they use he/him and they/them pronouns.*

REID: *Great! I was thinking about getting them cool "His" and "Theirs" key chains I saw at the bookstore.*

 WANT MORE INFO?
THINK: **SOMEONE WHOSE IDENTITY ENCOMPASSES TWO GENDERS.**

| **USAGE NOTE:** | This term is commonly used in the transgender, nonbinary, and gender |

nonconforming communities.

BINARY

▼ noun

Something having two parts.

SEE ALSO
GENDER BINARY

▼ adjective

Relating to or involving two things.

" *The use of binary systems is a bit simple and uninformative to me. Do we really only want to see the world in just black or white?"*

 WANT MORE INFO?
THINK: **A SYSTEM BUILT ON A PAIR OF OPPOSITES.**

▲ Binary

BIND

▼ *verb*

To flatten or conceal one's breasts/chest using constricting materials, typically using a BINDER, which is the healthiest and safest way to bind.

SEE ALSO
"Tucking & Binding 101," p. *163*

❝ *Hey, queer masc nation, I have some tips for you on how to bind properly. Check it out on my blog. Link in profile!"*

 WANT MORE INFO? *THINK:* **TO REDUCE THE APPARENT SIZE OF ONE'S BREASTS.**

 USAGE NOTE: This term is commonly used in the transgender, nonbinary, gender nonconforming, and drag communities. There are many blogs, videos, and picture tutorials that can be researched online to help achieve a safe and comfortable binding technique.

BINDER

▼ *noun*

An undergarment used to reduce the appearance and size of breasts.

SEE ALSO
"Tucking & Binding 101," p. *163*

❝ *Avoid using tape or ACE bandages to bind. Wear a binder instead."*

 WANT MORE INFO? *THINK:* **A COMPRESSION GARMENT FOR BREASTS/CHEST.**

 USAGE NOTE: This term is commonly used in the transgender, nonbinary, gender nonconforming, and drag communities.

BIO QUEEN

▼ *noun*

SEE **FAUX QUEEN**

BIPHOBIA

▼ *noun*

Aversion, fear, or hatred toward bisexuality.

RELATED
BIPHOBIC *adjective*
BIPHOBE *noun*

SEE ALSO
ACEPHOBIA, **FEMMEPHOBIA,** **HOMOPHOBIA,** **LESBOPHOBIA,** **QUEERPHOBIA,** **TRANSPHOBIA**

❝ *Straight and gay people can be biphobic. I've personally been verbally mistreated more than I like to admit.*❞

 WANT MORE INFO? *THINK:* **PREJUDICE AGAINST BISEXUAL PEOPLE.**

BIPOC

▼ *noun*

SEE **POC**

BIROMANTIC

▼ *noun*

A person who has a romantic attraction to more than one gender.

❝ *Andrew and I just clicked! He likes to hold hands, even when mine are sweaty, and we write each other the sweetest letters. I think this asexual's biromantic heart has been shot by cupid's arrow!*❞

 WANT MORE INFO? *THINK:* **THE ROMANTIC COUNTERPART TO BISEXUAL.**

USAGE NOTE: This term is commonly used in the asexual community.

BISCUITS

▼ *noun*

SEE **CAKES**

BISEXUAL

▼ adjective

Being attracted to more than one gender. Often, but not limited to, being attracted to the same gender and other genders. Often shortened to "bi."

▼ noun

A bisexual person. A label used to describe a sexual orientation where a person may have physical attractions to more than one gender.

RELATED
BISEXUALITY noun

SEE ALSO
PANSEXUAL

"I am eleven, I use she/her/hers pronouns, and I identity as bisexual."

 WANT MORE INFO? THINK: ATTRACTED TO JACK AND JILL AND JAI, TOO.

USAGE NOTE: Bisexual attraction is often misunderstood as a sexual preference that is limited to the gender binary. Bisexuality is a personal journey and not all bisexual people share the same type of attraction model.

DID YOU KNOW Bisexual Visibility Day is celebrated each year on September 23 to recognize bisexual identity, history, and PRIDE! The day was first celebrated in 1999 at the International Lesbian and Gay Association Conference in Johannesburg, South Africa, to strengthen the visibility of bisexuality worldwide.

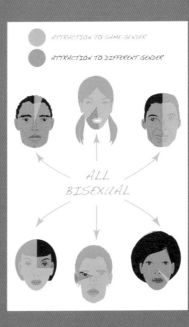

BITE ME

▼ idiom

An aggressive way to tell someone you do not want to be bothered.

"

KYLE: *Bite me, Xavian!*

XAVIAN: *Forget you, Kyle!*

 WANT MORE INFO?
***THINK:* "LEAVE ME ALONE!"**

BLACK GAY PRIDE

▼ noun

A movement that empowers the visibility of the Black gay, same gender–loving, and queer community. The terms "Black Pride" and "Black Pride Movement" can also be used.

"*I love Black Gay Pride! It's a celebration of Black identity, Black culture, and Black excellence.*"

 WANT MORE INFO?
***THINK:* A CELEBRATION OF BLACKNESS, GAYNESS, LOVE, AND UNITY.**

DID YOU KNOW Black Gay Pride became popular in the early 1990s when activists Welmore Cook, Theodore Kirkland, and Ernest Hopkins led a crowd of over eight hundred people in Washington, DC, to educate the Black community about HIV/AIDS. Black Pride events have evolved over the decades to celebrate being Black and LGBTQIA+, advocate for equality and social justice, and provide space to articulate the specific needs of the community. Today there are over thirty annual Black Pride celebrations across the country, including popular cities like Atlanta, Miami, Philadelphia, and Washington, DC.

BLACK TRIANGLE

▼ noun

A symbol adopted by the lesbian community to show pride in women's liberation and resistance against discrimination.

SEE ALSO

PINK TRIANGLE

"

MX. NEAL: *Stacey, that's beautiful! What are you creating?*

STACEY: *I am drawing a black triangle with the Venus and moon signs. They symbolize a mix of strength, tenacity, and balance.*

 WANT MORE INFO? *THINK:* SYMBOL FOR QUEER FEMINISM AND LESBIAN PRIDE.

DID YOU KNOW The black triangle was originally used in Nazi concentration camps to mark prisoners who were considered "asocial" or "work-shy." Lesbians were included in this category. The symbol was reappropriated by the lesbian community in the 1970s as a symbol of pride. Celebrating lesbian history ensures future generations will understand the ongoing resistance and activism women, feminists, and trans, nonbinary, and queer people have made in society. The Lesbian Herstory Archives, founded in 1970, preserves the records of lesbian lives and activities throughout the decades, storing photos, poems, films, posters, clothing, letters, oral contributions, and more of the lesbian community.

▲　　　**Black Triangle**

BLANCHE

▼ *noun*

SEE **MARY**

BLAPS

▼ *noun*

Irritable bowels. The term "blatts" can also be used.

" *My stomach is rumbling! I got the blaps."*

 WANT MORE INFO? *THINK:* DIARRHEA.

BLAQUEER

▼ *noun*

An empowering identifier for a Black person who identifies as queer. The term "BlaQ" can also be used.

SEE ALSO
QPOC or QTPOC

❝ *The separation of the words 'Black' and 'Queer' presents a false division, a convenient (forced) circumcision of self, that is not the reality for BlaQueer people across the world."*

—DR. T. ANANSI WILSON, *BLAQUEERFLOW*

 WANT MORE INFO?
THINK: **A TERM FOR QUEER BLACK EMPOWERMENT.**

USAGE NOTE: This term was coined by writer, activist, and motivational speaker Dr. T. Anansi Wilson, JD and is commonly used in the Black queer community.

DID YOU KNOW From prolific writers James Baldwin and Lorraine Hansberry to legendary modern dance pioneer Alvin Ailey; from civil rights trailblazer Bayard Rustin and trans activist Marsha P. Johnson and her impact on the 1969 Stonewall riots to the award-winning queer activists and Black Lives Matter cofounders, Patrisse Khan-Cullors and Alicia Garza—Black LGBTQIA+ artists and activists have played crucial roles in shaping American history for decades.

BLOCKERS

▼ *noun*

Medicine taken by transgender, nonbinary, or genderqueer youth to prevent puberty from starting. These drugs interrupt the production of hormones and delay the development of secondary sex characteristics, such as the deepening of the voice, development of facial and body hair, and menstruation. The term "puberty blockers" can also be used.

❝ *The primary use of blockers is for young people to have time to understand who they are. If you don't think you want breasts, blockers can put that development on hold.*"

 WANT MORE INFO?
THINK: **PUBERTY STOPPER.**

 USAGE NOTE: This term is commonly used in the transgender, nonbinary, and gender nonconforming communities.

DID YOU KNOW Blockers were first used to help young girls who experienced puberty at an early age. Blockers would halt menstruation in girls as early as age seven, and when the girl reached a more mature age, she would come off the blocker to resume puberty. Today, puberty blockers allow trans, nonbinary, and queer youth more time to explore their gender identity and present a body that feels more aligned with their gender expression; one can stop taking blockers at any time and continue going through puberty as their sex assigned at birth.

BLUE BOY

▼ *noun*

A police officer. The terms MATILDA and MEG can also be used.

❝ *What happened? Why are the blue boys in front of our school?*"

 WANT MORE INFO?
THINK: **THE COPS.**

BLUE DISCHARGE

▼ *noun*

A dated term for the discharge of a gay man from the United States Army.

❝ *My grandfather was given a blue discharge even though his personal life had nothing to do with his service for the US Army.*"

 WANT MORE INFO? *THINK:* **AN ARMY DISMISSAL BASED ON GAY OR QUEER RELATIONSHIPS.**

BODY-ODY-ODY

▼ *noun*

An attractive physique. The phrase "serving body" can also be used.

❝ *That's right! Embrace those curves! Show off that body-ody-ody!*"

 WANT MORE INFO? *THINK:* **EMBRACE YOUR BEAUTIFUL NATURAL CURVES AND BODY SHAPE.**

 USAGE NOTE: This term originated in ballroom culture and is commonly used in the larger queer and trans people of color (QTPOC) community.

BOI

▼ *noun*

A person of any gender expression who presents in a youthful, masculine way.

❝ *I'm a girl, he's a dude, they are enby but we all also identify as 'boi.'*"

 WANT MORE INFO? *THINK:* **A YOUNG-LOOKING, MASC-OF-CENTER PERSON.**

 USAGE NOTE: This term originated in the lesbian community. It has been appropriated by the larger LGBTQIA+ community.

DID YOU KNOW A wide range of gender identities can fall under this term including young femme gay males, masculine lesbians, transmasculine, intersex, and gender nonconforming folx (to name a few).

BOOBS

▼ *noun*

Breasts. The terms "boobies" or "bosom" can also be used.

❝ *OMG! My boobs are growing! I wear a B-cup bra size now."*

 WANT MORE INFO? *THINK:* **TOP-FRONT AREA OF A GIRL'S OR FEMME TGNC PERSON'S BODY.**

BOOM

▼ *exclamation*

A stern, dismissive signifier to punctuate the end of a statement.

❝ *Just admit you forgot it was due today! You had two weeks to turn in your part of the group assignment, Tiffany. Boom!"*

 WANT MORE INFO? *THINK:* **I SAID, WHAT I SAID . . . MIC DROP.**

DID YOU KNOW This term originated in Black American culture and is commonly used in the Black gay and queer community.

▲ Boom

BOOP

▼ *exclamation*

A sound effect used to signify agreement.

❝

JULES: *I want to get this Lululemon shirt with matching joggers. You think my mom and Nadine will let me buy it? They gave me their credit card, plus I've been working so hard in school.*
TEDDY: *Boop! Queen, you deserve it. Tell your parents to spend those coins!*

WANT MORE INFO?
THINK: **YAAAASSS!**

BOOTS

▼ *exclamation*

An emphatic word used to enhance an adjective. The superlative is BACKBOOTS.

❝ *I just want all the food! I'm hungry boots! What time is lunch?*❞

 WANT MORE INFO?
THINK: **AN ADJECTIVE INTENSIFIER.**

USAGE NOTE:	This term originated in the Black gay community.

BOOTY

▼ *noun*

SEE **CAKES**

BOSTON MARRIAGE

▼ *noun*

A dated term for a relationship in which two unmarried women live together long-term, without the company of a man.

❝ *People think Alice B. Toklas and Gertrude Stein were roommates?! Ha! Back then, that was called a Boston marriage. In the early 1900s, they were calling each other 'wifey' and 'baby precious'!*❞

 WANT MORE INFO?
THINK: **AN OLD-SCHOOL EUPHEMISM FOR LESBIAN ROOMMATES.**

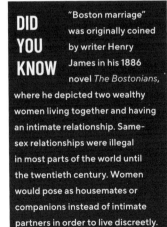

DID YOU KNOW "Boston marriage" was originally coined by writer Henry James in his 1886 novel *The Bostonians*, where he depicted two wealthy women living together and having an intimate relationship. Same-sex relationships were illegal in most parts of the world until the twentieth century. Women would pose as housemates or companions instead of intimate partners in order to live discreetly.

BOTTOM SURGERY

▼ *noun*

Reconstructive surgery performed on the genitals, often performed to better suit a person's gender identity. The term LOWER SURGERY can also be used.

SEE ALSO
TOP SURGERY

66 *Bottom surgeries can include vaginoplasty for male-to-female or male-to-nonbinary and phalloplasty or metoidioplasty for female-to-male or female-to-nonbinary."*

 WANT MORE INFO?
THINK: **MEDICAL PROCEDURE TO ALTER ONE'S PRIVATE PARTS.**

USAGE NOTE: This term is commonly used in the transgender, nonbinary, and gender nonconforming communities.

BOYFLUX

▼ *adjective*

Gender identity label for males who experience fluctuating levels and various intensities of maleness and/or masculinity. There are many ways to experience boyflux identity as this label is personal to each individual. People who identify as boyflux may identify as a boy/man and may also identify with another gender.

SEE ALSO
DEMIBOY

66 *Many people who identify as boyflux use the masculine pronouns he/him/his, but it is still always best to ask them their pronouns."*

 WANT MORE INFO?
THINK: **FEELING MASCULINE** *MOST* **OF THE TIME BUT** *NOT ALL* **THE TIME.**

BREEZY

▼ *noun*

An attractive girl or woman.

❝ *Every time she smiles at me, I can't stop blushing. Amanda McClinton is such a breezy!*❞

 WANT MORE INFO? *THINK:* **SUCH A CUTIE!** **#GIRLCRUSH**

 USAGE NOTE: This term originated in Black American culture and is commonly used in the Black lesbian community. It has also been appropriated by mainstream culture.

BRING OUT THE GAY

▼ *idiom*

To persuade a heterosexual person to explore homosexuality.

❝ *Lil Nas X can bring out the gay in anybody. It's a gift.*❞

 WANT MORE INFO? *THINK:* **TO TEMPT SOMEONE TO EXPLORE SAME-GENDER OR QUEER LOVIN'.**

BRO OR BRUH

▼ *noun*

A term of endearment used between two masculine people.

❝ *Bruh, what's up for the weekend? I'm gonna play* Halo Infinite *on Saturday with Ty and Aisha, wanna come?*❞

 WANT MORE INFO? *THINK:* **PAL, BUD, DUDE.**

 USAGE NOTE: This term originated in Black American culture. It has been appropriated by the larger LGBTQIA+ community and mainstream culture.

▲ **Bro or Bruh**

BUG

▼ *noun*

SEE **LUG**

BULL DAGGER

▼ *noun*

A lesbian characterized by masculine behavior and appearance. The term "bull dyke" can also be used.

SEE ALSO
DYKE, BUTCH, "The Lesbian Spectrum," *p. 255*

❝ *Before the words 'butch' or 'lesbian' the term 'bull dagger' was first used to describe a woman's attraction to other women or her masculine gender expression.*"

 WANT MORE INFO? *THINK:* **A SUPER-MASCULINE LEZZIE.**

 USAGE NOTE: The term "dyke" was once a derogatory slur for lesbians but has been reclaimed by some of the LGBTQIA+ community. It may still have negative connotations for some people.

> **DID YOU KNOW** The terms "bull dagger" and "bull dyke" can be traced back to the lesbian community in the 1920s, during the Harlem Renaissance. Popular lesbian blues singers like Ma Rainey and Bessie Smith were widely known as bull daggers and felt empowered by the term. Over time, bull dyke was shortened to dyke and used to hurt and insult queer women, particularly lesbians and bisexual women of color. Some members of the lesbian community reclaimed the word to restrict outsiders from harmfully using the word again.

BULL DYKE

▼ *noun*

SEE **BULL DAGGER**

BUNS

▼ *noun*

SEE **CAKES**

▼ Butch

BUTCH
———

▼ *adjective*

Denoting the vast and dynamic representation of masculine characteristics, regardless of gender. Both "femme" and "butch" are often paired with the adjectives "soft"/"hard" or "high"/"low" as a means of distinction.

SEE ALSO

FEMME, FUTCH, "The Lesbian Spectrum," *p. 255*

▼ *noun*

In the lesbian community, a person who possesses a masculine appearance and behaviors.

SEE ALSO

BABY BUTCH, SOFT BUTCH, STONE BUTCH

❝ *Lesbians can all be so different! You can be a handsome, super-macho butch lesbian. You can really like wearing makeup and dresses and be a femme lesbian. Or, you can even be a combination of both butch and femme, called a futch lesbian!"*

 WANT MORE INFO? *THINK:* **MASCULINE.**

 USAGE NOTE: This term originated in the lesbian community. It has been appropriated by the larger LGBTQIA+ community.

BUTCH/FEMME RELATIONSHIP

▼ *noun*

An intimate relationship between a butch lesbian and a femme lesbian.

SEE ALSO

BUTCH, FEMME, MAMA AND PAPA RELATIONSHIP

" *I love butch/femme relationships because my girlfriends never want to wear my clothes."*

 WANT MORE INFO?
THINK: **LESBIAN LOVERS—ONE MASCULINE, ONE FEMININE.**

USAGE NOTE: This term originated in the lesbian community. It has been appropriated by the larger LGBTQIA+ community.

DID YOU KNOW In 1940s working-class bar culture, the words "butch," "femme," and "kiki" described women who were attracted to other women before "lesbian" was widely used. In butch/femme relationships, partners assumed traditionally masculine and feminine gender roles. Kiki girls did not adhere to the butch/femme binary when it came to gender expression *or* attraction preference; they were often shunned within the lesbian community. Today, lesbian and queer relationships celebrate the diversity of attraction, gender identity, and gender expression.

▲ **Butch/Femme Relationship**

▲ **Butchkini**

BUTCHKINI

▼ *noun*

The bathing suit of choice for butch lesbians and other masculine queer people with breasts, like bois, tomboys, studs, transmasc, or AFAB genderqueer people: a sports bra and board shorts.

❝ *Dad, I need this rainbow butchkini for sleepaway camp next week! Please? I have been obsessing about it since I saw Ellen in theirs last year.*❞

 WANT MORE INFO?
THINK: **A BODY-POSITIVE SWIMSUIT FOR BUTCHES OR MASC-OF-CENTER PEOPLE.**

BUTCH QUEEN

▼ *noun*

A competition category in the ballroom scene for cisgender males.

SEE ALSO
CATEGORY, QUEEN

A gay, bisexual, or queer male who possesses both masculine and feminine traits.

❝ *That's right! I said it! Butch queen! Boy in the day, girl at night."* —**PARIS DUPREE,** *PARIS IS BURNING*

 WANT MORE INFO?
THINK: **A GAY MAN PERFORMING IN A BALL.**

 USAGE NOTE: This term originated in ballroom culture. It has been appropriated by the larger LGBTQIA+ community.

BYE, FELICIA

▼ *idiom*

This phrase is used as a dismissive signifier.

"

CHLOE: *Let's go skydiving tomorrow! Don't you think that will be fun?*

TOMMIE: *Bye, Felicia! Absolutely not.*

WANT MORE INFO?
THINK: **HECK, NO!**

USAGE NOTE: This term originated in Black American culture and is commonly used in the Black gay and queer community. It has been appropriated by mainstream culture.

DID YOU KNOW The phrase "Bye, Felicia" was first coined by rapper, actor, and producer O'Shea Jackson (better known as Ice Cube) in the popular 1995 film *Friday*.

The Genderbread Person

BE INFORMED ON **GENDER IDENTITY, EXPRESSION,** AND **SEXUAL ORIENTATION**

THE GENDERBREAD PERSON serves as a basic introduction to understanding the complexities of gender identity, gender expression, and a person's physical and romantic preferences. The concept was first created by members of the TGNC community, specifically Cristina González, Vanessa Prell, Jack Rivas, and Jarrod Schwartz. Over the years, the design has evolved and become popularized by educator, author, and activist Sam Killermann as an educational tool that breaks down the complex concepts of gender and sexuality into a comprehensive, visual format for learners of all ages.

Here you will find a version of the Genderbread Person enhanced with even more terms to account for the full spectrum of expression. Our queer community is so vast and brilliant—and the way we talk about identity is always changing—that there may be people who do not fit neatly into any of the labels provided here. Their existence is just as celebrated and just as valid as the descriptions presented below.

GENDER IDENTITY: *The internal understanding of one's gender and the self. Who you are at your core, who you know yourself to be.*

- ▶ Woman-ness
- ▶ Man-ness
- ▶ Trans-ness
- ▶ Androgynous
- ▶ Flux
- ▶ Genderless

GENDER EXPRESSION: *Outward characteristics—such as appearance, behaviors, and attitudes—that communicate a person's identity to society.*

- ▶ Feminine
- ▶ Masculine
- ▶ Androgynous
- ▶ Neutral
- ▶ Fluid

ANATOMICAL SEX: *The physical makeup of the human body, sometimes referred to as biological sex. Our understanding of anatomical sex is led by things like genitals, chromosomes, and hormones.*

- ▶ Female-ness
- ▶ Male-ness
- ▶ Sex assigned at birth: Male, Female, Intersex

ATTRACTION: *The physical and romantic ways in which humans are drawn to one another. Gender and sexuality are separate entities, and someone's gender expression, identity, or anatomical sex actually have nothing to do with who they're attracted to.*

- ▶ Aesthetic attraction
- ▶ Alloromantic
- ▶ Allosexual
- ▶ Androsexual
- ▶ Aromantic
- ▶ Asexual
- ▶ Bi-curious
- ▶ Biromantic
- ▶ Bisexual
- ▶ Demiromantic
- ▶ Demisexual
- ▶ Fluid
- ▶ Gay
- ▶ Gynesexual
- ▶ Heteroflexible
- ▶ Heterosexual
- ▶ Homoflexible
- ▶ Homoromantic
- ▶ Homosexual
- ▶ Lesbian
- ▶ Lesbiflexible
- ▶ Monosexual
- ▶ Non-monogamous
- ▶ Non-monosexual
- ▶ Omnisexual
- ▶ Pansexual
- ▶ Polyamorous
- ▶ Polysexual
- ▶ Queer
- ▶ Romantic orientation
- ▶ Same-gender loving
- ▶ Sexual orientation

Cc

CAKES

▼ *noun*

Enticing buttocks. The term BISCUITS, BOOTY, or BUNS can also be used.

66 *Wow, my cakes are looking great!"*

 WANT MORE INFO?
THINK: **A NICE BUTT.**

USAGE NOTE: This term originated in Black American culture. It has been appropriated by the larger LGBTQIA+ community and mainstream culture.

CALL WARDROBE

▼ *idiom*

An expression of dissatisfaction with someone's style of dress.

66 *Liz, what do you have on? No, for real . . . what is this? Yellow polka-dot boots, pink leg warmers, a green dress, and a fuzzy brown sweater? This is a hard, NO! CALL WARDROBE!"*

 WANT MORE INFO?
THINK: **TO POINT OUT SOMEONE'S ABSOLUTELY UNACCEPTABLE ATTIRE.**

A complaint.

66 *These people and their 'call wardrobe' cries about everything. The sodas are free, the food is free, and*

CALL
WARDROBE
CONT.

the WiFi is free. What's the problem?"

 WANT MORE INFO?
THINK: AN SOS SIGNAL.

CAMP

▼ *noun*

The spirit of extravagance, irony, or sometimes exaggerated bad taste.

RELATED
CAMPY *adjective*
CAMP IT UP *idiom*

❝ *Honestly, dressing camp is really cool. Just look at all the Lady Gaga, Beyoncé, and Elton John fashions! Being bold and extravagant is fun!"*

 WANT MORE INFO?
THINK: JOHN WATERS'S HAIRSPRAY.

USAGE NOTE: The term was commonly used in Polari, a coded slang used by British gay men during the rise of anti-LGBT laws.

DID YOU KNOW The word "camp" derives from the French word *se camper* meaning "to flaunt." Camp is often associated with aesthetic, homosexuality, beauty, art, and stylization that date back to the beau ideal seen in the Renaissance sculptures. King Louis XIV is cited as an embodiment of sophisticated high camp style, which was a sign of wealth and power in seventeenth-century France—fast-forward to twentieth-century drag culture, ballroom culture, and underground films like *Flaming Creatures*, and camp has undergone theatricalization, now associated with queer campiness.

CARRY

▼ *noun*

One who over embellishes or overdoes it, referred to as "a carry."

❝ *Did Ronnie just say he is having a bouncy house birthday party for Sasha? OMG! Yes, she is cute, sweet, and turning two, but she is a poodle and they are a carry!"*

WANT MORE INFO?
THINK: A BIT MUCH.

▼ *verb*

To be insulted or outdone.

❝ *Dang, you just got carried! Why did you let that third grader talk to you like that?"*

 WANT MORE INFO?
THINK: DISSED.

USAGE NOTE: This term originated in ballroom culture.

CARTA

▼ *idiom*

SEE **FACE**

CATEGORY

▼ *noun*

A division of ballroom competitions with strict rules surrounding a particular theme.

SEE ALSO
"History Lesson: The Ballroom Scene," *p.308*

 ❝ *The category is . . . Runway. Calling all Stars, Statements, and Legends. Let me see you walk, Miss Honey!"*

 WANT MORE INFO?
THINK: A ROUND OF WALKERS SERVING THEIR BEST LOOKS ON THE RUNWAY TO CLAIM AWARDS AND THE TITLE.

DID YOU KNOW In ballroom culture, competition categories were created to give gay and trans people of color the opportunity to embody unique identities—Butch Queens, Femme Queens, Butches, Women, Drag Queens, Trans Men, Female Figures, and Male Figures—and walk in popular categories like Realness with a Twist, Runway, Vogue Femme, Face, Bizarre, and Body, to name a few.

CD

▼ *noun*

SEE **CROSS-DRESSER**

CELESBIAN

▼ *noun*

A female celebrity known or reputed to be a lesbian.

❝ *There are just so many to name them all but Hayley Kiyoko, Taylor Schilling, Ali Krieger, Lena Waithe, Kate Moennig, and Samira Wiley are my favorite celesbians.*❞

 WANT MORE INFO? *THINK:* **A QUEER WOMAN IN POP CULTURE AND MEDIA.**

CH

▼ *exclamation*

A sound made by emphasizing a hard "ch" sound to dismiss an action or a thought, often accompanied by a smirk and/or an eye roll. Alternate spellings include "chu" or "chi," as the term is derived from CHILD. The term TUH can also be used.

❝

CHRISTOPHER: *I am so excited to go vegan! Only plant-based foods now until forevermore. Want to join me?*

QUINTON: *Chu! I am not about to live on just rabbit food. I love hamburgers toooooooo much!*

 WANT MORE INFO? *THINK:* **A HARD** *NO.*

USAGE NOTE: This term originated in the Black gay community. It has been appropriated by the larger LGBTQIA+ community and mainstream culture.

CHAPSTICK LESBIAN

▼ *noun*

A gay girl or woman who has a muted feminine sensibility. The term was coined as an alternative to "lipstick lesbian," for women who present in a feminine way but prefer casual clothes and ChapStick over feminine clothes and makeup.

SEE ALSO

ANDROGYNY, SOFT BUTCH, "The Lesbian Spectrum," *p. 255*

❝ *I like ChapStick lesbians. There's nothing cooler than watching her code and create a website in her favorite Urban Outfitters hoodie."*

 WANT MORE INFO? *THINK:* **THAT CUTE, ATHLETIC, SMART, SUPER-COOL GIRL YOU HAVE A CRUSH ON.**

USAGE NOTE: This term originated in the lesbian community.

This term is a reference to the popular early 2000s television show *The L Word* (and the new series *The L Word: Generation Q*).

❝ *I created my version of the chart, using every lesbian in Omaha!"*

 WANT MORE INFO? *THINK:* **THE LITTLE BLACK BOOK OF LESBIAN, BI, AND QUEER CRUSHES.**

The Chart   ▼

CHART, THE

▼ *noun*

An extensive diagram representing the relationships and physical connections between lesbian, bisexual, and queer girls or women within a community.

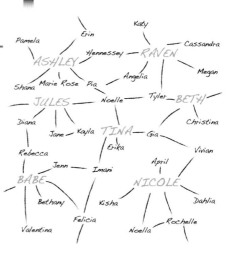

THE QUEENS' ENGLISH

CHILD

▼ exclamation

A term used to express dissatisfaction or dismissal of an action or thought. Alternate spellings include "chile" or "churld."

66 *Chile, this show is so boring and it's making me fall asleep. Can we see what's good on Disney+ or Hulu?"*

 WANT MORE INFO?
THINK: **"UH-UH, NO WAY!"**

USAGE NOTE: This term originated in Black American culture. It has been appropriated by the LGBTQIA+ community and mainstream culture.

▲ **Child**

CHILD BOO

▼ idiom

Used to signal a disagreement or lack of interest with a particular matter. The term "child, please" can also be used.

66 *Child boo! You know I am the best dancer at the studio! Look at how many followers I have on TikTok."*

 WANT MORE INFO?
THINK: **A DISAPPROVING SHAKE OF THE HEAD.**

USAGE NOTE: This term originated in Black American culture and is commonly used in the Black gay and queer community. It has been appropriated by mainstream culture.

CHILDREN, THE

▼ noun

Young gay and trans members of the ballroom scene.

Young members of the LGBTQIA+ community.

SEE ALSO

KIDS, THE, "History Lesson: The Ballroom Scene," *p. 308*

66 *The ballroom scene is a family support system for young QTPOC who need it. Ballroom houses—like House of Chanel, House of Amazon, and the Royal House of Nina Oricci—have house mothers and/or house fathers who serve as mentors to the younger queer members known as 'the children.'"*

 WANT MORE INFO? *THINK:* **YOUNG, WILD, AND FREE QUEER REVOLUTIONARIES.**

 USAGE NOTE: This term originated in ballroom culture. It has been appropriated by the larger LGBTQIA+ community and mainstream culture.

CHOP

▼ *verb*

To dismiss, eliminate, or reject.

66 *You just got chopped, Miss Girl! You are the weakest link. Goodbye!"*

 WANT MORE INFO? *THINK:* **REJECTED.**

USAGE NOTE: This term is commonly used in ballroom culture.

DID YOU KNOW "Chop" is used in the ballroom scene when judges decide to eliminate a walker from the competition. The term can be used by judges, opposing contestants, or members of the audience to provoke D-R-A-M-A.

CHOSEN FAMILY

▼ *noun*

Individuals who are not biologically or legally related who deliberately choose to support and nurture each other like family. The word CIRCLE can also be used.

SEE ALSO

DRAG FAMILY, HOUSE CULTURE

❝ *Coming out as nonbinary can be a very confusing process. But I was really able to feel rooted, energized, and supported by my chosen family."*

—DARIELLE FERNÁNDEZ

 WANT MORE INFO? *THINK:* **FAMILY NOT BY BLOOD, BUT BY HEART.**

DID YOU KNOW Many gay, trans, and queer people have experienced rejection from their biological families, making chosen families an important part of the LGBTQIA+ community. This social family unit plays a vital role in providing love, mentorship, and support to a young queer person, as well as providing access to LGBTQIA+ history and community resources.

▼　　　　Chosen Family

CHOSEN NAME

▼ *noun*

A name chosen by an individual that differs from their given name at birth. In the LGBTQIA+ community, a chosen name often helps in affirming an individual's gender identity and expression.

SEE ALSO

GIVEN NAME, DEADNAME

❝ *My chosen name and my pronouns make me feel whole. They validate who I am.*❞

 WANT MORE INFO?
THINK: **A PERSON'S NAME. PERIOD.**

USAGE NOTE: This term is commonly used in the transgender, nonbinary, and gender nonconforming communities. Some young queer people are unable to legally change their name because their guardian(s) will not grant permission. Other reasons can include costs, fees, and legal issues. Regardless, an individual's chosen name is their rightful name.

CHUB

▼ *noun*

A body label used to refer to a gay boy or man who is large, plump, or even overweight. The term "chubby" may also be used. This person may also identify as being part of the gay chub subculture.

SEE ALSO

"Help! What Type of Gay Am I?," *p. 203*

❝ *Yes, indeed, I am a chub! I'm an adorable lovable big teddy bear with a heart of gold.*❞

 WANT MORE INFO?
THINK: **HUSKY.**

USAGE NOTE: This term originated in the white gay male community.

▲ _____ Chub

CIRCLE

▼ *noun*

SEE **CHOSEN FAMILY, FAMILY**

CISGENDER

▼ *adjective*

Describing a person whose gender identity matches the gender they were assigned at birth. The term can be shortened to "cis."

❝ *My straight-as-straight-can-come parents assume that everyone experiences gender identity in the same way. We don't! My experience as a genderfluid twelve-year-old is just different, okay.*"

 WANT MORE INFO? *THINK:* **GENDER IDENTITY IS THE SAME AS ONE'S BIRTH CERTIFICATE.**

CISGENDER PRIVILEGE

▼ *noun*

The inherent rights and immunities granted to cisgender people. Can be abbreviated as "cis privilege."

SEE ALSO
MALE PRIVILEGE, PRIVILEGE, STRAIGHT PRIVILEGE, WHITE PRIVILEGE

❝ *Cisgender privilege is absolutely seen in sports. Why can't ALL girls play on the girls' sports teams? Yes, that includes trans girls! ALL GIRLS!*"

 WANT MORE INFO? *THINK:* **THE ENTITLEMENT OF CISGENDER PEOPLE.**

CISHET

▼ *adjective*

An abbreviation for

"cisgender heterosexual." The term "cishetero" can also be used.

"

MRS. GLEEN: *Well, well, well . . . look at all these supportive cishet men discussing diversity, sexuality, and gender equality! I'm impressed.*

MX. CHO: *Are my ears hearing what I think they're hearing? Good for you, Mark and Tom. I'll be looking forward to seeing you bring more diversity on our school's board and making real change here.*

 WANT MORE INFO? *THINK:* **CIS AND STRAIGHT.**

CISSEXISM

▼ *noun*

The belief that there are only two genders based on one's sexual anatomy (male

and female), that these genders are assigned at birth and are immutable. This belief results in the oppression of genderqueer, agender, nonbinary, and transgender people, among others.

 We are speaking out against cissexism. Equality is equality. Period."

WANT MORE INFO? *THINK:* **SOCIAL BELIEF THAT ONLY MALE AND FEMALE SEXES EXIST AND THEY CANNOT BE CHANGED.**

CIVIL UNION

▼ *noun*

SEE **DOMESTIC PARTNERSHIP**

THE QUEENS' ENGLISH

CLAPBACK

▼ *noun*

A quick, witty response to criticism.

"

HADIYAH: *Did you just take off your shoes, Lisa? It smells in here! Where is the air freshener?*

LISA: *It does smell awful in here, but I think it's because you opened you mouth and let out your dragon breath!*

NIKKI: *Okay, okay. Enough of the twin sibling spew. But good clapback this time, Lisa!*

 WANT MORE INFO?
THINK: **A SOCK-IT-TO-YA REBUTTAL.**

 USAGE NOTE: This term originated in Black American culture and is commonly used in the Black gay and queer community. It has been appropriated by mainstream culture.

CLOCK

▼ *verb*

To take notice of someone or something.

" *I clocked him as soon as he took out his Nintendo Switch at the lunchroom table. Principal Dean said, 'No electronics at school.'"*

 WANT MORE INFO?
THINK: **DO A DOUBLE TAKE.**

To take notice of someone and identify them as gay. The term READ can also be used.

" *My math teacher totally clocked me when my* All Boys Aren't Blue *book fell out of my book bag. He stopped me before fifth period and said that was one of his favorite books."*

 WANT MORE INFO?
THINK: **TO PEG SOMEONE AS QUEER.**

To recognize a transgender person as trans, usually when they are trying to appear cisgender. The term SPOOKED can also be used.

SEE ALSO
PASSING

❝I hate when there is no all-gender bathroom for me to use! I can't get clocked. It's not safe.❞

 WANT MORE INFO? *THINK:* **TO BE SEEN AS TRANS, DESPITE TRYING TO BLEND IN AS CIS.**

USAGE NOTE: This term may have negative connotations for many queer, transgender, and gender nonconforming people.

 DID YOU KNOW A large number of transgender students are denied access to restrooms that affirm their gender identity, so many trans youth avoid using public or school bathrooms in fear of being mistreated. Due to the harassment trans people have endured and the cultural pressure to appear cisgender, being clocked can often be a disappointing or scary experience for a trans person. Not all trans and gender diverse people, however, feel the need to "pass" as cisgender, and many are comfortable shaking up others' perceptions of gender norms.

CLOSET

▼ *idiom*

Mostly used in the phrase "in the closet" as a metaphor to describe individuals who do not publicly disclose their sexual orientation or gender identity.

RELATED
CLOSETED *adjective*

SEE ALSO
COME OUT, "Coming Out 101," *p. 38*

❝Freedom is too enormous to be slipped under a closet door.❞

—HARVEY MILK

 WANT MORE INFO? *THINK:* **UNABLE TO EXPRESS OR EMBRACE ONE'S QUEERNESS IN PUBLIC.**

CLOSET CASE

▼ *noun*

An individual who denies their sexuality or gender identity. The terms "closet queen" or "closet queer" can also be used.

SEE ALSO
"Coming Out 101," *p. 38*

66 *That closet case is never going to come out."*

 WANT MORE INFO? *THINK:* **COMPLETELY HIDING FROM ONE'S QUEERNESS.**

 USAGE NOTE: This term can be considered derogatory. Please be aware that this term can be considered mature.

COERCIVE PASSING

▼ *noun*

The coercion of a queer individual by an outside force to pass as or claim a gender or sexual orientation that might not align with the individual's identity.

SEE ALSO
INVISIBILITY, ERASURE

66 *We must support and empower our LGBTQIA+ youth. Their identity is valid just like any other child. We DO NOT need to change them! Coercive passing is absolutely unnecessary and we must work to end this by prioritizing educational resources on the spectrum of identity and eliminating society's negative attitudes toward the queer community."*

 WANT MORE INFO? *THINK:* **ACTIVELY PUSHING SOMEONE TO APPEAR AS SOMETHING THEY ARE NOT.**

COERCIVE SURGICAL GENDER REASSIGNMENT

▼ *noun*

The forcible alteration of someone's phenotype (the

physical expression of an individual's sexual organs) without the individual's consent or because the person was misinformed and/or denied the proper medical services. This tends to happen to intersex children.

❝ *Coercive surgical gender reassignment is an unnecessary procedure that forces the surgical reshaping of a person's body when there is absolutely nothing wrong with being intersex."*

 WANT MORE INFO? *THINK:* **SURGICALLY ASSIGNING A GENDER TO AN INTERSEX PERSON WHO HAS NO AGENCY.**

COIFFED

▼ *adjective*

Carefully fashioned and exquisite in presentation. The term is most commonly used in reference to lavishly styled hair but can also be used in other contexts.

SEE ALSO
DONE, LAID

❝ *I love getting my hair done by Mrs. Fernanda. She always leaves my hair silky and coiffed."*

 WANT MORE INFO? *THINK:* **STYLE SO DIVINE IT'S EASY, BREEZY, AND BEAUTIFUL.**

▲ Coiffed

COIN

▼ *noun*

Money.

❝ *Girl, I will call you back because I need do my chores. My nana pays me twenty dollars every time I make her bed and sweep the floor. I need these coins to buy my electric scooter!"*

 WANT MORE INFO? *THINK:* CASH.

 USAGE NOTE: This term originated in Black American culture and is commonly used in the Black gay and queer community. It has been appropriated by mainstream culture.

COME FOR

▼ *verb*

To point out someone's faults or flaws.

❝ *Mama is about to come for you! You still haven't cleaned your room yet?"*

 WANT MORE INFO? *THINK: "I'LL GET YOU, MY PRETTY!"*

 USAGE NOTE: This term originated in the Black gay community and is commonly used in the larger queer and trans people of color (QTPOC) community. It has been appropriated by mainstream culture.

COME OUT

▼ *idiom*

In the LGBTQIA+ community, this phrase is most commonly used in reference to a person sharing their sexual orientation, romantic orientation, gender expression, and/or gender identity publicly. The phrase "come out of the closet" can also be used.

> SEE ALSO
> **CLOSET, OUT, "Coming Out 101," *p. 38***

❝ *The most important thing is for you to come out when you feel ready."*

WANT MORE INFO?
THINK: ADMITTING, ACCEPTING, AND EMBRACING WHO WE ARE TO OURSELVES AND OTHERS.

DID YOU KNOW National Coming Out Day (NCOD) is observed each year on October 11. It was first celebrated in 1988 to observe the anniversary of the 1987 National March on Washington for Lesbian and Gay Rights. Robert Eichberg and Jean O'Leary are credited as the founders of this day of awareness. Artist Keith Haring designed the first poster for NCOD—an image that is still highly recognized.

COME THROUGH

▼ *idiom*

An accolade used to affirm something fabulous.

❝ *Come THROUGH with this baked mac and cheese! I can't believe you made this, it's so good!"*

 WANT MORE INFO?
THINK: VERY IMPRESSED.

USAGE NOTE: This term originated in the Black gay community and is commonly used in the larger queer and trans people of color (QTPOC) community. It has been appropriated by mainstream culture.

Come Through ▼

COMMENTATOR

▼ noun

The emcee for a ballroom ball or other event. This person uses creativity, leadership, and improvisational skills to keep a competition energized and organized.

"

COMMENTATOR *(into bejeweled microphone): Walk for meeee. Destroy for meeee. Kat! Kat! Kat to kat to kat! Kitty kat! Hold that pose for me!*

 WANT MORE INFO? *THINK:* **ANNOUNCER OF A COMPETITION.**

DID YOU KNOW A commentator is often considered the crown jewel of a ball because of the dynamic level of showmanship the host position requires. They are usually a leader within the ballroom community and set the tone for competitions. Most commentators are skilled freestylers and DJs. Well-known commentators include Jack Mizrahi, Selvin Khan, Kevin JZ Prodigy, Junior LaBeija, and Jay Blahnik, to name a few.

▲   Commentator

COMMITTED

▼ adjective

Dedicated to presenting a particular behavior or style.

" *Have you seen Ru Paw's Instagram? Ha! That kitty is committed to a fierce look every time!"*

 WANT MORE INFO? *THINK:* **"I PLEDGE MY HONOR TO THIS CHOICE AND ONLY THIS CHOICE, SO HELP ME."**

CONTOUR

▼ *verb*

To enhance or sharpen the structure and features of one's face with the aid of cosmetics.

❝ *I want to contour like Sasha Velour!"*

 WANT MORE INFO?
THINK: CHEEKBONES FOR DAYS.

▲　Contour

CONVERSION THERAPY

▼ *noun*

A social, pseudoscientific, and sometimes religious approach that attempts to forcibly change a person's sexuality and/or gender expression from anywhere on the queer spectrum to heterosexual and/or cisgender.

❝ *If the American Psychological Association is against conversion therapy because it is harmful and actually doesn't work, then we should actively listen."*

 WANT MORE INFO?
THINK: A "MEDICAL" TREATMENT USED TO "MAKE QUEER PEOPLE STRAIGHT."

CROSS-DRESSER OR CROSSDRESSER

▼ *noun*

A person who dresses as another gender. The term CD can also be used.

RELATED
CROSS-DRESS *verb*

SEE ALSO
TRANSVESTITE

❝ *Dan is a cross-dresser not because he is gay or wants to change his gender, but because he feels pretty as a woman.*❞

 WANT MORE INFO?
THINK: "I AM SINCERE IN MY PREFERENCE FOR MY MEN'S CLOTHES—I DO NOT WEAR THEM TO BE SENSATIONAL. I THINK I AM MORE ALLURING IN THESE CLOTHES."
—MARLENE DIETRICH

USAGE NOTE: It should not be assumed that cross-dressing and sexual orientation are related. A person who identifies as a cross-dresser does not identify as transgender.

DID YOU KNOW In the late 1800s, public decency laws banned citizens from appearing publicly in clothes that did not align with their assigned gender at birth. By the 1960s, cross-dressing laws allowed police officers to actively target the gay community. Women were arrested for wearing fewer than three pieces of "female" clothing, and men faced jail time if caught in dresses or skirts.

CROSS ORIENTATION

▼ *noun*

Describes a person who has a romantic attraction and a physical attraction that is different. The term MIXED ORIENTATION can also be used.

❝ *Someone can be physically attracted to just boys, but romantically attracted to boys, girls, nonbinary people, and no label people. This is called cross orientation.*❞

WANT MORE INFO?
THINK: SOMETIMES WE ARE BOTH PHYSICALLY AND ROMANTICALLY ATTRACTED TO THE SAME TYPES OF PEOPLE AND SOMETIMES WE ARE NOT.

CROSS-SEX HORMONE THERAPY

▼ *noun*

SEE **HORMONE REPLACEMENT THERAPY**

CUB

▼ *noun*

A young gay, bisexual, or queer man with a large or stocky body and visible facial and body hair.

SEE ALSO
"Help! What Type of Gay Am I?," p. 203

❝ *I love to see cubs being mentored by bears. It's important for gay youth to learn about the history and culture of the queer community."*

 WANT MORE INFO?
THINK: YOUNG GAY BOY WHO WILL GROW UP TO BE A BEAR.

 USAGE NOTE: This term originated in the white gay male community.

▲   **Cub**

CULTURAL APPROPRIATION

▼ noun

The adoption of a marginalized culture's styles, traditions, and/or words by members of a more dominant culture without permission or awareness of their origin.

SEE ALSO
APPROPRIATE, MISAPPROPRIATE, REAPPROPRIATE

❝ Have you seen Amandla Stenberg's 'Don't Cash Crop on My Cornrows' video? She calls out the abuse and misuse of Black culture. It's a lesson in Cultural Appropriation 101. Basically, if you ain't Black but want to rock braids, vogue dance on TikTok, and rap to every popular song, take a moment and remember what Amandla said. There is a difference between cultural appreciation and cultural appropriation. Honor the culture!❞

 WANT MORE INFO? *THINK:* **VIOLATION OF INTELLECTUAL AND ARTISTIC PROPERTY OF A PARTICULAR CULTURE.**

CULTURALLY QUEER

▼ adjective

Describing a person's identity that is culturally embedded in queer history, traditions, lifestyles, and pride.

❝ Because many of us have been part of the queer community since we were babies, we have grown up in a culturally queer community, like going to Pride marches, consuming queer art, and being raised by our queer parents and friends.❞ — ÁNGEL MARTIN

 WANT MORE INFO? *THINK:* **IMMERSED IN LGBTQIA+ CULTURE.**

Culturally Queer

CUT

▼ *verb*

To speak with sharpness or harshness intended to hurt another's feelings.

SEE ALSO
READ

 66 *Why are you always trying to cut someone when we are playing video games? Just play fair or don't play at all!"*

WANT MORE INFO?
THINK: TO VERBALLY ASSAULT.

CUTE FOR YOU

▼ *idiom*

A phrase used as a compliment or affirmation that something—be it related to style, attitude, or some other decision—is specifically suited for a particular person. This compliment can be given in a condescending or snarky tone, making it either a playful tease or a backhanded compliment.

 66 *Oh, purple is cute for you, but I like the dress better in this glittery gold."*

WANT MORE INFO?
THINK: NICE FOR YOU, BUT NOT FOR ME.

 USAGE NOTE: This term is commonly used in the Black gay community and the larger queer and trans people of color (QTPOC) community.

CYBERBULLYING

▼ *verb*

A form of bullying—negative and harmful comments, posts, and other content—that is experienced online, such as on social media, in gaming spaces, in general apps, on online forums, and via computer, tablet, and phone SMS/text messages.

SEE ALSO
"Gaybashing Must Stop!" p. 171

"Somebody made another meme of me tripping down the stairs and now everyone is laughing at me. I have anxiety and feel embarrassed, but I'm not going to tell a teacher because they don't think cyberbullying is a real thing."

 WANT MORE INFO? *THINK:* **DELIBERATELY SHARING MEAN CONTENT ONLINE TO HURT SOMEONE'S FEELINGS.**

Common Pronouns 101

PRONOUNS ARE PERSONAL identifiers that validate and support a person's gender identity. The pronouns listed below are singular pronouns—pronouns that refer to a single individual.

While this list is not exhaustive, the pronouns below are commonly used to represent a range of gender identities, including male, female, transgender, genderqueer, genderfluid, nonbinary, gender nonconforming, and other expressions.

SUBJECT	OBJECT	POSSESIVE	REFLEXIVE
He	Him	His	Himself
She	Her	Hers	Herself
They	Them	Theirs	Themselves
Sie	Sie	Hirs	Hirself
Ze	Hir	Hirs	Hirself
Zie	Zir	Zirs	Zirself
Xe	Xem	Xyrs	Xemself
Ey/e	Em	Eirs	Eirself/Emself
Ve	Ver	Vers	Verself
Ve	Vem	Vir	Virself
Fae	Faer	Faers	Faerself
Tey	Ter	Ters	Terself

Physical characteristics may not always determine a person's pronouns, so it is best to respectfully ask someone's pronouns if you are unsure. Do not feel ashamed to ask! Your thoughtfulness is appreciated. It is important to understand that many gender-inclusive pronouns are used to limit binarism or otherwise assume someone's gender. It is not uncommon for a person to use more than one set of pronouns, like she/they or he/she, and/or use neopronouns like ze, xe, or fae to affirm their identity. Pronouns are powerful identifiers, and misgendering someone is problematic and taken very seriously. If you use the wrong pronoun to identify someone, offer a sincere apology, brush it off, and keep working at it until it becomes second nature. Let's all continue to encourage, learn, and celebrate the many ways human identity is expressed.

Dd

DADDY

▼ noun

A man, butch lesbian, or masc-identifying person who practices the role of provider and protector in a queer relationship. Typically, this partner exhibits an attractive, confident attitude and is the dominant one in the partnership.

> SEE ALSO
> **BUTCH/FEMME RELATIONSHIP, MAMA AND PAPA RELATIONSHIP, ZADDY**

❝ My mom always calls her girlfriend 'Daddy' and then they get all mushy! Gosh, get a room!"

 WANT MORE INFO?
THINK: THE CHARMING AND GOOD-LOOKING ONE IN CHARGE.

DAIRY

▼ adjective

Describing a Caucasian gay, bisexual, or queer person.

❝ Almost ninety degrees and sunny today, huh? I'm gonna need extra SPF 50 for this dairy skin."

 WANT MORE INFO?
THINK: WHITE.

USAGE NOTE: This term may be considered a stereotype or derogatory.

DANDY

▼ adjective

Stylish and well-groomed. This term was originally used to describe fashionable men who were thought to be gay or queer in some capacity. The term has since evolved to also include stylish, buttoned-up butch lesbians.

▼ noun

A dandy person, regardless of gender.

" Suspenders and a bow tie? Yes, please! Dandy, if I do."

 WANT MORE INFO? *THINK:* **WELL-GROOMED, MASCULINE PEOPLE WHO FAVOR SUITS AND TIES.**

DAPPER

▼ adjective

Well-groomed and trim in style and appearance. Traditionally used to describe men, this term has been adopted by the lesbian community as well.

" It's time for the WNBA All-Stars Orange Carpet event! Dap, dap to them dapper girls looking so fresh in those fitted suits."

 WANT MORE INFO? *THINK:* **BUTTONED-UP AND HANDSOME.**

DEAD

▼ adjective

Not important; over, done.

" You are still on that topic? Girl, it's dead."

 WANT MORE INFO? *THINK:* **IRRELEVANT.**

Disbelieving or shocked.

66 *Oh, no! A pop quiz, again? I am literally dead."*

 WANT MORE INFO?
THINK: STUNNED.

USAGE NOTE: This term originated in Black American culture and is commonly used in the Black gay and queer community. It has been appropriated by mainstream culture.

DEADNAME

▼ *noun*

The former name of a transgender, nonbinary, or genderqueer person who has changed their name to affirm their gender identity.

▼ *verb*

To publicly use a transgender person's birth name instead of their chosen name.

66 *I want to change schools, now! I hate being misgendered or deadnamed. If I'm at a new school, they won't do that because they won't know the old me!"*

 WANT MORE INFO?
THINK: THE BIRTH NAME OF A TRANS OR NONBINARY INDIVIDUAL THAT IS NO LONGER USED.

USAGE NOTE: This term has negative connotations for many queer and trans people. Please ask for and use a person's chosen name and pronouns.

DID YOU KNOW Transgender students are able to change their name or gender marker on their school documents under the Family Educational Rights and Privacy Act (FERPA). This law protects the privacy of student educational records, and parents or legal guardians can amend their child's records if the information is inaccurate, misleading, or in violation of the student's rights of privacy.

DEATHDROP

▼ *noun*

SEE **DIP**

DEMI

▼ *adjective*

A French prefix meaning "half" or "partial."

❝ *'Demi' is often used as a signifier to describe a sexuality or gender identity that is not solely on one end of the spectrum but floats somewhere in between the binary."*

 WANT MORE INFO?
THINK: PART, SEMI, SORT OF.

DEMIBOY

▼ *noun*

Gender identity label for people who only partially identify with the terms "boy," "man," or "male." They may or may not identify with another gender in addition to feeling partly male. The terms DEMIMAN and DEMIMALE can also be used.

❝ *Every time I fill out a student survey form, I have to mark my gender as 'other' and I write in 'demiboy.'"*

 WANT MORE INFO?
THINK: A PERSON WHO IDENTIFIES PARTLY AS BOY/MAN/MALE.

USAGE NOTE: This term is commonly used in the intersex, transgender, nonbinary, and gender nonconforming communities.

DEMIFEMALE

▼ *noun*

SEE **DEMIGIRL**

DEMIGENDER

▼ *adjective*

An umbrella term for nonbinary gender identities.

When "demi" is used as a prefix to a particular gender identity, it creates a new label for people who only identify partially with that gender identity.

❝ *As kids, we're told to be either a boy or girl. I want to explore who I am and I feel that I could identify as demigender.*"

 WANT MORE INFO? *THINK*: **DESCRIBING SOMEONE WITH A PARTIAL CONNECTION TO A SPECIFIC GENDER.**

USAGE NOTE: This term is commonly used in the intersex, transgender, nonbinary, and gender nonconforming communities.

Demigender

DEMIGIRL

▼ *noun*

Gender identity label for people who only partially identify with the terms "girl," "woman," or "female." They may or may not identify with another gender in addition to feeling partly female. The terms DEMIWOMAN and DEMIFEMALE can also be used.

❝ *Hi, coders! I'm Jess and I'm excited to be your youth assistant this summer. I'm from Boise, Idaho, I identify as a demigirl, and I use she/zie pronouns.*"

 WANT MORE INFO? *THINK*: **A PERSON WHO IDENTIFIES PARTLY AS GIRL/WOMAN/FEMALE.**

USAGE NOTE: This term is commonly used in the intersex, transgender, nonbinary, and gender nonconforming communities.

DEMIMALE

▼ *noun*

SEE **DEMIBOY**

DEMIMAN

▼ *noun*

SEE **DEMIBOY**

DEMINONBINARY

▼ *adjective*

Gender identity label for people who only partially identify as nonbinary. They may identify with another gender, often a binary gender, in addition to feeling partly nonbinary.

❝As deminonbinary, I have the ability to release myself from trying to fit in. I use she/her pronouns and sky/skyself noun-self pronouns. I feel good about how I express my identity.❞

 WANT MORE INFO?
THINK: **A PERSON WHO IDENTIFIES AS PARTLY NONBINARY.**

USAGE NOTE: This term is commonly used in the transgender, nonbinary, and gender nonconforming communities.

DEMISEXUAL

▼ *adjective*

Experiencing physical attraction only when a strong emotional connection is present.

▼ *noun*

A demisexual person. This is a label used to describe a sexual orientation where a person may only show physical affection toward others if there is a strong emotional bond.

❝I'm a demisexual person. I don't want to hug or hold hands unless I know I am REALLY connected with that person. I usually feel *butterflies in my stomach when that happens."*

 WANT MORE INFO? THINK: TRUST AND CONNECTION ARE MOST IMPORTANT IN BUILDING A RELATIONSHIP.

▲   Demisexual

DEMIWOMAN

▼ *noun*

SEE **DEMIGIRL**

DETRANSITION

▼ *verb*

To reverse the process

of transitioning from one gender to another. A transgender person may stop any medications or reverse surgery in order to return—in some capacity— to a previously assigned gender.

❝ *Barnes and Noble's book of the month pick is* Detransition, Baby: A Novel *by Torrey Peters.*

 WANT MORE INFO? THINK: RETURN TO PRE- TRANSITION GENDER.

USAGE NOTE: The process of detransitioning may not always indicate that the person does not identify as transgender or gender nonconforming. The decision may have been made to ensure a person's well-being and safety.

DFAB

▼ *adjective*

SEE **AFAB**

DIE

▼ verb

To be extremely surprised, happy, or shocked. Often used in the phrases "I die," "I would die," or "I'm dying."

SEE ALSO
DEAD

66

SHARON: *I heard someone is going to pull the fire alarm at seventh period so we can get early dismissal from school today!*

DEON: *Oh my goddess, I would diiiiie! That means we'll miss Mrs. Mackintosh's social science test! YEEEEEEEEESSSSSSSSS!*

 WANT MORE INFO?
***THINK*: TO BE THUNDERSTRUCK!**

DIESEL DYKE

▼ noun

An overtly masculine lesbian who is characterized by an occupation or hobby involving machinery.

66 *Hands down, the coolest diesel dykes are Dykes on Bikes."*

 WANT MORE INFO?
***THINK*: A LESBIAN IN WORK BOOTS AND HEAVY, DURABLE CLOTHES.**

USAGE NOTE: This term originated in the white lesbian community. The term "dyke" was once a derogatory slur for lesbians but has been reclaimed by some of the LGBTQIA+ community. It may still have negative connotations for some people.

DID YOU KNOW Dykes on Bikes (DOB) is a lesbian motorcycle club that was founded during the San Francisco Pride Parade in 1976. DOB now has twenty-two chapters around the world, and these women bikers take particular pride in their strength and masculinity. DOB is the annual riding leader in the San Francisco Pride Parade as well as many other Pride parades and festivals around the world.

DIP

▼ *noun*

An elemental part of vogue dance, popular in ballroom culture, when a walker drops to the floor while maneuvering their body—keeping time with the music—into a pose with the back arched and one leg tucked beneath them. The term DEATHDROP is often used in mainstream and commercial dance settings.

 Oh, girl, she did the fiercest dip! Even her ponytail levitated!"

🤔 **WANT MORE INFO?**
THINK: YOUTUBE LEIOMY

MALDONADO—THE WONDER WOMAN OF VOGUE—IT'LL CHANGE YOU.

 USAGE NOTE: This term originated in ballroom culture. It has been appropriated by mainstream culture.

DISABLISM

▼ *noun*

Discrimination, prejudice, and unfair treatment against disabled people.

 Many able-bodied people don't understand the concerns and challenges people with disabilities face daily. Disablism is unfair and it hurts us."

🤔 **WANT MORE INFO?**
THINK: UNEQUAL TREATMENT OF PEOPLE BECAUSE OF A DISABILITY.

DISABILITY JUSTICE

▼ *noun*

The complex way disability, race, gender, and class overlap or intersect; the importance of focusing on the presence of disabled communities within the larger framework of society and work to dismantle the complexity of ableism.

❝ *We are students for DISABILITY JUSTICE! Disability rights are civil rights!"*

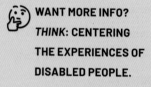 **WANT MORE INFO?** *THINK:* **CENTERING THE EXPERIENCES OF DISABLED PEOPLE.**

CHLOE O. DAVIS

DID YOU KNOW The term "disability justice" was coined in 2005 by three disabled queer women of color, Patty Berne, Mia Mingus, and Stacey Milbern, to center the views of disabled people and directly address ableism. Disability Pride Month is celebrated during the month of July to commemorate the Americans with Disabilities Act (ADA) and empower the voices of disabled people and our diverse humanity.

DISCREET

▼ *adjective*

Being private with one's sexual orientation or gender identity.

SEE ALSO
CLOSET

66 *Look, this has to be discreet. I don't want anyone at camp to know I'm trans. You promise not to tell anyone? I can trust you, right?"*

 WANT MORE INFO? *THINK:* **KEEP IT A SECRET . . . SHHHHH.**

DISCRIMINATION

▼ *noun*

Unequal and unfair treatment against a particular person, group, or community based on race, gender, class, ability, gender, sexual orientation, among other categories.

66 *I know it may feel uncomfortable sometimes. But . . . umm, when we have conversations about discrimination in school, we, uh, learn how to better respect each other. Everyone should feel valued, right?"*

WANT MORE INFO?
THINK: CREATING
BARRIERS THAT MAKE IT
HARDER FOR SOMEONE
TO ACHIEVE THEIR BEST.

DID YOU KNOW For generations, youth have been at the forefront in advocating for equality, inclusion, and safety. From the civil rights lunch counter sit-ins of the 1960s to the rise of Black Lives Matter marches in the 2010s/2020s, and from the Vietnam War protests in the 1960s/1970s to March for Our Lives in 2018, youth-led activism has made substantial impacts, changing the world for the good. Our youths' passion and courage to fight against racial discrimination, gender inequality, socioeconomic health disparities, xenophobia, and ableism is a superpower that should be celebrated.

DISHONORABLE DISCHARGE

▼ *noun*

The dismissal of someone from the armed forces because of immoral behavior. In the past, many gay, bisexual, and queer servicepeople were discharged because of their sexuality. The term DONALD DUCK can also be used.

❝ *Did you read about the men who were kicked out of the army back in the sixties who are fighting to change their dishonorable discharges to 'honorable'? Their lives were ruined. They deserve to be recognized and receive benefits.*❞

 WANT MORE INFO?
THINK: NO GAY SAILORS
ALLOWED.

DIVA

▼ *noun*

A person who is recognized for being extraordinary, fabulous, and unapologetically fierce. While this term was originally used for women, it can be used to describe people of all gender identities.

❝The LGBTQIA+ community would like to present the Iconic Diva Award to . . . Regina King, Lady Gaga, Selena Gomez, and Michelle Obama, for speaking out and standing in solidarity with trans girls' and women's rights!❞

 WANT MORE INFO?
THINK: SINGING BEYONCÉ'S LYRIC, "I'M A, I'M A, A DIVA!"

Someone who is demanding, conceited, or high-maintenance.

❝Gray is being a diva. I know they are the classroom leader this week, but this bossy I-don't-care-what-anyone-thinks attitude needs to go!❞

 WANT MORE INFO?
THINK: A DIG FOR SOMEONE WHO IS DIFFICULT.

DIVA FEMME

▼ *noun*

SEE **HIGH FEMME**

DMAB

▼ *adjective*

SEE **AMAB**

DOING SHOWS

▼ *idiom*

Blatantly acting out of character. The term STUNT can also be used.

" *We have a substitute teacher today? Oh, no! They won't stand a chance! I bet Kevin is going to come in here doing shows."*

 WANT MORE INFO?
THINK: BEING *EXTRA*.

USAGE NOTE: This term originated in ballroom culture.

DO IT

▼ *verb*

To encourage someone to continue to display greatness or to pay a compliment.

" *You're already doing high school curriculum in the seventh grade? Oh, do it, girl! Talk about brainpower!"*

 WANT MORE INFO?
THINK: TO GIVE A VERBAL HIGH FIVE.

USAGE NOTE: This term originated in Black American culture and is commonly used in the Black gay and queer community. It has been appropriated by mainstream culture.

DOMESTIC PARTNERSHIP

▼ *noun*

A relationship between two people who live and share a domestic life together but are not married. The term CIVIL UNION can also be used.

" *Before marriage equality, the only option for my dads to be together was through a domestic partnership. They have been legally married for nine years, but really together for sixteen years."*

 WANT MORE INFO?
THINK: COMMON-LAW MARRIAGE FOR THE GAYS.

DOMINANT

▼ *adjective*

The authoritative or influential role in a relationship. Often abbreviated as DOM.

SEE ALSO

MAMA AND PAPA RELATIONSHIP, SUBMISSIVE

---

66 *Some people think the dominant partner has to be masculine, supporting traditional gender roles, but that isn't necessarily the case. Femininity can be just as dominant."*

 WANT MORE INFO? *THINK:* **THE BOSS.**

DONALD DUCK

▼ *noun*

SEE **DISHONORABLE DISCHARGE**

DONE

▼ *adjective*

Being completely over an idea, person, or situation.

66 *I am done. I am not about to wait another two hours to get on this roller coaster! Why didn't we get the Fast Track passes?"*

 WANT MORE INFO? *THINK:* **IRRITATED.**

A refined and polished state.

66 *OMG! This is where you live? Your house is done! Plus, you have a pool. I want to come over EVERY weekend."*

SEE ALSO

LAID

 WANT MORE INFO? *THINK:* **FANCY.**

 USAGE NOTE: This term is commonly used in the Black gay community and the larger queer and trans people of color (QTPOC) community.

DONOR-CONCEIVED PERSON

▼ *noun*

SEE **ASSISTED REPRODUCTION**

DON'T DO ME

▼ *idiom*

A phrase used to tell someone in a playful or sarcastic way to not openly insult or judge you. The phrases "don't come for me" and "don't do it" can also be used.

 Look, don't do me, Alex. I'm going to eat this chocolate cake. Actually, two pieces, and I dare you to go upstairs and tell. Double-dare you!"

 WANT MORE INFO? *THINK*: **"BACK OFF!"**

 USAGE NOTE: This term originated in ballroom culture. It has been appropriated by the larger LGBTQIA+ community and mainstream culture.

DON'T GO THERE

▼ *idiom*

An expression used to tell someone not to expose unwarranted information or to avoid a particular subject or situation. The phrase "don't even" can also be used.

 Don't go there. Mind your business, Miss Thing!"

 **WANT MORE INFO?** *THINK*: **"DON'T PUSH MY BUTTONS."**

USAGE NOTE: This term originated in Black American culture and is commonly used in the Black gay and queer community. It has been appropriated by mainstream culture.

▲   **Don't Do Me**

DOWN

▼ *idiom*

An intensifier that makes anything increase in value or priority.

❝Louboutins on the feet? Rollie on the wrist? Oh, he is dressed down and giving executive realness. Dooowwwwn!❞

 WANT MORE INFO? *THINK:* **A DEGREE OF EMPHASIS.**

USAGE NOTE: This term originated in ballroom culture and is commonly used in the larger queer and trans people of color (QTPOC) community.

▼ *adjective*

In agreement.

❝

IBINABO: *Who wants to walk to the store with me?*
DASH: *I'm down.*
BRITTANY: *I'm down, too. But can we stop by McDonald's first? I want some fries.*

 WANT MORE INFO? *THINK:* **ALL IN.**

USAGE NOTE: This term originated in Black American culture. It has been appropriated by mainstream culture.

DOWN LOW or DL

▼ *noun*

A person, often a man, who is discreet about one's physical and/or romantic relationship; a person who intentionally hides one's queerness. A person "on the down low" strives to appear as heterosexual to the public. Often used in the phrases "on the down low" or "on the DL."

SEE ALSO
CLOSET

❝Look, I know I told you I'm gay, but you gotta keep things on the down low. I'm not ready to tell my parents or anyone else yet.❞

WANT MORE INFO?
THINK: GAY OR QUEER
ATTRACTION—BUT ONLY
BEHIND CLOSED DOORS.

 USAGE NOTE: This term originated in the Black gay male community and was coined by author J. L. King. It has been appropriated by mainstream culture.

DOXX

▼ *verb*

Exposing someone's personal and/or confidential information online without permission.

SEE ALSO

DEADNAME

❝ *I can't believe Terry doxxed me online. She outed me as trans using my deadname on Facebook. It's a nightmare."*

 WANT MORE INFO?
THINK: THE MALICIOUS
ACT OF DROPPING
INFORMATION.

DID YOU KNOW Doxxing is short for "dropping documents," which is computer hacker shorthand for revealing an individual's or business's sensitive documents. It was brought into the queer community when a lawsuit was filed by feminist activist Cathy Brennan against a journalist working for lesbian media website AfterEllen. Brennan believed she was defamed in an article saying she harassed, outed, and "doxxed" transgender women.

▲ Doxx

DRAG

▼ *noun*

The art of dressing up in clothing or costume that embodies an exaggerated portrayal of gender stereotypes. Drag is frequently performed for entertainment purposes, honoring femininity, masculinity, and queerness. Often used in the phrase "in drag."

❝ *Drag Culture History 101: Drag was first used in theater to describe how men would wear women's clothes to portray female characters.*"

 WANT MORE INFO? *THINK:* **CAMPY CROSS-DRESSING FOR ENTERTAINMENT.**

▼ *verb*

To insult someone harshly.

❝ *He called Mrs. Anderson a hippo in front of the entire class! Why did he have to drag her like that?*"

 WANT MORE INFO? *THINK:* **TO DRAG THROUGH THE MUD.**

To feel sluggish and tired.

❝ *I am dragging right now, but I can't sleep until I finish this paper. It was due today but Mr. Wang told me if I brought it in first thing tomorrow morning, he'd let it pass!*"

 WANT MORE INFO? *THINK:* **MUST. GET. SLEEP.**

DRAG PAGEANT

▼ *noun*

A form of pageantry—typically for female impersonators and transgender women—that mimics the traditional beauty pageant. In recent years, pageants have become more inclusive for male impersonators and transgender men, as well.

" When I do drag pageants, I transform into my alter ego, Valencia Diamond. She always wins the crown."

 WANT MORE INFO?
THINK: BEAUTY CONTEST FOR QUEER GENDERBENDERS.

DID YOU KNOW Drag pageants started out as small events held at local gay bars and clubs. In 1972, Nashville began the Miss Gay America Pageant—a pageant for female impersonators themed after the Miss America contest. Now trans and queer people have been breaking barriers and competing in mainstream pageants; Kataluna Enriquez made history as the first trans person to win the Miss Nevada USA crown.

DRAG DAUGHTER

▼ *noun*

A drag performer who has been taken under the wing of a more experienced drag queen mentor, called a DRAG MOTHER.

" Laganja Estranja, Gia Gunn, and Shangela Laquifa Wadley are drag daughters of the incredible queen Alyssa Edwards."

 WANT MORE INFO?
THINK: DRAG MOTHER + DRAG DAUGHTERS = DRAG FAMILY

▼   **Drag Pageant**

DRAG FAMILY

▼ *noun*

An intimate community of drag queens, typically comprised of a family tree of queens: a drag mother and all of her drag daughters. Roles within a drag family are used to imply close friendship between drag performers.

SEE ALSO

CHOSEN FAMILY, DRAG MOTHER, DRAG DAUGHTER, HOUSE CULTURE

 I wouldn't know how to pad, lip-sync, or contour without my loving drag family. These girls are my life."

WANT MORE INFO? *THINK:* **A QUEEN AND ALL OF HER DRAG DAUGHTER MENTEES.**

DRAG KING

▼ *noun*

A person—typically a woman or female-identifying—who entertains while dressed in masculine drag, personifying and/or exaggerating masculine stereotypes.

I think it's about time for RuPaul's Drag Race to introduce some drag kings. Inclusion is everything, right?"

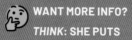 **WANT MORE INFO?** *THINK:* **SHE PUTS ON HER TROUSERS, SUSPENDERS, BLAZER, AND TOP HAT.**

DID YOU KNOW American drag king performance can be traced back to 1868, when male impersonator Annie Hindle rose to fame. In the 1920s, blues singer Gladys Bentley performed as a drag king with a chorus line of drag queens. In the 1950s, Stormé DeLarverie was a popular drag performer at the first racially integrated drag establishment in America. In the modern drag community, performing in male drag is often seen as an homage to masculinity.

DRAG MOTHER

▼ *noun*

An experienced drag queen who supports and educates an amateur queen and teaches her about drag culture (and how to slay).

66 *My drag mother showed me the ropes of the business, and I vow to do the same for someone else someday."*

 WANT MORE INFO?
THINK: **A MENTOR FOR YOUNG DRAG QUEENS.**

DRAG QUEEN

▼ *noun*

A person—typically a man or male-identifying—who entertains while dressed in feminine drag, personifying and/or exaggerating feminine stereotypes.

66 *Bianca Del Rio, Bob the Drag Queen, Trixie Mattel, Lady Bunny, Divine, and, of course, Mother Pepper LaBeija and The Lady Chablis are all iconic drag queens. These girls definitely don't play around when it's time to beat, battle, and strut."*

 WANT MORE INFO?
THINK: **RUPAUL, THE**

FIRST DRAG QUEEN TO BE HONORED WITH A STAR ON THE HOLLYWOOD WALK OF FAME.

DID YOU KNOW Drag is often associated with the history of theater, dating back to classical Chinese theater and Shakespearean productions. Theater was considered unfit for women and they were banned from performing, so men played both male and female characters. In the modern drag community, performing in female drag is often seen as an homage to femininity.

125

THE QUEENS' ENGLISH

DRAG SHOW

▼ *noun*

A live performance or show featuring drag performers who typically entertain through dancing, singing, or lip-syncing to popular songs. Other performance components include stand-up comedy, skits, visual art, and political activism.

❝ *DragCon is three days of the best celebrity drag queens, jaw-dropping drag shows, and is the ultimate drag celebration!*❞

 WANT MORE INFO? *THINK:* **PRIDE MONTH MUST-DO ACTIVITY FOR THE WHOLE FAMILY!**

DRAG SISTER

▼ *noun*

One or more than one drag daughters who are supported by the same drag mother.

A friend within the drag community who uses "sister" as an indicator of a close relationship.

❝ *Queen Mayhem Miller has a squad of drag sisters who are not to be messed with.*❞

 WANT MORE INFO? *THINK:* **BESTIES WITHIN THE DRAG COMMUNITY.**

DRAMA

▼ *noun*

An extreme level of emotion or scandal.

❝ *DRAMA ALERT!!!! Jonathan just broke up with Murphy.*❞

 WANT MORE INFO? *THINK:* **EXTRA, EXTRA, READ ALL ABOUT IT!**

DRAMA AND KAFLAMA

▼ *idiom*

A heightened version of DRAMA.

❝ *Miss Thing came to the ball getting her tens with drama and kaflama!"*

 WANT MORE INFO? THINK: DOING WAY TOO MUCH!

 This term originated in ballroom culture.

DRESSED TO THE NINES

▼ *idiom*

An expression describing someone who is dressed exquisitely. This person usually demonstrates exceptional taste in fashion and style.

❝ *I love opening the door for the sweet little church ladies dressed to the nines with their big, beautiful hats, lace gloves, and pearls around the neck. What can I say, I'm a true gentleman."*

 WANT MORE INFO? THINK: FLAWLESS ATTIRE.

▲   **Dressed to the Nines**

DUCKWALK

▼ *verb*

A vogue dance move that emphasizes a deep squat walk.

SEE ALSO
VOGUE FEMME

❝ *Omari teaches a fierce vogue class. We learn vogue femme, and you know we have a duckwalk battle."*

 WANT MORE INFO? THINK: DANCING LIKE A DUCK— BUT LOOKING FABULOUS.

 This term originated in ballroom culture.

DUST

▼ *noun*

A term used to dismiss someone or something completely.

❝ *Every time he asks to borrow my pencils, he never gives them back. So, when he asked again yesterday, I paid him dust.* ❞

 WANT MORE INFO? *THINK:* DENIED!

USAGE NOTE: This term originated in Black American culture and is commonly used in ballroom culture.

▲ _____ Dust

DUSTED

▼ *adjective*

To be chic, refined, or perfect. Often used to refer to makeup.

❝ *Stepping out tonight with my bestie looking dusted. Our selfies are about to flood your timelines.* ❞

 WANT MORE INFO? *THINK:* THE OPPOSITE OF BUSTED.

DYKE

▼ *noun*

A lesbian, bisexual, or queer female.

A masculine, aggressive lesbian, bisexual, or queer girl/woman.

RELATED
DYKEY *adjective*

SEE ALSO
BULL DAGGER, "The Lesbian Spectrum," *p. 255*

66 *When we use the word 'dyke' in the lesbian community, most of the time it's okay! But if you use the word and you're not a lesbian, then there is a BIG problem."*

 WANT MORE INFO?
THINK: **A LESBIAN.**

USAGE NOTE: This term was once a slur for butch women and lesbians but has been reclaimed by some of the LGBTQIA+ community. It may still have negative connotations for some people. Please be aware that this term can be considered mature.

DID YOU KNOW Bull dyke or dyke, traditionally meaning butch lesbian, dates back to as early as the 1920s. Later, it became a slur directed toward masculine lesbians but has since been reappropriated by many in the lesbian community as an empowering descriptor for queer women or gender nonconforming people who are typically attracted to women.

DYKON

▼ *noun*

A woman—usually gay, but not always—who is considered an icon within the lesbian community.

SEE ALSO
BICON, GAY ICON

66 *Dykons? Clea DuVall, Sarah Paulson, k.d. lang, Wanda Sykes, Jenny Shimizu—shall I go on? Oh, well I can include the straight dykons like Hillary Clinton, Oprah, and Pink, too."*

 WANT MORE INFO?
THINK: **QUEER (OR QUEER-FRIENDLY) WOMEN WHO ARE GAME CHANGERS.**

USAGE NOTE: The term "dyke" was once a derogatory slur for lesbians but has been reclaimed by some of the LGBTQIA+ community. It may still have negative connotations for some people.

DYSPHORIA

▼ noun

A state of feeling unhappy, uneasy, and/or insecure with one's personal state of being.

SEE ALSO

GENDER-AFFIRMING CARE, GENDER DYSPHORIA

 Be gentle and encourage Cam when you see them. They're dealing with some serious dysphoria and have been super stressed lately."

WANT MORE INFO?
THINK: THE OPPOSITE OF EUPHORIA.

D **is for** **Dictionary**
Look at you having fun reading one!

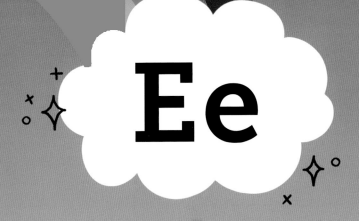

Ee

EAT IT

▼ *idiom*

In ballroom culture, this phrase is used to display confidence or to be exceptional. The phrase "Oh, you ate that" can also be used.

66 *Honey, eat it allllll up! Go for the glory!"*

 WANT MORE INFO? *THINK:* **SHINING YOUR LIGHT OH, SO BRIGHT!**

ENBY

▼ *adjective*

The phonetic pronunciation of the abbreviation for nonbinary, or "nb," a gender identity that is open to a full spectrum of gender expressions, not limited by masculinity and femininity. An enby person may express masculinity, femininity, both, or neither.

SEE ALSO

GENDER NONCONFORMING, GENDERQUEER, NONBINARY

66 *Being nonbinary feels different for each person, but there are some great enby YouTube channels where people are openly sharing their stories and it's great to hear their experiences."*

ENBY
CONT.

WANT MORE INFO?
THINK:

#PROUDTOBENONBINARY

USAGE NOTE: The term "enby" is commonly used in the nonbinary, genderqueer, genderfluid, and gender nonconforming communities, though some nonbinary people may find it offensive. The abbreviation "nb" is not often used because it was once a common reference for a "non-Black person."

ENDO

▼ *noun*

An abbreviated form of endocrinologist, a doctor who specializes in medical interventions for patients who need assistance with hormone balance, including, but not limited to, transgender and nonbinary patients.

SEE ALSO

GENDER-AFFIRMING CARE

❝ *I take great pride in being an endo for the queer community. My patients are important to me and their happiness is my priority."*

WANT MORE INFO?
THINK: A KEY HEALTH
PROVIDER SUPPORTING
THE MEDICAL CARE
OF QUEER AND TRANS
BODIES.

EQUALITY

▼ *noun*

The quality or state of being equal—having equal rights, opportunities, and status.

❝ *The fight for equality has been relentless and exhausting, but we will not give up!* ❞

 WANT MORE INFO?
THINK: EQUAL
TREATMENT FOR ALL
PEOPLE.

DID YOU KNOW
The Human Rights Campaign (HRC) is America's largest organization that advocates for lesbian, gay, bisexual, transgender, and queer equality while educating the public on LGBTQIA+ issues. HRC's mission is to improve the lives of queer people and their families by encouraging more inclusive policies in laws, work environments, ideological spaces, and other supportive avenues worldwide.

▼ Equality

THE QUEENS' ENGLISH

ERASURE

▼ *noun*

Elimination or absence from data or history.

SEE ALSO
INVISIBILITY

❝ *Queer theory very rarely engages with bisexuality, thus supporting—whether intentional or not—its erasure.*❞

 WANT MORE INFO? THINK: LACK OF REPRESENTATION.

DID YOU KNOW Karla Rossi created a magazine called *Anything That Moves: Beyond the Myths of Bisexuality* to confront the issues of bi-erasure and biphobia in America. The magazine was published from 1990 to 2002 as an extension of the San Francisco Bay Area Bisexual Network. Rossi used the publication to promote bisexual visibility by highlighting diverse voices and experiences while redefining the traditional concepts of sexuality and gender. Today, young celebrities and activists like Tyler Blackburn, Shannon Purser, Avery Cyrus, and others are using their social media platforms to increase awareness and openly speak out about being bisexual.

EVERYTHING

▼ *adjective*

Describing something or someone fabulous, giving 100 percent approval.

❝ *Ooh la la! This lip gloss is everything! It smells like cotton candy, too. Wanna try it?*❞

 WANT MORE INFO? THINK: TENS ACROSS THE BOARD!

USAGE NOTE: This term originated in the Black gay community and is commonly used in the larger queer and trans people of color (QTPOC) community.

EX-GAY

▼ *noun*

A person who identified as gay at one point in time, but no longer identifies as such.

SEE ALSO

YESTERGAY

66 *New Jersey, Colorado, Maine, Oregon, Illinois, New Mexico, and so many other states have signed their gay conversion therapy ban! Therapy will not turn someone into an ex-gay. Queerness does not need a cure!*"

 WANT MORE INFO? *THINK:* NOT GAY ANYMORE.

USAGE NOTE: This term has negative connotations as it limits sexuality to a hetero/homo binary, denying the reality of a fluid sexuality.

EXTRA

▼ *adjective*

Displaying excessive behavior. Often seen as XTRA.

66 *You are soooooo extra! Why do you always have to be the center of attention? Just chill!*"

 WANT MORE INFO? *THINK:* DRAMATIC, NARCISSISTIC, AND/OR OVER THE TOP.

USAGE NOTE: This term originated in Black American culture and is commonly used in the Black gay and queer community. It has been appropriated by mainstream culture.

Equality and *Justice* for All **LGBTQIA+** *Queens!*

#transrights #blacklivesmatter #stopasianhate #daca #genderequality #LGBTQStudentsAreProtected

Finding My Identity: "Who Am I"

OUR **IDENTITY** IS THE
CORE PART OF OUR MAKEUP.
IT IS WHAT MAKES US **UNIQUE**.

SELF-DISCOVERY IS AN important step in finding our full identity. This is a process of learning more about ourselves, exploring who we are, and evolving into who we want to be. It is common to have stages in your life when you question your identity. You may be uncertain about how you feel about others, unsure of how you want to express yourself, or curious about exploring new labels. This is all normal!

Having time to fully discover all the unique parts of you—gender, gender expression, attraction, feeling, ability, even personality and values—is necessary. Do not ever feel rushed when trying to find the labels or words that feel right to you. Feel safe and empowered to ask the question, "Who am I?" and discover all the ways you can feel your most authentic self. Some labels will feel right and some will not.

Did you know feeling unsure about your identity is more common than you think? There are many young people who question their identity and are exploring the spectrum of expressions and attractions. Research has shown that more than 60 percent of youth have questioned their identity at some point during their adolescent phase.

HERE IS A guide sheet that you can use at your leisure to help you unpack the questions you may have about your identity and explore the many layers of who you are.

Get curious and find new labels
that make you feel good!

WHAT COULD BE MY GENDER IDENTITY? Look through the dictionary and find gender identities that you connect with and/or are interested in exploring. Pick as many as you want! Remember, we are exploring and discovering what feels right!

WHAT COULD BE MY GENDER EXPRESSION? Your gender expression is the outward characteristics—such as appearance, behaviors, and attitudes—that communicate your identity to society. Look through the dictionary and find gender expressions that you connect with and/or are interested in exploring. You can also use some of the highlighted spreads throughout the dictionary to assist you. Remember, there is no wrong answer. We are finding all the unique parts of ourselves.

WHO AM I ATTRACTED TO? Attraction can be multilayered. You can be attracted to the same gender, opposite gender, multiple genders, all genders, or no gender. Think about who you are attracted to and who you would desire to be attracted to you. Also explore how you express your attraction. Is it romantically, physically, both, or neither? Look through the dictionary and find sexual orientations, romantic orientations, and other attraction identities that you connect with and/or are interested in exploring. Remember, your attractions are valid and should be respected by others.

WHAT WORDS WOULD I LIKE TO USE TO IDENTIFY MYSELF, BUT I'M AFRAID TO USE? It is okay to give yourself permission to discover more of your identity. Use this section to safely navigate through fear, anxiety, and confusion about who you are. Remember, exploring your identity is an important part of growing up. Sending you some positive energy and encouragement on your journey to finding what feels right!

Your identity is always valid.
It may feel disappointing if no one
else accepts it, but remember that it
is more important that you accept it
and strive to live in your truth.

FAB

▼ **adjective**

An abbreviation of "fabulous."

RELATED
FABULOUSNESS *noun*
FABULOSITY *noun*

❝ *So fab, so fierce, so me!* ❞

 WANT MORE INFO? *THINK: WONDERIFIC.*

FACE

▼ **idiom**

An acknowledgment of beauty and fierceness. Often used in the phrase "giving face."

❝ *Avery is giving face in these pictures. Those cheekbones, that smile, yas!* ❞

 WANT MORE INFO? *THINK: GORGEOUS.*

▼ **noun**

In ballroom culture, a prominent competition category where a competitor is judged on the smoothness, symmetry, and beauty of their face. The term CARTA can also be used.

❝ *Werk!!! A modeling agent from Wilhelmina saw him slay face last night at the ball and he instantly got signed!* ❞

WANT MORE INFO?
THINK: **COMPETITION CATEGORY THAT IS A MUST-SEE AT A GAY BALL.**

USAGE NOTE: This term originated in ballroom culture. It has been appropriated by mainstream culture.

▲ Face

FACIAL FEMINIZATION SURGERY (FFS)

▼ *noun*

A series of surgical procedures that alters masculine facial features to make them appear more feminine.

 FFS can be rewarding but it is not for everyone. Being part of a support group was an important part of finding the right surgeon and preparing myself emotionally."

 WANT MORE INFO?
THINK: **SPECIALIZED COSMETIC FACIAL SURGERY FOR PEOPLE TO APPEAR MORE FEMININE.**

USAGE NOTE: This term is commonly used in the transgender, nonbinary, and gender nonconforming communities.

FAG BAG

▼ *noun*

SEE **BEARDED LADY**

FAGGOT

▼ *noun*

A gay man. While it originated as a slur, some

members of the LGBTQIA+ community have reclaimed the insult, using it as a term of endearment or powerful personal identifier. Often shortened to "fag."

❝ *Look at those fags over there kissing! I love gay PDA!"*

 WANT MORE INFO? *THINK:* **OFTEN AN OFFENSIVE TERM FOR A GAY MALE.**

USAGE NOTE: This term originated as a derogatory slur for gay men but has been reclaimed by some of the LGBTQIA+ community. It may still have negative connotations for some people. Please be aware that this term can be considered mature.

DID YOU KNOW The use of the word "faggot" in American English slang goes back to 1914 and was popularized in the Black culture of New York during the 1920s and 1930s. Many people referred to the popular Hamilton Lodge Ball—a Harlem Renaissance–era party known for celebrating gay love and freedom of expression—as the "Faggots' Ball."

FAG HAG

▼ *noun*

A woman—usually straight—who enjoys the friendship of and spends great amounts of time with gay men. The term FRUIT FLY can also be used.

> SEE ALSO
> **FAGGOT, FAG STAG, GOLDILOCKS**

❝ *The fag hag pledge: Every girl needs a gay best friend!"*

 WANT MORE INFO? *THINK:* **FEMALE BEST FRIEND TO GAY GUY.**

USAGE NOTE: Like the word "fag," "fag hag" originated as a derogatory slur for gay men but has since been reclaimed by some of the LGBTQIA+ community. It may still have negative connotations for some people. Please be aware that this term can be considered mature.

FAG STAG

▼ noun

A male—usually straight—who enjoys the friendship of and spends great amounts of time with gay males. Also known as FRUIT FLY.

SEE ALSO
FAGGOT, FAG HAG, FRUIT FLY

❝ *I'm obsessed with my sister's gay best friend, Matt. My sister says I'm a fag stag, but I'm cool with that. His fashion advice has gotten me so many compliments and I feel more confident when I talk to girls.*❞

 WANT MORE INFO?
THINK: STRAIGHT GUY WHO WATCHES *QUEER EYE* WITH HIS GAY BFF.

 USAGE NOTE: The term "fag" originated as a derogatory slur for gay men but has been reclaimed by some of the LGBTQIA+ community. It may still have negative

connotations for some people. Please be aware that this term can be considered mature.

FAIRY

▼ noun

A gay, bisexual, or queer male who has a light and airy demeanor and deeply identifies with feminine expression.

❝ *I like getting gel nail polish designs, I'm obsessed with Taylor Swift, and EVERY piece of clothing I own has sparkle and glitter. Yes, I live the fairy life.*❞

 WANT MORE INFO?
THINK: A QUEER BOY WHOSE INTERESTS ARE CONSIDERED STEREOTYPICALLY FEMININE.

 USAGE NOTE: The term "fairy" originated as a derogatory slur for gay men but has been reclaimed by some of the LGBTQIA+ community. It may still have negative connotations for some people.

Fairy ▲

FAMILY

▼ *noun*

Used to acknowledge and refer to members within the lesbian, gay, bisexual, transgender, and queer community, and those in supporting social communities.

SEE ALSO
CHOSEN FAMILY

66 *Wow, I'm reading Zuri's blog on Black history and she is shouting out family! It mentions gay literary powerhouse James Baldwin,* *trans media mogul Janet Mock, lesbian comedian Danitra Vance, bisexual activist Angela Davis, and nonbinary actor Carl Clemons-Hopkins. I love learning more about Black queer history!"*

 WANT MORE INFO? THINK: TOGETHERNESS, SUPPORT, AND LOVE WITHIN THE LGBTQIA+ COMMUNITY.

DID YOU KNOW "Family" was first popularized by the Black gay community and was used as a coded word to ask if someone was same-gender loving or gay. Today, "family" is used widely among the LGBTQIA+ community, regardless of ethnicity.

FATHER OF THE HOUSE

▼ *noun*

SEE **HOUSE FATHER**

FAUX QUEEN

▼ *noun*

A girl or woman who entertains, either recreationally or professionally, while dressed in exaggerated female attire and makeup. The term BIO QUEEN can also be used.

❝ *My best friend and I were addicted to drag culture. The only thing we watched for a whole year was* RuPaul's Drag Race . . . *no, seriously! So, I became a faux queen and he became a drag queen. We do shows for our friends at least once a week.*"

 WANT MORE INFO? *THINK:* A FEMALE FEMALE IMPERSONATOR.

 USAGE NOTE: The term "faux queen" is typically preferred over "bio queen," as the implication of biology may be considered derogatory to transgender, nonbinary, and gender nonconforming queens.

FEATURE

▼ *verb*

To give attention to something.

SEE ALSO
NOT FEATURING

❝ *Yaran is still featuring that trophy? Okay, we get it! You won the spelling bee, but it was last week! Can we move on?*"

 WANT MORE INFO? *THINK:* TO SHOW OFF.

 USAGE NOTE: This term originated in ballroom culture and is commonly used in the larger queer and trans people of color (QTPOC) community.

FEELING IT

▼ *idiom*

To have a self-confident demeanor. The phrases "feeling yourself" or "feeling myself" can also be used.

Exploring the deepest and most honest part of yourself.

66 *You're feeling it now that your braces are off, huh? Keep smiling, boo!"*

 WANT MORE INFO?
THINK: **A STRONG DOSE OF SELF-ADMIRATION.**

USAGE NOTE: This term originated in Black American culture. It has been appropriated by the larger LGBTQIA+ community and mainstream culture.

▲   **Feeling It**

FEMALE

▼ *adjective*

A biological sex or identity expression often associated with the display of feminine physicality, demeanor, and behavior.

▼ *noun*

A female-identifying person.

> SEE ALSO
> **"The Genderbread Person,"** *p. 73*

66 *The future is female. The world is nothing without her."*

 WANT MORE INFO?
THINK: **ASSOCIATED WITH GIRLS, WOMEN, AND FEMMES.**

FEMALE FIGURE

▼ *noun*

A competition category in ballroom culture. This competition involves any individual who represents the femme form in their performance, and may include cisgender women, transgender women, and drag queens.

❝ *The Female Figure performance prize is going for two thousand dollars tonight. Get that money!"*

 WANT MORE INFO? *THINK:* BALLROOM CATEGORY FOR FEMMES.

FEMALE-TO-MALE

▼ *noun*

A person who is assigned female at birth but has transitioned or is in the process of transitioning to male. The term is often abbreviated as "FTM."

▼ *adjective*

Describing a person who has undergone an FTM transition.

SEE ALSO
AFAB, FEMALE-TO-NONBINARY/GENDER NEUTRAL/NEUTROIS, MALE-TO-FEMALE, MALE-TO-NONBINARY/GENDER NEUTRAL/NEUTROIS, STP, TRANSMASCULINE

❝ *Elliot Page, Sasha Knight, Laith Ashley, Zach Barack, Logan Rozos, Chella Man, Gottmik, and Ashton Mota are all proud FTM transgender powerhouses."*

WANT MORE INFO?

THINK: A TRANS MAN.

USAGE NOTE: This term may be considered outdated by some members of the LGBTQIA+ community. The use of "AFAB," or "assigned female at birth," is widely accepted because it does not imply an individual's gender identity has changed, instead acknowledging the binding nature of being assigned a specific gender at birth. The use of this term relies on an individual's preference. Please ask for a person's chosen name and pronouns.

FEMALE-TO-NON-BINARY/GENDER NEUTRAL/NEUTROIS

▼ *noun*

A person who is assigned female at birth and identifies as nonbinary, gender neutral, or neutrois. The term is often abbreviated as "FTN."

▼ *adjective*

Describing a person who has undergone an FTN transition.

SEE ALSO

AFAB, FEMALE-TO-MALE, MALE-TO-FEMALE, MALE-TO-NONBINARY/GENDER NEUTRAL/NEUTROIS

 I may look femme to you, but 'girl' is not my identity. I don't feel like a boy, either. I identify as FTN or nonbinary."

WANT MORE INFO?

THINK: AFAB AND IDENTIFIES AS NONBINARY, GENDER NEUTRAL, OR NEUTROIS.

USAGE NOTE: This term may be considered outdated by some members of the LGBTQIA+ community. The use of "AFAB," or "assigned female at birth," is widely accepted because it does not imply an individual's gender identity has changed, instead acknowledging the binding nature of being assigned a specific gender at birth. The use of this term relies on an individual's preference. Please ask for a person's chosen name and pronouns.

147

THE QUEENS' ENGLISH

FEMININE- PRESENTING

▼ *adjective*

Describing a gender expression—outward expression, behavior, style, or physical look—that is feminine. The term "femme-presenting" can also be used.

SEE ALSO
FEMME

❝ *There might be a time when I want to dress completely femme-presenting and that doesn't mean that in that moment I'm identifying as a woman, it just means that's what I want to wear in that moment.*❞

—DEMI LOVATO

 WANT MORE INFO? *THINK:* **A PERSON'S OUTWARD AND EXTERNAL GENDER EXPRESSION IS FEMININE, NOT THAT THEIR GENDER IDENTITY IS FEMALE.**

FEMINIZING HORMONE THERAPY

▼ *noun*

A process in which hormones are used to produce physiological changes within the body to exhibit physical female attributes. The term HORMONE REPLACEMENT THERAPY can also be used.

SEE ALSO
BLOCKERS, MASCULINIZING HORMONE THERAPY

❝ *My doctor said that estrogen, testosterone blockers, and progesterone are certain types of medicine used for feminizing hormone therapy.*❞

 WANT MORE INFO? *THINK:* **MEDICAL THERAPY USED FOR FEMALE/FEMME GENDER AFFIRMATION.**

 USAGE NOTE: This term is commonly used in the transgender, nonbinary, and gender nonconforming communities.

FEMME

▼ adjective

Denoting the vast and dynamic representation of feminine characteristics, regardless of gender. Both "femme" and "butch" are often paired with the adjectives "soft"/"hard" or "high"/"low" as a means of distinction.

SEE ALSO
BUTCH

" *He rocked that 'FEMME VIBE' crop top. I saw it at H&M last week. Yes, kween!"*

 WANT MORE INFO? *THINK:* **ACTING, DRESSING, OR BEHAVING IN A TRADITIONALLY FEMININE MANNER.**

In the lesbian community, a queer woman who possesses a feminine appearance and behaviors. This term can be associated with girls, women, and femme-of-center people.

SEE ALSO
HIGH FEMME, LIPSTICK LESBIAN

" *Just because I'm a femme lesbian and I like to wear dresses, doesn't mean I'm less queer than a masc-of-center lesbian in flannel."*

 WANT MORE INFO? *THINK:* **THE OPPOSITE OF BUTCH.**

USAGE NOTE: This term originated in the lesbian community. It has been appropriated by the larger LGBTQIA+ community and mainstream culture.

DID YOU KNOW The *Oxford English Dictionary* credits bisexual poet Lord Byron with one of the earliest uses of the word "femme" in 1814. By the mid-twentieth century, the term was used widely in working-class bar culture to label and identify lesbian women—it became the feminine counterpart to "butch." By the 1980s, "femme" was widely used to describe gay men in addition to lesbians. Today, the transgender, nonbinary, and genderqueer communities also use "femme" as a label to articulate gender identity and/or gender expression.

FEMME FOR FEMME

▼ *idiom*

Expression referring to romantic relationships between two queer femme people. This can also be referred to as "femme on femme" or abbreviated as "F4F."

> *Femme for femme relationships should be respected. Please lose the stereotypical view of a butch/femme relationship. That goes for you, too, heteros!"*

SEE ALSO

BUTCH/FEMME RELATIONSHIP, STUD FOR STUD, MASC FOR MASC

 WANT MORE INFO? THINK: A PARTNERSHIP BETWEEN TWO LIPSTICK LESBIANS.

USAGE NOTE: This term originated in the lesbian community. It has been appropriated by the larger LGBTQIA+ community.

FEMME-OF-CENTER

▼ *adjective*

Referring to gender identities that lean toward femininity.

SEE ALSO
MASC-OF-CENTER

66 *Femme and femme-of-center, butch, and masc are labels queer people use to support our gender expressions and identities. I cannot deal with cishet people using our words— they don't need to call themselves femme or masc to be understood and accepted.*"

 WANT MORE INFO? *THINK:* **ON THE FEMININE SIDE.**

USAGE NOTE: This term is commonly used in the transgender, nonbinary, and gender nonconforming communities.

FEMMEPHOBIA

▼ *noun*

Aversion, fear, or hatred toward femmes.

RELATED
FEMMEPHOBIC adjective
FEMMEPHOBE noun

SEE ALSO
ACEPHOBIA, BIPHOBIA, HOMOPHOBIA, LESBOPHOBIA, MISOGYNY, QUEERPHOBIA, TRANSPHOBIA

66 *A lot of my gay friends get bullied at school because of femmephobia. It's just not right!*"

 WANT MORE INFO? *THINK:* **DISLIKE OF OR PREJUDICE AGAINST FEMMES.**

151

THE QUEENS' ENGLISH

FEMME QUEEN

▼ *noun*

A competition category in the ballroom scene for transgender women and the up-and-coming transfeminine children.

> SEE ALSO
> **BUTCH QUEEN, CATEGORY, QUEEN**

Refers to a drag queen or femme-presenting person.

❝ *Femme Queen Performance has been an important factor and foundation of ballroom culture since it began, a category reserved for trans women."* —NOELLE DELEON

 WANT MORE INFO?
THINK: A TRANS OR FEMME-PRESENTING WOMAN.

 USAGE NOTE: This term originated in ballroom culture. It has been appropriated by the larger LGBTQIA+ community.

FHT

▼ *noun*

SEE **FEMINIZING HORMONE THERAPY**

FIERCE

▼ *adjective*

Exceptional, powerful, intense.

❝ *Snap, snap, snap, snap! FIERCE! FIERCE! FIERCE!"*

 WANT MORE INFO?
THINK: SPECTACULAR.

 USAGE NOTE: This term originated in ballroom culture. It has been appropriated by the larger LGBTQIA+ community and mainstream culture.

FILIPINX

▼ *adjective*

A gender-neutral, inclusive alternative to Filipino or Filipina, identifying people of Filipino American descent.

> 66 *I'm a queer Filipinx first-generation immigrant and I'm proud of every part of my identity. I want other Asian queer teens to know that your queerness and your culture are both powerful parts of you. Never be ashamed of that."*

 WANT MORE INFO?
THINK: **AN EMPOWERING TERM FOR *ALL* PEOPLE OF FILIPINO AMERICAN DESCENT.**

DID YOU KNOW On June 12, 1898—during the Spanish-American War—Filipinos declared their independence from Spanish rule. The month of June celebrates both Pride Month and Philippines Independence Day! Queer Filipinx Americans like the founder of Gender Proud, Genna Rocero; cofounder of National Queer Asian Pacific Islander Alliance, Ben de Guzman; former Chairperson and Commissioner of the New York City Commission on Human Rights, Carmelyn Malalis; Broadway's hit musical *Here Lies Love*; and founder of Broadway Barkada, Billy Bustamante; are devoted to making impactful and progressive change in both the Filipino community and LGBTQIA+ community at large.

FIRE

▼ *adjective*

Outstanding, energetic, hot. The terms NASTY and "fiyah" can also be used.

> 66 *Zendaya looks fiyah on the magazine cover! Absolutely gorgeous."*

 WANT MORE INFO?
THINK: **SIZZLING.**

USAGE NOTE: This term originated in Black American culture and is commonly used in the Black gay and queer community. It has been appropriated by the larger LGBTQIA+ community and mainstream culture.

FISH

▼ *adjective*

Looking super femme. In the ballroom scene and drag community, it identifies a person who looks like a woman. The term "fishy" can also be used.

❝ *You mean the drag queen Galaxy? She's so fish and femme!"*

A girl or a woman.

❝ *I'm gay. I definitely don't want that fish."*

 WANT MORE INFO? *THINK:* **SINGING AT THE TOP OF YOUR LUNGS, "YOU MAKE ME FEEL LIKE A NATURAL WOMAN!"**

 USAGE NOTE: This term originated in Black American culture. It has been appropriated by the larger LGBTQIA+ community.

FLAMING

▼ *adjective*

Extremely flamboyant.

RELATED
FLAMER *noun*

❝ *She is fierce, flaming, and on fiyah! Jeans tighter than ballet tights and a cloak as plush as a velvet throne. I bow down, kween!"*

 WANT MORE INFO? *THINK:* **ALL HAIL THE QUEENS JONATHAN VAN NESS AND BILLY PORTER!**

 USAGE NOTE: This term may be considered a stereotype or derogatory.

FLANNEL

▼ *noun*

A garment—usually a button-up shirt—using soft plaid or tartan material. A stereotypically lesbian piece of clothing.

▼ *adjective*

Describing a plaid piece of clothing.

❝ *I looked in my girlfriend's closet and all she owns are flannels, jeans, hiking boots, and Birkenstocks.*❞

 WANT MORE INFO? *THINK:* **THE UNOFFICIAL MASC LESBIAN DRESS CODE.**

▲ **Flannel**

FLEXIBLE

▼ *adjective*

Describing a person who predominantly identifies as one specific sexual orientation, but is open to exploring attractions and relationships that are outside that identity.

SEE ALSO
HETEROFLEXIBLE, HOMOFLEXIBLE, LESBIFLEXIBLE

❝ *Learning new words like 'demi,' 'bi,' and 'flexible' gave me labels that identified the fluidity of my attraction to others.*❞

—CHLOE O. DAVIS

 WANT MORE INFO? *THINK:* **AN ATTRACTION-IDENTITY DESCRIPTOR THAT IS OPEN TO EXPERIENCING QUEER RELATIONSHIPS OUTSIDE OF THE PRIMARY ONE.**

FLIT

▼ *noun*

A gay person.

RELATED
FLITTY *adjective*

❝ *Back in the day, there were so many coded words used to describe being gay! Flit, Mary, Nancy, Friends of Dorothy, fairy, nelly, fruit, queen, and more!"*

 WANT MORE INFO? *THINK:* **SAME-SEX ATTRACTION.**

> **DID YOU KNOW** The word "flit" as it is defined here first appeared in print in J. D. Salinger's *The Catcher in the Rye*: "A flitty-looking guy with wavy hair came out and played the piano."

FLOWER

▼ *noun*

An effeminate male or delicate queer person.

❝ *Some young queer boys go through a flower stage where they start to mimic their mother's or a prominent female figure's behavior and speech."*

 WANT MORE INFO? *THINK:* **AN ELEGANT FEMME.**

FLUID

▼ *adjective*

An identity descriptor that expresses the fluctuating nature of one's sexual orientation, gender identity, and/or gender expression over time.

Folx   ▼

"I'm fluid. I change. I float. I move along the spectrum of self-expression in every way."

 WANT MORE INFO?
THINK: NOT FIXED; CHANGING OVER TIME.

FOLX

▼ *noun*

A way to write "folks" that implies inclusivity and celebrates queerness, similar to the use of the lettver *X* in the terms LATINX, MX., and WOMXN.

"Queer youth folx are strong and more than enough! We will carry on the fight for social justice to achieve the true equality we all deserve."

 WANT MORE INFO?
THINK: AN INCLUSIVE IDENTIFIER FOR THE QUEER COMMUNITY.

FOOLISHNESS AND DEBAUCHERY

▼ *idiom*

Describes someone acting in an outlandish or comical way for others' amusement.

"You are foolishness and debauchery! My stomach hurts from laughing so hard."

 WANT MORE INFO?
THINK: COMIC RELIEF.

USAGE NOTE: This term originated in Black American culture and is commonly used in the Black gay and queer community.

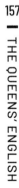

FOR BLOOD

▼ *idiom*

To go to the extreme; to do something full out, with no regrets. This term is most often used in the phrase "go for blood."

❝ *The kids go for blood at Afropunk: piercings,* mohawks, dashikis, and tattoos. Unapologetically Black and beautiful. Brooklyn, stand up!*"*

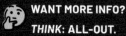 **WANT MORE INFO?** *THINK:* **ALL-OUT.**

USAGE NOTE: This term originated in ballroom culture. It has been appropriated by the larger LGBTQIA+ community and mainstream culture.

FOR POINTS

▼ *idiom*

An emphatic phrase used to acknowledge something or someone highly exceptional.

❝ *Ah, this strawberry lemonade goes for points! It quenches my thirst EVERY TIME!"*

 WANT MORE INFO? *THINK:* **SCORING BIG POINTS FOR A JOB WELL DONE.**

USAGE NOTE: This term originated in ballroom culture and is commonly used in the larger queer and trans people of color (QTPOC) community.

FOR THE BIRDS

▼ *idiom*

A response to an undesirable situation, experience, or comment.

❝ *This game is for the birds. We have not scored a point yet! Geeeezzzzz! Our team stinks."*

 WANT MORE INFO? *THINK:* **AN EXPRESSION OF DISTASTE.**

FOR THE GODS OR TO THE GAWDS

▼ *idiom*

A phrase used to praise something exceptional.

> 66 *This one right here is for the kids who slay. We be up on YouTube talking makeup all day. Slay to the gawds! Slay, slay to the GAWDS!"*
> —TATIANA WARD, "BEAT FACE HONEY"

WANT MORE INFO?
THINK: BOW DOWN TO THE BEST.

USAGE NOTE: This term originated in ballroom culture and is commonly used in the larger queer and trans people of color (QTPOC) community.

FREE AGENT

▼ *noun*

In ballroom culture, this is a person who performs in ball competitions without being represented by a house or team. The term "007" can also be used.

❝ *You know she doesn't perform as Infiniti anymore; she is a free agent now."*

 WANT MORE INFO?
THINK: **A FREELANCER IN THE BALLROOM SCENE.**

FRIEND OF DOROTHY

▼ *idiom*

A dated term used to inconspicuously identify another gay or queer person.

❝ *Hey, Ralph, the friends of Dorothy are coming over for tea at noon. Care to join?"*

 WANT MORE INFO?
THINK: **CODE FOR**

A MEMBER OF THE LGBTQIA+ COMMUNITY.

 USAGE NOTE: This term originated in the gay male community.

DID YOU KNOW The term "friend of Dorothy" gained contemporary usage as a reference to actress Judy Garland's role of Dorothy in *The Wizard of Oz*. Garland was adored by the gay community and remains a gay icon.

FRUIT

▼ *noun*

Used to refer to a gay man, but can be used to identify a lesbian, bisexual, transgender, and/or queer individual. The terms "fruitcake" and "fruit basket" can also be used.

RELATED
FRUITY *adjective*

❝

SEBASTIAN: *Fruits come in all different shapes and sizes*
ANNA: *Yeah, no two are exactly alike!*

WANT MORE INFO?
THINK: A GAY.

USAGE NOTE: The term was commonly used in Polari, a coded slang used by British gay men during the rise of anti-LGBT laws. Later, it was used as a derogatory slur for a queer person but has been reclaimed by some of the LGBTQIA+ community. It may still have negative connotations for some people.

FRUIT FLY

▼ *noun*

SEE **FAG HAG, FAG STAG**

FTM

▼ *adjective*

SEE **FEMALE-TO-MALE**

FTM ▲

FTN

▼ *adjective*

SEE **FEMALE-TO-NONBINARY/ GENDER NEUTRAL/ NEUTROIS**

FULL OUT

▼ *idiom*

Giving maximum output.

 You have to dance the routine full out, with feeling! Kick your face! Leave it all on the floor! Don't you want to win top solo?"

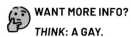 **WANT MORE INFO?**
THINK: GO HARD OR GO HOME.

Full-Spectrum ▲

FULL-SPECTRUM

▼ *adjective*

Total, intergenerational, culturally diverse inclusion within the LGBTQIA+ community across gender and sexuality spectrums. Typically used in the phrase "full-spectrum community," the term is used to create space for marginalized groups within the gay community.

SEE ALSO
RAINBOW

❝ We need language and spaces dedicated to bringing everyone in our queer family—in all its diverse glory—together in an effort to create and support a full-spectrum community.❞

 WANT MORE INFO?
THINK: **ALL-INCLUSIVE.**

FUTCH

▼ *noun*

A lesbian, bisexual, or queer female who presents herself as a mix of feminine and masculine; a portmanteau of "femme" and "butch."

SEE ALSO
SOFT STUD, SOFT BUTCH, "The Lesbian Spectrum," p. 255

p. 255

❝A futch lesbian is the dopest!❞

 WANT MORE INFO?
THINK: **A BUTCH GIRL AND FEMME GIRL UNITED IN ONE BODY.**

 USAGE NOTE: This term originated in the lesbian community.

Tucking & Binding 101

HOW DO YOU **EXPRESS** YOUR GENDER?

HERE ARE A few do-it-yourself practices for producing an appearance that matches your gender expression or desired drag performance persona. A few friends created this safe, easy-to-follow, step-by-step tutorial to tucking and binding.

Always talk to your parent, trusted adult, and/or doctor before you start tucking and binding. It is best to research the benefits and risks of gender-affirming practices.

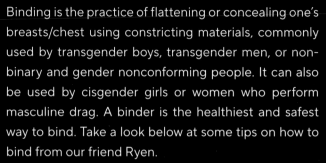

How to Bind

Binding is the practice of flattening or concealing one's breasts/chest using constricting materials, commonly used by transgender boys, transgender men, or non-binary and gender nonconforming people. It can also be used by cisgender girls or women who perform masculine drag. A binder is the healthiest and safest way to bind. Take a look below at some tips on how to bind from our friend Ryen.

1. Based on your body type, select a properly sized binder. You can buy a binder online or apply for a program that gives away free binders. Do not use tape or bandages.

2. Step into the binder as opposed to pulling it over your head. It's much easier! If you feel uncomfortable with the binder on your skin, wear a shirt underneath it.

3. Adjust your chest/breasts outward and down for a natural and flat look in the binder.

4. Put a shirt on over your binder and double-check everything is adjusted.
   PRO TIP: Dark-colored shirts mask a lot!

5. To ensure safety, inform your parents, guardians, or doctor that you are wearing binders. Also, do not sleep in or wear a binder for long periods of time, because it may cause lack of oxygen, bruising, or tissue damage.

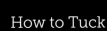

How to Tuck

Tucking is a practice of concealing one's genitals and is commonly used by transgender girls, women, or non-binary and gender nonconforming people. Cisgender boys and men who perform in drag also conceal their genitals. Take a look below for some tips on tucking and taping from Genderosity and Brenda Dharling.

OLD WAY, *courtesy of Genderosity*

1. If needed, shave the genitals with a good quality razor. You want the area nice and smooth.

2. Put testicles in hip cavities and pull the penis back between your legs.

3. Put napkin over shaft of penis to protect it from the tape.

4. Take duct tape strips and tape the covered penis using a front-to-back taping technique.

5. Repeat until satisfied.

NEW WAY, *courtesy of Brenda Dharling*

1. If needed, shave genitals with a good razor and make sure you use a shaving cream or gel. Get that hair off!

2. Put testicles in hip cavities. Here is where the tucking begins. If it's your first time, it may feel uncomfortable. But you will get the hang of it over time.

3. Pull penis back to anus. Remember tight, tight, tight.

4. Pull up gaff/tucking pants. Make sure you choose a pair that works best for you. Spandex and microfiber are a good choice to keep everything nice and tight.

History Lesson: Gays in the Military

HOMOSEXUALITY WAS ILLEGAL in all branches of the American military and subject to severe punishment dating back as early as the Revolutionary War. Men were discharged from the armed forces if found engaging in same-sex relationships throughout the eighteenth and nineteenth centuries. By the mid-1940s, women who served in the Women's Army Corps (WAC) were also discharged if found engaging in intimate same-sex affairs.

In 1975, Sergeant Leonard Matlovich—a gay man who dedicated his life to the air force and received a Bronze Star and a Purple Heart—became the face of the gay rights movement with his groundbreaking *Time* magazine interview and cover. The cover of the magazine showed Matlovich in his US Air Force military uniform with a caption reading, "'I Am a Homosexual': The Gay Drive for Acceptance." This marked the beginning of a broader cultural conversation around equal rights in the military.

The US military banned openly gay, lesbian, bisexual, and transgender people from service until 1993, insisting "Homosexuality is incompatible with military service." President Bill Clinton signed Don't Ask Don't Tell (DADT) into law, allowing gay, lesbian, and bisexual people to serve in the military, as long as they kept their sexual orientation to themselves.

In 2011, President Barack Obama repealed DADT, asserting that any person, regardless of sexual orientation or gender identity, could serve openly and freely in the US military without limitation. However, under President Donald Trump's administration and the Transgender Military Ban, the fight for transgender and intersex equality in the armed forces was an ongoing battle. In 2021, President Joe Biden lifted the transgender ban, ensuring all LGBTQIA+ people are able to serve in the Unites States military.

Gg

GAFF

▼ noun

A clothing item used for people assigned male at birth (AMAB) to smooth out the appearance of their genitals, especially when wearing slim-fitting clothing or practicing tucking.

SEE ALSO
TUCK, "Tucking & Binding 101," *p. 163*

"

MOM: *Quinn, we are running late. You need to come down and eat breakfast!*
QUINN: *I need ten more minutes! I'm having trouble*

putting my T-tape and gaff on.
MOM: *Do you want me to pull up the YouTube video again to help you?*

 WANT MORE INFO?
THINK: **TIGHT UNDERGARMENT USED TO TUCK YOUR AMAB PRIVATE PARTS.**

USAGE NOTE: This term is commonly used in the transgender, nonbinary, gender nonconforming, and drag communities.

GAG

▼ verb

To be in a state of total surprise or disbelief. The

terms SCREAM or DIE can also be used.

RELATED
GAGGED *adjective*

❝ I had them all gagging when I spelled 'hippopotomonstrosesquip-pedaliophobia' correctly! Ha! Fear? No, I laugh in the face of long words."

 WANT MORE INFO? *THINK:* **CHOKING ON EMOTION.**

 USAGE NOTE: This term originated in ballroom culture. It has been appropriated by the larger LGBTQIA+ community and mainstream culture.

GAGA

▼ *noun*

SEE **WHAT'S THE T**

GAL PAL

▼ *noun*

A term typically used by people outside the queer community to describe two girls or women in what they view as a "close" relationship without acknowledging them as lesbians.

❝ Kristen Stewart always has a close gal pal for some reason. She and Dylan Meyer must be such good friends."

 WANT MORE INFO? *THINK:* **THE WAY A STRAIGHT PERSON MIGHT REFER TO A LESBIAN COUPLE.**

▼   Gag

GAWD

▼ *exclamation*

A nonreligious and non-blasphemous spelling of the word "God." Most times used as an intensifier to show a supreme reaction.

SEE ALSO
LAWD; YES, GAWD!

"

JAMAL: *Yes, GAWD!*
TYRONE: *Yes, queen! Didn't I tell you you'd look good in this?!*

 WANT MORE INFO? THINK: EXCLAMATION POINT, EXCLAMATION POINT, EXCLAMATION POINT!

▼ Gay

GAY

▼ *adjective*

Homosexual. Experiencing same-sex or same-gender attraction.

Queer, not completely heterosexual.

▼ *noun*

A homosexual or same-gender loving person. Often used to describe a male, but it's an identifier for many others.

" *The hardest thing about coming out wasn't that I was gay but finding the right words to tell my Mexican family I am gay. Most of the Spanish words are negative and repulsive like 'maricon.' That's not me. I'm myself, I'm just E."*
—ERNESTO

 WANT MORE INFO? *THINK:* **A PERSON WHO EXISTS SOMEWHERE ON THE SEXUALITY**

SPECTRUM OTHER THAN HETEROSEXUAL.

USAGE NOTE: This term is commonly used as an inclusive identifier for anyone who does not strictly identify as heterosexual. The use of this term relies on an individual's preference.

DID YOU KNOW The first recognized gay organization in America was the Society for Human Rights, founded in 1924 by Henry Gerber in Chicago, Illinois, to reform anti-homosexual laws. In 1950, Harry Hay and other gay men in Los Angeles founded the Mattachine Society to protect and improve the rights of gay people. Both organizations added momentum to the gay rights movement and inspired other organizations and activists to join the fight for equality.

GAY-BASHING

▼ *noun*

The harassment and mistreatment of LGBTQIA+ people. Verbal, physical, and emotional mistreatment all fall under the umbrella of gay-bashing.

SEE ALSO

"Gaybashing Must Stop!" *p. 172,* "Hate Crime Epidemic," *p. 408,* **HOMOPHOBIA**

▼ *verb*

Engaging in the activity of mistreating gay, lesbian, or queer people.

❝ *Gay-bashing must STOP! This October, let's go purple on Spirit Day to support all LGBTQIA+ youth. Let's build better schools where queer students have the opportunity to explore identity, express themselves, and live freely as they are."*

 WANT MORE INFO? *THINK:* QUEER BULLYING AND HATE CRIMES.

GAYBASHING MUST STOP!

PREVENT BULLYING: Together, Let's Use Our Superpowers!

CALLING ALL students, teachers, administrators, coaches, parents, families, and school communities. Show your support to **CREATE POSITIVE CHANGE!**

October is National Bullying Prevention Month.

NATIONAL BULLYING PREVENTION MONTH was founded in 2006 by PACER's National Bullying Prevention Center to raise awareness about childhood bullying and encourage school districts across the United States to eradicate this kind of treatment. Many LGBTQIA+ students experience bullying in school because of their gender identity, gender expression, romantic attraction, and sexual orientation. Queer youth are often teased, physically mishandled, and discriminated against, causing emotional frustration and hindering their learning performance. Queer youth also experience mistreatment in online spaces, known as cyberbullying. When the school community—principals, teachers, counselors, parents, coaches, staff, and other students—sees bullying behavior, they must intervene and stop it immediately. This not only provides a sense of protection to LGBTQIA+ students, but also sends a message to the student body that this behavior is not tolerated. Creating a "Safe Schools Policy" implementing teacher training on anti-bullying and building safe schools for LGBTQIA+ students is imperative to their learning. Organizations like StopBullying, It Gets Better, GSA, GLSEN, and many others have created effective anti-bullying prevention strategies to help both schools and communities achieve unbiased and welcoming spaces.

GAYBIE OR GAYBY

▼ *noun*

A young gay or queer person.

❝ *We are having an online discussion for gaybies who need support and guidance on how to come out to their parents.*❞

 WANT MORE INFO?
THINK: LGBTQIA+ YOUTH.

A child of a gay or queer parent or parents.

SEE ALSO
QUEERSPAWN

❝ *We are so emotional right now! Kurt and I just got our adoption papers finalized. We're getting our gayby!*❞

 WANT MORE INFO?
THINK: A KID WITH LGBTQIA+ PARENTS.

A close friend who identifies as gay or queer.

❝ *I love a good debate with my gaybies. Everyone's opinion is always respected.*❞

 WANT MORE INFO?
THINK: YOUR LGBTQIA+ BESTIE.

GAYBORHOOD

▼ *noun*

A neighborhood primarily made up of LGBTQIA+ residences, businesses, and entertainment.

SEE ALSO
"USA Gayborhoods," *p.* 406

❝ *There are gayborhoods in cities all across the US! In Philadelphia, down to New Orleans, and over to Salt Lake City. Just follow the rainbow!*❞

 WANT MORE INFO?
THINK: THE CASTRO, WEST HOLLYWOOD, BOYSTOWN, AND NEW YORK'S TRIFECTA: THE

VILLAGE, CHELSEA, AND HELL'S KITCHEN.

GAY CHRISTIAN

▼ *noun*

A queer person who practices Christianity.

SEE ALSO
"Religion and LGBTQIA+ Believers," *p. 352*

❝ *Churches that welcome gay Christians believe that it is unjust to close their church doors to anyone who is in search of God's word.*❞

 WANT MORE INFO?
THINK: "YOU CAN BE PART OF THE LGBTQIA+ COMMUNITY AND STILL BELIEVE IN GOD AND HIS GOSPEL PLAN." —DAVID ARCHULETA

DID YOU KNOW The Naming Project, a Christian ministry that celebrates LGBTQIA+ youth, was founded by Jay Wiesner and Ross Murray in 2003 to provide a safe and inclusive spiritual space for queer Christian teens to grow and learn. Wiesner and Murray also created a faith-based summer camp for LGBTQIA+ seventh to twelfth graders and allies to explore the beautiful truth about who they are and fully understand God's unconditional love for them—empowering youth to know that sexuality and spirituality can be discussed and explored together.

Gay Christian ▼

GAY DAD

▼ noun

A gay man or masc-identifying person who is supportive in the development and well-being of younger LGBTQIA+ people. The term "gay father" can also be used.

AALIYAH: *Let's throw a big surprise party at the Center to celebrate our gay dads.*
MARQUIS: *Man, if it wasn't for James stepping up and being a father to me, I'd be so lost.*

 WANT MORE INFO?
THINK: **A GAY MENTOR.**

USAGE NOTE:	This term originated in the gay male community. It has been appropriated by the larger LGBTQIA+ community.

GAYDAR

▼ noun

The perceived ability to intuitively identify if a person is gay, bisexual, or queer. The term "queerdar" can also be used.

YE: *How did you know he was gay? He doesn't look or even dress gay.*
COREY: *Gayness can't be put in a box! It's experienced differently for each person. But, if you must know . . . my gaydar is 20/20.*

 WANT MORE INFO?
THINK: **A SKILL FOR IDENTIFYING GAYS.**

GAY GAMES

▼ noun

International sporting events that celebrate LGBTQIA+ people.

My uncle participated in the 1986 Gay Games in San Francisco and he promised to watch me complete in the games when I get older. I can't wait to make him proud and continue the legacy."

 WANT MORE INFO? *THINK:* **THE GAY OLYMPICS.**

DID YOU KNOW The Gay Games started in 1982, by Tom Waddell, Brenda Young, and other activists, as a nine-day international sporting and cultural event specifically for LGBTQIA+ athletes. The games were first held in San Francisco, but since its inception, other host cities like Vancouver, Sydney, Chicago, Paris, and Hong Kong have invited competitors eighteen-plus from all over the world to compete—even from countries where being gay or queer is illegal—and experience the celebration of LGBTQIA+ athletic acceptance and inclusion. Today, the Gay Games feature over thirty-five sporting disciplines—including aquatics, ball games, racquet sports, track and field, and marathons—and the Funding Support Program (Gay Games Scholarship) supports underfunded participants from around the world in competing, bringing more access and diversity to the games.

GAY HUSBAND

▼ *noun*

A gay man or masc-identifying person who has formed a close platonic friendship with a woman or femme-identifying person and has playfully been adopted as a "husband."

AUNT SANDRA: *Wait, I am confused? Your dinner date is with Juan? I thought he was gay!*

AUNT KELLY: *Oh, he absolutely is. He's my gay husband.*

 WANT MORE INFO? *THINK:* **A GAL'S MASC GAY BESTIE.**

GAY ICON

▼ *noun*

A public figure—queer or not—who is exalted by the LGBTQIA+ community.

SEE ALSO

BICON, DYKON

❝ We salute our gay icons for their individuality, their fabulosity, and for supporting our queer community with a little extra love each and every day.❞

 WANT MORE INFO? *THINK:* **DEAR LADY GAGA, THANK YOU FOR BRINGING US "BORN THIS WAY." LOVE, QUEER NATION.**

GAY LITERATURE

▼ *noun*

A genre of literature written for and by the LGBTQIA+ community. Themes, characters, and plots are centered around queer lifestyles. The term "queer literature" can also be used. Lesbian-themed literature is referenced as "lesbian literature."

❝ *I was looking on Amazon for some queer literature for youth and found* The Best at It, Ivy Aberdeen's Letter to the World, *and* This Is Our Rainbow. *Go check it out!"*

 WANT MORE INFO? THINK: QUEER FICTION, NONFICTION, ROMANCE, SCI-FI, YA, AND HORROR BOOKS.

DID YOU KNOW Queer literature represents stories and identities across the spectrum that celebrate LGBTQIA+ culture. Both classic and modern queer literature written by award-winning authors Oscar Wilde, Virginia Woolf, Leslie Feinberg, Edmund White, and Essex Hemphill (to name a few) have explored queer identity and imagination in great depths, centering the focus on articulating the nuances and diversity of sexuality, gender, and expression. Queer literature provides a platform for youth, and adults alike, to experience LGBTQIA+ characters, plots, and feelings, shows authentic examples of what it's like to be queer, and reflects LGBTQIA+ identity, history, and culture. Queer literature is a necessary resource that affirms the LGBTQIA+ community, and Lambda Literary is a staple queer organization that garners national visibility for LGBTQIA+ books, publishers, and bookstores.

GAY MARRIAGE

▼ *noun*

SEE **MARRIAGE EQUALITY**

GAYMER

▼ *noun*

A queer individual who is part of the gaming community—one who plays video, tabletop, and/or computer games. The term "gay gamer" can also be used.

❝ *Hey, are you going to the GaymerX convention this year? My favorite Twitch and YouTube gaymers will be there!"*

 WANT MORE INFO? THINK: LGBTQIA+ YOUTH WHO LOVE *FORTNITE*, *CALL OF DUTY*, *THE SIMS*, *MINECRAFT*, AND OF COURSE, *ROBLOX*!

DID YOU KNOW

Gaming has a history of misogyny and homophobia. GaymerX, a nonprofit organization, was created in 2012 to champion queer gamers and game developers, with the goal of creating a safer space within the gaming community for LGBTQIA+ players. Over the decade, LGBTQIA+ game designers have actively advocated for more queer representation, encouraging the gaming market to be more inclusive. In 2023, the queer-friendly video game, *The Sims 4*, created gender-affirming features—medical wearables, binders, and shapewear, among others—allowing players to create characters with transgender, nonbinary, and genderqueer expressions and identities.

GAY MOTHER

▼ *noun*

A lesbian or femme-identifying person who is supportive in the development and well-being of younger LGBTQIA+ people. The term "gay mom" can also be used.

❝ *I am helping my gay mom work on a mural for the LGBT youth center. She is such an amazing artist! I want to learn everything from her.*❞

 WANT MORE INFO? THINK: A GAY MENTOR.

GAY PRIDE

▼ *noun*

SEE **PRIDE**

GAYSIAN

▼ *noun*

A gay, bisexual, or queer person of Asian descent.

❝ *High five to Vicky Du and her short documentary* Gaysians! *It tells the stories of five queer and trans Asian American people navigating life, family, and culture. It's incredible representation!*❞

 WANT MORE INFO? THINK: QUEER. ASIAN. HERE.

USAGE NOTE: This term may be considered a stereotype or derogatory.

GCS

▼ *noun*

SEE **GENDER AFFIRMATION SURGERY**

GENDER

▼ *noun*

In a historical context, this refers to the characteristics associated with masculinity and femininity.

❝ *Everyone keeps asking my mom if she is having a girl or a boy! Why does the* baby's gender have to be a boy or girl? Why can't the baby just be a baby until they develop their own gender?"

 WANT MORE INFO? *THINK:* **BLUE FOR BOYS. PINK FOR GIRLS.**

In a modern context, this refers to a broader range of characteristics that go beyond the gender binary.

SEE ALSO
GENDER EXPRESSION, GENDER IDENTITY, "The **Genderbread Person,**" *p. 73*

66 *Gender and sex are often used interchangeably, but they are not the same! Gender relates to a person's identity and self-expression, while sex relates to a person's reproductive organs. The two do not have to be aligned in a traditional sense in order to be legit."*

 WANT MORE INFO? *THINK:* **A COMPLEX AND**

LAYERED EXPRESSION OF A PERSON.

▼ *verb*

To assign masculine or feminine characteristics to a person, place, or thing.

66 *Drew likes pink, but he never feels comfortable wearing it because society has gendered the color as feminine. Just let colors be colors!"*

 WANT MORE INFO? *THINK:* **TO IMPOSE MALE-NESS OR FEMALE-NESS ON SOMEONE OR SOMETHING.**

DID YOU KNOW Some youth begin to express transgender or nonbinary feelings before they even start school. When schools implement gender diversity practices, concepts, and language during the primary grades, it creates an inclusive and nondiscriminatory learning environment that is beneficial to all students. Allowing students the ability to choose colors, play games, and sing songs that feel right to them, not because it's a "girl" or a "boy" thing, is a great way to empower children to be themselves.

GENDER-AFFIRMING CARE

▼ *noun*

Health care treatments and services that support one's gender identity. Examples of care may include medication, therapy, surgery, education, medication, counseling, and community support, among others.

❝ *Gender-affirming care can give a young queer person the confidence they need to be themselves.* ❞

 WANT MORE INFO? *THINK:* **"TRANSGENDER MINORS HAVE A RIGHT TO GENDER-AFFIRMING CARE."**

gender. However, in recent years, several states have restricted access to gender-affirming care for transgender, nonbinary, and gender nonconforming youth. States like Alabama, Florida, Texas, and Arkansas view some gender-affirming care, like blockers, as unethical and prohibit health-care specialists from providing this treatment to minors. Even families can receive legal disciplinary actions if they are found seeking gender-affirming care for their children. With the Biden administration's Equality Act, along with organizations like the National Center for Transgender Equality and Transgender Legal Defense & Education Fund, plus LGBTQIA+ advocates across the country, people are working tirelessly to fight for transgender youth rights.

DID YOU KNOW Some youth may feel that their assigned sex at birth or physical body type does not align with their gender identity and want to explore gender-affirming care. Health-care specialists prescribe medication, therapy, and counseling, as well as educational resources, to help queer youth feel more aligned with their

GENDER AFFIRMATION SURGERY

▼ *noun*

A medical procedure for a transgender, nonbinary, or gender nonconforming person that alters the physical body in order for the physical appearance to reflect their gender identity. The terms "gender confirmation surgery," GCS, sex reassignment surgery, and SRS can also be used. The TGNC community often use the words PRE-OP and POST-OP when referring to gender affirmation surgery.

66 *My parents said they are in support of me getting my gender affirmation surgery when I turn sixteen. I just want to feel more aligned with my gender identity."*

WANT MORE INFO?
THINK: A WAY OF CONNECTING THE MIND AND THE BODY TO AFFIRM A PERSON'S GENDER.

USAGE NOTE: Using the terms "gender confirmation surgery" or "gender affirmation surgery" over "sex reassignment surgery" may be more affirming for transgender, nonbinary, and gender nonconforming people.

DID YOU KNOW In America, evidence of gender affirmation surgery (then called sex reassignment surgery) was apparent as early as the 1940s. Transgender woman Christine Jorgensen was the first American documented to undergo the procedure.

Genderbend ▲

GENDERBEND

▼ *verb*

To go against, or "bend," expected gender norms physically, behaviorally, or otherwise.

> RELATED
> **GENDERBENDER** *noun*

66 *Genderbending is using your outward expression to absolutely disagree with and undermine society's old-fashioned ways of thinking about gender. You can be who you want to be."*

 WANT MORE INFO?
THINK: **TO EMBRACE MASCULINITY, FEMININITY, AND ANDROGYNY, BLURRING THE LINES BETWEEN "GIRL" AND "BOY."**

GENDER BINARY

▼ *noun*

The enforced societal system of male and female identities—two distinct identities that each come with a set of expected, gendered roles.

RELATED
GENDER BINARISM *noun*

SEE ALSO
BINARY

❝ *The gender binary is so limiting. It hinders my way of existing. I don't want to adhere to a gender role or stereotype. I just want to be me."*

 WANT MORE INFO? *THINK:* **A WAY OF THINKING ABOUT GENDER IN BLACK AND WHITE.**

Gender Binary ▲

GENDER DIVERSITY

▼ *noun*

The presence of gender identities that are inclusive of expressions outside the binary.

Fair and equitable treatment to all gender identities.

❝ *Research has shown that more schools around the country are seeking ways to address the increasing gender diversity seen in youth-aged students. Schools that implement gender-inclusive practices are committed to celebrating diversity and creating a safe and inclusive environment for all students."*

 WANT MORE INFO? *THINK:* **YOUR IDENTITY IS WELCOMED!**

GENDER DYSPHORIA

▼ *noun*

A profound dissatisfaction with one's physical and/or mental state, caused by discrepancies between one's gender identity and gender assigned at birth.

SEE ALSO
DYSPHORIA

❝ *Signs of gender dysphoria may include social isolation, depression, and anxiety in addition to being super uncomfortable in one's body. Here at the clinic, we offer outpatient therapy to help you unpack these complicated feelings.*❞

 WANT MORE INFO? *THINK:* **A DEEP DISCONNECT BETWEEN BODY AND GENDER IDENTITY.**

DID YOU KNOW Many artists, creatives, and performers are advocating for award shows to embrace gender diversity. Some movie, television, or theater award shows have non-gendered categories and other shows ask the person being nominated to choose their preferred binary category (e.g. "Leading Actress" or "Supporting Actor"). Many nonbinary, genderqueer, and agender people feel having to choose a gendered category that does not authentically represent their identity is challenging and unfair. Trans nonbinary Broadway performer Justin David Sullivan made a public statement saying, "I hope the award shows across the industry will expand their reach to be able to honor and award people of all gender identities." In 2023, Broadway performers Alex Newell and J. Harrison Ghee were the first nonbinary actors to win Tony Awards, through both were nominated in "Actor" categories.

GENDER EXPANSIVE

▼ *noun*

An umbrella term that refers to gender identities that do not conform to society's dominant view of the gender binary.

❝ *'Gender expansive' is the term to use instead that*

allows folks creativity and freedom to not fit into a societal norm."

—JACKIE GOLOB

 WANT MORE INFO? *THINK:* HONORING THE MANY WAYS NON-CISGENDER IDENTITIES ARE EXPRESSED.

GENDER EXPRESSION

▼ *noun*

Outward characteristics—such as appearance, behaviors, and attitudes—that communicate a person's identity to society.

SEE ALSO

"The Genderbread Person," *p. 73*

❝ Gender expression is fluid. It's a bit of this and a dash of that. Just ask the Genderbread Person."

 WANT MORE INFO? *THINK:* HOW A PERSON

EXPRESSES THEIR GENDER THROUGH COOL HAIRCUTS, CLOTHES, HOBBIES, AND OVERALL PERSONALITY.

GENDER-FLUID OR GENDERFLUID

▼ *adjective*

Not confined to a fixed gender expression or presentation.

❝ Identifying as genderfluid—not limited by masculinity and femininity—is so empowering!"

 WANT MORE INFO? *THINK:* GENDER EXPRESSION AND/OR IDENTITY THAT FLOWS BACK AND FORTH AND ALL AROUND THE GENDER SPECTRUM.

USAGE NOTE: This term is commonly used in the transgender, nonbinary, and gender nonconforming communities

GENDERFLUX

▼ *adjective*

An identifier for people who experience a range of intensity within a particular gender identity.

❝*I am genderflux. I identify mostly as female, but the intensity of my femininity changes over time. I have felt ultrafeminine, I have felt nonbinary and femme, and I've also felt super butch, but still female.*❞

 WANT MORE INFO?
THINK: YOUR GENDER IS A LAMP WITH A DIMMER SWITCH—THE LIGHT ITSELF DOESN'T CHANGE, BUT THE DIMNESS AND BRIGHTNESS FLUCTUATE OVER TIME.

 USAGE NOTE: This term is commonly used in the transgender, nonbinary, and gender nonconforming communities.

GENDER IDENTITY

▼ *noun*

The internal understanding of one's gender and the self. This identity may or may not correlate with one's assigned sex at birth and may not be directly correlated to one's outward gender expression.

SEE ALSO
"The Genderbread Person," *p. 73,* **"Finding My Identity: 'Who Am I,'"** *p. 136*

❝*It's important for parents, teachers, and counselors to accept the gender identity and language queer youth use to label themselves. Their pronouns, chosen names, and their choice in expressing their gender are all valid.*❞

 WANT MORE INFO?
THINK: THE INTERNAL FEELINGS A PERSON HAS ABOUT THEIR GENDER.

Gender Identity ▲

GENDERISM

▼ *noun*

Grouping individuals into distinct masculine and feminine categories based on the belief that there are or should be only two genders. The term "gender binarism" can also be used.

> SEE ALSO
>
> **GENDER BINARY**

❝ *We are taught genderism as early as kindergarten, where name tags and bathrooms are separate based on kids' male-ness and female-ness.*"

 WANT MORE INFO?
THINK: A PERVASIVE BELIEF THAT THE WORLD IS MADE UP OF ONLY TWO DIFFERENT GROUPS OF PEOPLE: MEN AND WOMEN.

GENDERLESS

▼ *adjective*

Not identifying with any gender. The terms AGENDER or NONGENDER can also be used.

SEE ALSO
NEUTROIS, NULL GENDER

❝*Mx. Ollis's language arts class is my favorite. Ze always asks us to use genderless language in our discussions. This way all the students feel included and welcomed in the classroom.*❞

 WANT MORE INFO? THINK: NOT FEMALE, NOT MALE, NOT BOTH, OR NEITHER.

USAGE NOTE: This term is commonly used in the transgender, nonbinary, and gender nonconforming communities.

DID YOU KNOW Using genderless or gender-neutral language in schools, camps, sports, and other youth activities allows for a more inclusive environment for transgender, nonbinary, genderfluid, and gender nonconforming (TGNC) youth. For example, instead of saying "boys and girls," you can say "students," "athletes," "campers," and "players," among others. Gender-neutral practices help normalize the idea that everyone is included and equally prioritized regardless of their gender identity. Public school districts, as well as charter, private, and independent schools across the country, are implementing gender-neutral platforms and professional development trainings, and incorporating discussions with youth around gender identity, gender expression, and sexual orientation. These initiatives will assist in providing a safe, positive, and fun environment for everyone to learn and grow.

GENDER-NEUTRAL DRESS CODE

▼ *noun*

A dress code policy in a school or other institution without gender-specific rules.

❝*A gender-neutral dress code supports body*

positivity and a feminist cause—allowing everybody to wear whatever they want without being targeted as 'distracting' or 'inappropriate.'"

 WANT MORE INFO? *THINK: A DRESS CODE THAT DOESN'T REPRIMAND STUDENTS FOR THEIR WARDROBE CHOICES.*

GENDER NEUTRALITY

▼ *noun*

The movement to end gender discrimination through means of gender-neutral language, the end of gender-based segregation, and other social causes.

❝ *Gender neutrality is practiced by introducing more gender-neutral restrooms, the ability to select a gender-neutral option on ID cards,*

passports, and other government forms, and implementing fewer gender-specific groupings. These initiatives will help us build a more equal and loving society."

 WANT MORE INFO? *THINK: "A GENDER-EQUAL SOCIETY WOULD BE ONE WHERE THE WORD 'GENDER' DOES NOT EXIST: WHERE EVERYONE CAN BE THEMSELVES."* —GLORIA STEINEM

DID YOU KNOW In April 2022, under the Biden administration, US citizens were first able to select an X gender marker—unspecified or another gender identity other than "male" or "female"—on their US passport application.

GENDER NONCONFORMING

▼ *adjective*

Expressing one's gender in a way that does not fit neatly into the gender binary. Often abbreviated as "GNC." The term "GENDER VARIANCE" can also be used.

> SEE ALSO
> **GENDERQUEER, NONBINARY**

66 *I'm gender nonconforming. Like, some days I feel like a man, but then other days I feel like a woman. I don't really—I think my energies are really all over the place. Any opportunity I have to break down stereotypes of the binary, I am down for it, I'm here for it."*

—JONATHAN VAN NESS

 WANT MORE INFO? *THINK:* **NOT BOUND TO A MALE OR FEMALE GENDER IDENTITY. COULD USE SHE/THEY, HE/THEY, AND ZE/ZEM PRONOUNS.**

USAGE NOTE: "Gender nonconforming," "gender variance," and "gender diverse" are often used as umbrella terms for people who identify outside the gender binary. It is always important to ask how a person identifies, however, because every person's preference is unique.

GENDERQUEER

▼ *adjective*

Not identifying with the conventional labels of female or male. This person may relate to both genders, express gender ambiguity, or refrain from expressing any gender at all.

> SEE ALSO
>
> **GENDER NONCONFORMING, NONBINARY**

66 *I'm a genderqueer Taurus Sun, Pisces rising, who loves skateboarding, gaming, manga, LEGO sets, astrology, and new moons."*

 WANT MORE INFO?
THINK: NOT BOUND BY THE GENDER BINARY.

USAGE NOTE: This term is commonly used in the transgender, nonbinary, and gender nonconforming communities.

GENDER QUESTIONING

▼ *adjective*

An identifier for an individual who is curious about or exploring their gender identity or gender expression.

> SEE ALSO
>
> **"Finding My Identity: 'Who Am I,'"** *p. 136,* **"Common Pronouns 101,"** *p. 101*

66 *Sometimes I feel like I am a girl and use she/her pronouns. Sometimes I feel nonbinary and want to use they/them pronoun. I don't know what to label myself yet. I'm still in a place where I am gender-questioning my identity."*

 WANT MORE INFO?
THINK: EXPLORING ONE'S GENDER TO SEE WHAT FEELS RIGHT.

GENDER VARIANCE

▼ *adjective*

SEE **GENDER NONCONFORMING**

GET INTO THIS

▼ *idiom*

To bring attention to something—a specific idea, attitude, or fashionable item.

❝

FARAH: *Oh, that's a cute Ivy Park jumpsuit!*

NATASHA: *Thank you, friend! GET INTO THIS!*

FARAH: *You flexing! Just make sure your big sis doesn't find out you took it out her closet.*

 WANT MORE INFO?
THINK: "COME ON, DON'T YOU LOVE IT?!"

 USAGE NOTE: This term is commonly used in the Black gay community and the larger queer and trans people of color (QTPOC) community.

GET IT

▼ *idiom*

Giving a compliment or pushing someone to do something great.

❝ *GET IT, GET IT, GET IT, POP IT. Yes, girl! You betta dance!"*

 WANT MORE INFO?
THINK: "DO IT!"

 USAGE NOTE: This term originated in Black American culture and is commonly used in the Black gay and queer community.

GILLETTE BLADE

▼ *noun*

A dated term that originated in the 1950s referencing a bisexual woman, leading others to infer that her sexuality cuts both ways.

❝ *Gillette blades, bicycles, AC/DC, swinging both ways … there have been so many labels used over the years to describe bisexuality."*

USAGE NOTE: This term may be considered a stereotype or derogatory and have negative connotations as it limits bisexuality to the gender binary. It is inappropriate to use this label if a person has not self-identified as such.

GIRL OR **GURL**

▼ *noun*

A term of endearment for a friend or loved one, regardless of gender. Often used in conversation to grab someone's attention. The terms BABY GIRL, "gurr," or "girrrl" can also be used.

SEE ALSO

GIRL, PLEASE; SISTER

 Girrrl! Wait until I tell you what happened at recess. You are not going to believe it!"

USAGE NOTE: This term originated in Black American culture and is commonly used in the Black gay and queer community. It has been appropriated by the larger LGBTQIA+ community and mainstream culture.

GIRL CRUSH

▼ *noun*

A straight girl's intense, platonic admiration for another girl. Girl crushes are typically not physical or romantic by nature and tend to be between straight females.

 Wesley is such a boss. Her nuclear energy research project was flawless, and she always has the funkiest style. I have such a girl crush!"

195

THE QUEENS' ENGLISH

GIRLFAG

▼ *noun*

A cisgender girl who is attracted to a gay guy.

"

CLIFF: *I have a girlfag!*

MORRIS: *Shut up, no, you don't.*

CLIFF: *I do! Johanna told me at lunch, "Cliff, I know you're gay, but I want to be your girlfriend sooooo bad!"*

MORRIS: *I'm screaming!*

 WANT MORE INFO? *THINK*: **A STRAIGHT GIRL CRUSHING ON A GAY BOY.**

USAGE NOTE: This term originated in the gay male community. The term "fag" originated as a derogatory slur for gay men but has since been reclaimed by some of the LGBTQIA+ community. It may still have negative connotations for some people. Please be aware that this term can be considered mature.

GIRL, PLEASE

▼ *idiom*

A term of dismissal to show disinterest. The phrase, "girl, bye" can also be used.

" *Girl, please. I am not about to help you with your chores. You should have done them yesterday when you were supposed to!"*

 WANT MORE INFO? *THINK*: **ABSOLUTELY NOT.**

USAGE NOTE: This term originated in Black American culture and is commonly used in the Black gay and queer community. It has been appropriated by the larger LGBTQIA+ community and mainstream culture.

GIRL, WHA?

▼ *idiom*

A response to express misunderstanding.

" *Girl, wha? I can't hear what you are saying from underneath this hair dryer!"*

WANT MORE INFO?
THINK: "COME AGAIN?"

A phrase used to express surprise.

" *Girl, wha? You're lying! You got an autographed poster from Ariana Grande!"*

 WANT MORE INFO? *THINK:* A FLABBERGASTED RESPONSE.

USAGE NOTE: This term originated in Black American culture and is commonly used in the Black gay and queer community. It has been appropriated by the larger LGBTQIA+ community and mainstream culture.

GIRLS, THE

▼ *noun*

Good friends. This term is often used by gay men to refer to their closest friends.

" *The girls are going over to Niles's house to watch Love, Victor. Want to come?"*

 WANT MORE INFO?
THINK: THE BESTIES.

GIVEN NAME

▼ *noun*

A person's legal name that was assigned at birth.

SEE ALSO
CHOSEN NAME, DEADNAME

" *On these official documents you are required to use your complete given name—first, middle, and last names."*

 WANT MORE INFO?
THINK: THE NAME ON SOMEONE'S BIRTH CERTIFICATE.

GIVING FACE

▼ *idiom*

SEE **FACE**

GIVING ME LIFE

▼ *idiom*

An expression used to announce extreme excitement.

SEE ALSO
GOT MY LIFE

" *These reruns of* The Golden Girls *are giving me life! That Blanche. I bet she and I would kiki all day."*

 WANT MORE INFO?
THINK: EXTRAORDINARY ENTHUSIASM.

 USAGE NOTE: This term is commonly used in the Black gay community and the larger queer and trans people of color (QTPOC) community.

GLAMAZON

▼ *noun*

A tall and beautiful woman or femme.

" *Look at all these glamazons on* Teen Vogue! *I want to be a model some day!"*

 WANT MORE INFO?
THINK: ULTRAGLAM, ULTRAFEMININE, TALL BEAUTIES.

Glamazon ▲

GNC

▼ *noun*

SEE **GENDER NONCONFORMING**

GO BE WITH HER OR GO BE WITH IT

▼ *idiom*

An expression jokingly suggesting that someone go and connect with who or whatever attracts their attention.

"*I can't believe you have been watching Netflix for more than twelve hours. Geez, go be with it!*"

 WANT MORE INFO? *THINK:* **TWO MAGNETS CONNECTING.**

GOLDEN RULE

▼ *noun*

SEE **ABSOLUTE CODE**

GOLDILOCKS

▼ *noun*
A woman who enjoys the company of gay men who identify as bears.

"*Aw, look at Goldilocks and the three bears.*"

 WANT MORE INFO? *THINK:* **A GIRL WHO LOVES HER GAY TEDDY BEARS.**

GO OFF

▼ *idiom*
A command to deliver a

top-quality presentation. The superlative phrase is "go all the way off."

SEE ALSO
EAT IT

"*I need you to go off on the last four measures of this song. Sing every riff and run you know. We're gonna win this competition.*"

 WANT MORE INFO? *THINK:* **"GIVE ME ALL YOU'VE GOT!"**

To get upset.

"*I am about to go off in 2.2 seconds if that dog across the street doesn't stop barking! I need my beauty sleep!*"

 WANT MORE INFO? *THINK:* **TO TURN INTO THE HULK.**

 This term is commonly used in ballroom culture and the queer and trans people of color (QTPOC) community.

GOT MY LIFE

▼ *idiom*

An expression of total happiness, enjoyment, and fulfillment.

❝ *When Rihanna came out with Fenty Beauty, I got my life. Launching forty shades of foundation—for all skin tones—was legendary!"*

 WANT MORE INFO? *THINK:* **TOTALLY EUPHORIC.**

USAGE NOTE: This term originated in the Black gay community. It has been appropriated by the larger LGBTQIA+ community and mainstream culture.

GRANOLA

▼ *adjective*

Super health-conscious and environmentally aware—may practice a holistic lifestyle. This term is not limited to queer people.

❝ *Here are five healthy food tips for my granola community: Eat more seeded food; drink more functional beverages; try recycled ingredient foods and international foods; replace cow's milk with oat milk; and, don't forget plant-based omega-3 fatty acids are your friend!"*

 WANT MORE INFO? *THINK:* **HIPPIE-DIPPIE.**

 Granola ▲

GRAY-ASEXUAL OR GRAYSEXUAL

▼ *noun*

An asexual person who has positive views about physical attraction and connection, but may not have physical feelings or attraction toward others. People who identify with gray asexuality are often referred to as "a grace," "a gray ace," or "being gray-A."

SEE ALSO
ASEXUAL, ACEFLUX

❝ Asexual is 'No, I don't want a kiss.' Graysexual is 'Maybe, I might want a kiss.' Allosexual is 'Yes, I want to kiss.'"

 WANT MORE INFO?
THINK: **AN UMBRELLA TERM FOR THOSE WHO IDENTIFY AS SOMEWHERE ON THE ASEXUAL SPECTRUM.**

USAGE NOTE: This term originated in the asexual community.

GRAY QUEEN

▼ *noun*

A gay, bisexual, or queer person, often a man, employed in the financial services industry.

❝

DAUGHTER: *Wow, Dad! Is this you in the magazine?*
FATHER: *Yes, that's your papa bear! I am listed as one of the top LGBTQIA+ leaders in finance. Proud to be among the other gray queens.*
DAUGHTER: *Ha! Gray queens? Dad, I think the gay community has a word for everything!*

 WANT MORE INFO?
THINK: **QUEERS ON WALL STREET.**

USAGE NOTE: This term originated in gay male culture in the 1950s, when professional attire in the financial district was a gray flannel suit.

GUG

▼ *noun*

SEE **LUG**

GYM BUNNY

▼ *noun*

A gay, bisexual, or queer person, often a man, who spends excessive time in the gym. The terms MUSCLE MARY and "gym rat" can also be used.

> SEE ALSO
>
> **"Help! What Type of Gay Am I?,"** *p. 203*

❝ *I like working out and getting ripped. My goal is to beat Bryson and break the four-hundred-meter school record. I need gym bunny focus to do that!"*

 WANT MORE INFO? *THINK:* **SOMEONE WHO IS AT THE GYM SEVEN DAYS A WEEK.**

USAGE NOTE: This term originated in the gay male community.

GYNESEXUAL

▼ *adjective*

Experiencing attraction toward femininity.

> RELATED
>
> **GYNESEXUALITY** *noun*

> SEE ALSO
>
> **ANDROSEXUAL**

▼ *noun*

A gynesexual person.

❝ *I identify as agender and gynesexual. I don't identity with a binary gender, or any gender actually, and I'm attracted to people who are females, trans girls, nonbinary femme-of-center people, as well as guys who are feminine."*

 WANT MORE INFO? **THINK: ATTRACTED TO FEMME PEOPLE.**

USAGE NOTE: This term is commonly used in the nonbinary, genderfluid, and gender nonconforming communities.

HELP! WHAT TYPE OF GAY AM I?

MANY GAY MEN use a specific set of animal identifiers based on body type and age to identify other gay men. It is sometimes referred to as the "Animal Kingdom." These are playful labels based on stereotypes found within the gay male community.

BEAR	Big and broad, often with a belly, but sometimes built
CUB	Big and broad, often with a belly, but sometimes built
OTTER	Thin and athletic
PUP	Slender
WOLF	Lean, muscular
GYM BUNNY/ GYM RAT	Sculpted
JOCK	Muscular and athletic
CHUB	Very big
TWINK	Slender

HAIR	AGE	THINK
Lots	Age	A sturdy, hairy gay guy
Lots	Young or young-looking	Young gay boy who will grow up to be a bear
Lots	Any	Gay guy who is athletic, hairy, and at the gym several times a week
None	Any	A baby gay
Some	Any	A muscular, hairy, attractive guy
Doesn't matter	Bunny is under fifty; rat can be any age	Someone who works out at the gym seven days a week
Doesn't matter	Any	A super-duper athletic guy
Doesn't matter	Any	A guy who is pleasingly plump
None	Young	Baby-faced, skinny gay boy
None	Young	A twink with muscle

Hh

HARD FEMME

▼ *noun*

A queer person whose appearance is feminine and presents as strong, tough, and/or resilient.

❝ *Batwoman, Poison Ivy, Harley Quinn, and Nia Nal aka 'Dreamer' are all part of the hard femme club, baby!"*

 WANT MORE INFO? *THINK:* **FEMININITY WITH A KISS OF TOUGHNESS.**

 USAGE NOTE: This term originated in the lesbian community. It has been appropriated by the larger LGBTQIA+ community.

HATE CRIMES

▼ *noun*

Crimes, typically violent in nature, committed against a particular identity or group because of prejudice.

SEE ALSO

ACEPHOBIA, BIPHOBIA, FEMMEPHOBIA, HOMOPHOBIA, QUEERPHOBIA, LESBOPHOBIA, TRANSPHOBIA, "Hate Crime Epidemic," *p. 408*

❝ *The violence committed against queer people—especially trans women of color—is a national epidemic.*

Hate crimes can be deadly and we need more laws in place to protect us."

 WANT MORE INFO? *THINK:* **HATE TURNED PHYSICAL AND OFTEN DEADLY.**

DID YOU KNOW In 2009, President Barack Obama signed the Matthew Shepard and James Byrd, Jr., Hate Crimes Prevention Act into law. The act expanded upon the existing federal hate crime law to further protect Americans from crimes committed on the basis of gender, sexual orientation, or disability. Unfortunately, hate crimes are still prevalent in society today. On June 12, 2016, the Pulse nightclub shooting in Orlando, Florida, marked the deadliest hate crime committed on the LGBTQIA+ community in US history. A shooter opened fire on club patrons on a Latin-themed night, killing forty-nine people and wounding fifty-three others. Research has shown that hate crimes targeting the LGBTQIA+ community continue to rise yearly.

HAVE A SEAT

▼ *idiom*

A phrase expressing dissatisfaction with a person or action. The superlative phrase is "have several seats."

 I am going to need you to fall back and have several seats. You are getting on my nerves!"

 WANT MORE INFO? *THINK:* **"STOP WHAT YOU ARE DOING, IMMEDIATELY."**

USAGE NOTE: This term is commonly used in the Black gay community and the larger queer and trans people of color (QTPOC) community.

HE/HIM/HIS

▼ *pronouns*

A set of pronouns typically used for masculine-identifying people.

> SEE ALSO
>
> **"The Genderbread Person,"** *p. 73,* **"Common Pronouns 101,"** *p. 101*

❝ *Hi, I'm Clark. It's nice to meet you. I use he/him/his pronouns. What are your pronouns?"*

 WANT MORE INFO? *THINK:* **MASC IDENTIFIERS.**

CHLOE O. DAVIS

HENNY

▼ *noun*

SEE **HONEY**

HERMAPHRODITE

▼ *noun*

A dated, problematic term used for intersex individuals.

SEE **INTERSEX**

❝

MOM: *Hermaphrodites are people born with both male and female sexual organs, right?*
JOSHUA: *Mom, don't say hermaphrodite! The proper word is "intersex," and it's a little more complicated than that.*

 WANT MORE INFO? *THINK:* **A MISLEADING AND STIGMATIZING SYNONYM FOR "INTERSEX."**

USAGE NOTE: This term is considered derogatory.

HERSTORY

▼ *noun*

A common feminization of the word "history."

❝ *Queer Herstory 101: The Daughters of Bilitis was the first lesbian civil and political rights organization in America.*❞

 WANT MORE INFO? *THINK:* **GIRLS, WOMEN, FEMMES, AND TGNC PEOPLE'S HISTORY.**

DID YOU KNOW The Daughters of Bilitis formed in San Francisco in 1955 as a reaction to police raids targeting lesbian bars and harassing queer patrons. Lesbian couple Del Martin and Phyllis Lyon founded the club in an effort to create a safe social setting for lesbians to find community and empowerment. They also created *The Ladder*—the first nationally distributed lesbian publication that ignited other historical lesbian publications like *Curve*, *Lesbian News*, *Aché*, and *Phoenix Rising*.

HETEROFLEXIBLE

▼ *adjective*

Describing a person who is predominantly heterosexual but is open to experiencing gay or queer relationships. This person is not likely to identify as bisexual.

SEE ALSO
HOMOFLEXIBLE, LESBIFLEXIBLE, SAME-SEX ATTRACTION

❝ *I haven't had a queer relationship yet, but I do consider myself to be open and heteroflexible.*❞

 WANT MORE INFO? *THINK:* **OPEN TO EXPLORING NONHETERO RELATIONSHIPS.**

USAGE NOTE: The use of this term relies on an individual's preference. Do not assume that an individual wants to be identified by this term.

HETERONORMATIVITY

▼ *noun*

A belief that people are given specific gendered roles within a societal binary and that these roles, along with heterosexuality, are automatically assumed as the norm.

❝ *I have two moms and they are great! I don't know what it's like to have a dad and honestly, I don't care. But I do care when people mistreat my family because they think we are 'not normal.' People have to understand that heteronormativity—must have a mom and dad—is not actually the norm because it's not my norm.*"

 WANT MORE INFO?
THINK: **A SYSTEM OF PERVASIVE SOCIETAL NORMS ROOTED IN HETEROSEXUALITY.**

HETEROSEXUAL

▼ *adjective*

Physically attracted to people of "the opposite sex." This term relies on the gender binary, male and female, and assumes there are only two genders: male and female. This term can be abbreviated as "het," "hetty," or "hetero."

▼ *noun*

A heterosexual person.

RELATED
HETEROSEXUALITY *noun*

❝ *My best friend is hetero. She was actually the first person I came out to. She said she would always love and support me; nothing will ever change that.*"

 WANT MORE INFO?
THINK: **STRAIGHT.**

HIGH FEMME

▼ *noun*

A queer person whose appearance is extremely feminine. In the Black lesbian community, the term DIVA FEMME can also be used.

> SEE ALSO
>
> **"The Lesbian Spectrum,"**
> **p. 255**

❝ *I was afraid I would be ignored because I present as high femme nonbinary."*

—COURTNEY STODDEN

 WANT MORE INFO? *THINK:* **A SUPER-GIRLY LESBIAN.**

USAGE NOTE: This term originated in the lesbian community. It has been appropriated by the larger LGBTQIA+ community.

HIJRA

▼ *noun*

A third gender specifically identified in the country of India. A person whose identity is neither male nor female or is transitioning to another gender.

❝ *Many hijras live in communities in north India where gender nonconforming people support one another like family."*

 WANT MORE INFO? *THINK:* **INDIA'S RESPECTED KINNAR AND ARAVANI COMMUNITIES.**

DID YOU KNOW Laxmi Narayan Tripathi, a hijra and activist for minority sexualities, was instrumental in advocating for gender recognition beyond male and female in India. In April 2004, the Indian Supreme Court officially recognized transgender rights.

HIV/AIDS

▼ *noun*

Acquired immunodeficiency syndrome (AIDS) is a spectrum of conditions caused by infection with human immunodeficiency virus (HIV). Over time, this results in the complete failure of the immune system and an inability to fight infections.

SEE ALSO
A-WORD, "History Lesson: HIV/AIDS," p. 213

❝ *For World AIDS Day, our whole classroom wore red ribbons to bring awareness to those in need and living with HIV/AIDS."*

 WANT MORE INFO? *THINK*: A GLOBAL HEALTH-CARE PANDEMIC.

HIV-NEGATIVE

▼ *adjective*

SEE **NEG**

HIV-POSITIVE

▼ *adjective*

SEE **POZ**

History Lesson: HIV/AIDS

THE HIV/AIDS PANDEMIC is one of the most serious public health challenges in modern history. America announced its first findings of what would eventually be called HIV/AIDS in June of 1981. The Centers for Disease Control and Prevention reported that five young men in Los Angeles had a rare lung infection, and within a short period of time, they had all died. The disease spread rapidly across the country and seemed to be afflicting scores of gay men in major metropolitan areas. As HIV spread, so did discrimination against the gay community. The Reagan administration delayed its response to the crisis. At one point, a proposal was made to quarantine people with HIV, but the proposal was denied. The Gay Men's Health Crisis (GMHC) was one of the first and few organizations that provided immediate assistance to gay men living with HIV/AIDS and raised funds for research. People were fearful and a harsh stigma was placed on those with the disease due to the lack of information made publicly available about HIV/AIDS.

As medical research began to catch up, and the understanding that AIDS was the result of an HIV infection that could only be contracted in distinct ways, activists began a dynamic movement to change the scope and stigma of HIV/

AIDS in America. Education about the disease, safe sex, and other preventative measures and treatments became widely available. HIV testing was offered in medical clinics and gay community centers. Activists and organizations like ACT UP demanded that pharmaceutical companies, medical researchers, and government officials understand the fatality of the disease and work harder to find treatment.

More than 82 million people have been infected with HIV worldwide, and the disease has taken over 40 million lives. While there is still no cure, through the efforts of activists, educators, medical research, pharmaceutical advancements, and government assistance, people living with HIV are able to enjoy long and healthy lives. Groundbreaking antiretroviral therapy can prevent sexual HIV transmission and preserve the health of people living with HIV.

WANT TO LEARN MORE?

Visit kidshealth.org, pedaids.org,
or gileadhiv.com for more information.

National HIV Testing Day is an annual event on June 27, during Pride Month. This is a campaign to encourage people to get tested for HIV and know their status.

World AIDS Day is celebrated annually on December 1. This day is dedicated to bringing international awareness to the ongoing crisis.

HOMO

▼ *noun*

SEE **HOMOSEXUAL**

HOMOFLEXIBLE

▼ *adjective*

Describing a person who is predominantly gay or lesbian but open to experiencing relationships with people of other gender expressions. This person is not likely to identify as bisexual.

SEE ALSO

**HETEROFLEXIBLE,
LESBIFLEXIBLE**

"

NATE: *Dee, are you flirting with her?!*

DEE: *I don't know? I'm gay but I think I like her. Maybe I'm homoflexible?*

 WANT MORE INFO? *THINK:* **GAY BUT OPEN TO RELATIONSHIPS WITH PARTNERS OF A DIFFERENT GENDER.**

 USAGE NOTE: The use of this term relies on an individual's preference. Do not assume that an individual wants to be identified by this term.

HOMONORMATIVITY

▼ *noun*

A term that addresses the problems of privilege and erasure within the LGBTQIA+ community as its members intersect with race, capitalism, sexism, transmisogyny, and cissexism.

" *The queer community claims to be inclusive and intersectional, but homonormativity begs to differ. According to the media, queer people are all white, middle class, cisgender, gay males. Where is the other diverse representation? I want to see it!"*

 WANT MORE INFO? *THINK:* **IGNORANCE TOWARD MINORITY GROUPS WITHIN THE LGBTQIA+ COMMUNITY.**

HOMOPHOBIA

▼ *noun*

Aversion, fear, or hatred toward homosexuality and queerness.

RELATED
HOMOPHOBE *noun*
HOMOPHOBIC *adjective*

SEE ALSO
ACEPHOBIA, BIPHOBIA, FEMMEPHOBIA, LESBOPHOBIA, QUEERPHOBIA, TRANSPHOBIA

❝ Did you read the sign that homophobe is holding? It says, 'Homosexuals are possessed by demons.' Well, that's extreme."

 WANT MORE INFO? THINK: DISLIKE OF OR PREJUDICE AGAINST GAY PEOPLE.

HOMOROMANTIC

▼ *adjective*

Describes a person who has a romantic or emotional attraction to people of the same gender.

▼ *noun*

A homoromantic person. This label is used to describe a romantic orientation where a person is only affectionate toward the same gender.

❝ I am a girl, and I identify as pansexual and homoromantic. I mean, I'm attracted to girls and guys and enbies, whoever. But my heart only truly beats for girls—cis or trans—I just love girls."

 WANT MORE INFO? THINK: A PERSON SEEKING SAME-GENDER LOVE.

 USAGE NOTE: This term is commonly used in the asexual community.

HOMOSEXUAL

▼ *adjective*

Physically attracted to people of "the same sex." As

with HETEROSEXUAL, this term relies on the gender binary, and assumes there are only two genders: male and female. Many LGBTQIA+ people prefer using broader identifiers such as "gay" or "queer" as a means of acknowledging genders outside the gender binary.

▼ *noun*

A homosexual person. This label is often used to describe a sexual orientation where a person is attracted to the same sex or gender.

RELATED
HOMOSEXUALITY noun

❝ *Everybody's journey is individual. If you fall in love with a boy, you fall in love with a boy. The fact that many Americans consider it a disease says more about them than it does about homosexuality.*"

—JAMES BALDWIN

WANT MORE INFO?
THINK: **ADAM AND STEVE OR ALLY AND EVE.**

HONEY

▼ *noun*

A term of endearment. The term HENNY can also be used.

SEE ALSO
CHILD, GIRL, MISS THING

❝ *Listen, honey, take it from an eighth grader, never eat the lunch on Friday. It's always the left-over lunch from Monday.*"

 WANT MORE INFO?
THINK: **DARLING.**

HORMONE REPLACEMENT THERAPY

▼ noun

Medical treatments where doses of hormones are administered to individuals to assist in affirming a person's gender identity. Often abbreviated as HRT. The terms CROSS-SEX HORMONE THERAPY, TRANSGENDER HORMONE THERAPY, or GENDER- AFFIRMING THERAPY can also be used.

> **SEE ALSO**
> **FEMINIZING HORMONE THERAPY, MASCULINIZING HORMONE THERAPY**

66 *Feminizing hormone therapy and masculinizing hormone therapy are two of the most common HRTs used for transgender or nonbinary individuals.*"

WANT MORE INFO?
THINK: ADMINISTERED DOSES OF HORMONES TO SUPPORT A PERSON'S GENDER TRANSITION.

USAGE NOTE: This term is commonly used in the transgender, nonbinary, and gender nonconforming communities.

DID YOU KNOW Hormone replacement therapy or gender-affirming hormone therapy is a common practice for transgender, nonbinary, and gender conforming adolescents, usually sixteen and older. It helps TGNC individuals transition safely into the physical bodies that affirm their gender identity—and has an extremely positive effect on their confidence and mental development—allowing them to live authentically and grow into the adult they are meant to be.

HORMONES

▼ noun

A general reference to medications used to assist in affirming a person's gender identity.

66 *Hey, Asa? I started*

hormones this month, so, I, uh, want you to know that you'll start to notice some physical changes in me. You've been such a huge support to me and I needed to tell someone."

 WANT MORE INFO? *THINK:* **GENERIC TERM FOR HORMONES USED IN HRT.**

USAGE NOTE: This term is commonly used in the transgender, nonbinary, and gender nonconforming communities.

HOUSE CULTURE

▼ *noun*

Another name for ballroom culture, referring to the social houses that provide a safe space for LGBTQIA+ people—particularly Black and Latinx—within the ballroom community. Each house adopts a family name (usually named after a major fashion label or LGBTQIA+ icon) and is typically governed by a house mother and/or house father who acts as a mentor and leader. House parents foster a community that becomes family for queer and trans people who may have been rejected by their biological family due to their gender identity or sexuality.

SEE ALSO

BALL, BALLROOM SCENE/ CULTURE, CHOSEN FAMILY, "History Lesson: The Ballroom Scene," *p. 308*

❝ *You know what a house is? I'll tell you what a house is. A house is a gay street gang. Now, where street gangs get their rewards from street fights, a gay house street-fights at a ball. And you street-fight at a ball by walking in the categories."*
—DORIAN COREY

 WANT MORE INFO? *THINK:* **MULTIGENERATIONAL CHOSEN FAMILY FOR GAY, QUEER, AND TRANS PEOPLE.**

HOUSE FATHER

▼ *noun*

In ballroom culture, this is a social patriarch of a particular house. This leader (of any gender) maintains the image of the house and presides over its members. The term FATHER OF THE HOUSE can also be used.

SEE ALSO

"History Lesson: The Ballroom Scene," *p. 308*

66 *My house father takes all of us to church on Sunday. He says, 'Gospel music is good for the soul!' Then afterward, we go to Melba's for some good soul food!"*

 WANT MORE INFO?
THINK: **THE HEAD MAN IN CHARGE OF A CHOSEN FAMILY.**

DID YOU KNOW Legendary house father Larry Ebony founded the House of Ebony in 1978 to support Black gay youth abandoned by their biological families. The house was noted for their three-story Brooklyn brownstone that many said housed up to fifty children at a time. House Father Larry Ebony believed, "You always had our ballroom family, your house."

House Mother ▼

HOUSE MOTHER

▼ *noun*

In ballroom culture, this is the social matriarch of a particular house. This leader (of any gender) maintains the image of the house and presides over its members. She is usually an iconic member of the ballroom scene. The terms MOTHER OF THE HOUSE and "House Muva" can also be used.

> *SEE ALSO*
> **"History Lesson: The Ballroom Scene,"** *p. 308*

> 66 *After walking for years and destroying every category, they finally announced her as the house mother."*

 WANT MORE INFO?
THINK: **THE HEAD WOMEN IN CHARGE OF A CHOSEN FAMILY.**

DID YOU KNOW Legendary mother Crystal LaBeija, a prominent Latinx drag queen, founded the House of LaBeija in New York City in 1972. Mother LaBeija wanted to create a drag scene that specifically featured Black and Latinx queens who felt marginalized by the predominantly white gay balls. House of LaBeija is noted for pioneering house culture for the drag community and today Crystal LaBeija and her successor Pepper LaBeija are considered some of the most iconic mothers in ballroom culture history.

HOUSE SYSTEM

▼ *noun*

SEE **BALLROOM CULTURE**

HOW BAD ARE YOU?

▼ *idiom*

A phrase used to challenge one's opponent.

"

KEVIN AVIANCE: *Your little dip at the end was cute. But it don't hold a candle to my duckwalk.*

WILLIE ESPERANZA: *Oh, really? You think you're it? How bad are you?!*

 WANT MORE INFO? *THINK:* MOONWALKS INTO THE SONG "BAD" BY MICHAEL JACKSON.

USAGE NOTE:	This term is commonly used in ballroom culture.

HPV

▼ *noun*

Human papillomavirus, a sexually transmitted infection. Depending on the strain, HPV may cause warts and, if left untreated, can lead to cervical cancer.

" *HPV is one of the most common STDs that affect today's youth. There may be a chance, if you are sexually active, that you have been exposed to one or more strains. Definitely talk to an adult you trust and with your doctor. Don't be ashamed."*

 WANT MORE INFO? *THINK:* THE MOST COMMON STD—MOST OF THE TIME IT ISN'T A BIG DEAL, BUT IT'S IMPORTANT TO GET IT CHECKED OUT.

HRT

▼ *noun*

SEE **HORMONE REPLACEMENT THERAPY**

HUNDRED-FOOTER

▼ *noun*

A lesbian who is easy to spot from one hundred feet away, based on stereotypically butch physicality, behavior, and demeanor.

❝ *I don't need binoculars to see that's a hundred-footer right there. Her hair is shorter than my brother's fade, and judging from those cargo shorts, I guarantee she's never seen a tube of lipstick in her life.*"

 WANT MORE INFO?
THINK: **WHEN YOU CAN TELL SHE'S A LESBIAN FROM ACROSS A CROWDED ROOM.**

USAGE NOTE: This term originated in the lesbian community.

HYFEE

▼ *adjective*

Acting in a snooty manner.

❝ *You're acting hyfee today. Your nose is up so high the sun might burn it off.*"

 WANT MORE INFO?
THINK: **STUCK-UP AND UNPLEASANT ATTITUDE.**

HYPERFEMINIZATION

▼ *noun*

Exaggeration of femininity, typically characterized by sex appeal, physical objectification, and passiveness.

RELATED
HYPERFEMINIZE *verb*

SEE ALSO
HYPERSEXUALIZATION

❝ *Hyperfeminization is so evident in professional sports. Female volleyball players wear bikinis and tennis players wear short skirts, while male athletes wear uniforms with much more coverage.*"

 WANT MORE INFO?
THINK: **KIM KARDASHIAN, CARDI B, THE VICTORIA'S SECRET FASHION SHOW.**

HYPERMASCULINIZATION

▼ *noun*

Exaggeration of masculinity, typically characterized by physical strength and machismo.

RELATED
HYPERMASCULINIZE *verb*

SEE ALSO
HYPERSEXUALIZATION, TOXIC MASCULINITY

❝ Society chastises boys for crying, then turns around and is dissatisfied when they are detached from their emotions. To be honest, hypermasculinization is crippling. ❞

 WANT MORE INFO? *THINK:* THE BULKY, ANGRY DUDES FROM WWE.

HYPERSEXUALIZATION

▼ *noun*

The act of making something extremely sexual in nature; linked to sexual objectification.

RELATED
HYPERSEXUALIZE *verb*

❝ The hypersexualization of young Black girls is a growing problem! Let them be children and grow naturally into their bodies like any other little girl. DO NOT OBJECTIFY THEIR BODIES! ❞

 WANT MORE INFO? *THINK: MAKING SOMETHING "SEXY" WHEN IT DOES NOT NEED TO BE.*

History Lesson: LGBTQIA+ Youth Homelessness

HOMELESSNESS IS A harsh reality for many LGBTQIA+ youth in the United States. Several hundred thousand queer youth face the hardships of homelessness each year. Queer young people are often overrepresented in the homeless community in comparison to their cishet counterparts.

Many young LGBTQIA+ people leave their homes with nowhere to turn due to family rejection or abuse because of their gender identity or sexual orientation. Some queer youth age out of the foster system and are unable to find proper housing. Transgender kids experience difficulty and are often denied admission into shelters that do not support their gender. During the 2020 COVID-19 pandemic, these young people encountered unsafe environments and experienced many obstacles that kept them from receiving the aid and care they needed. With a huge number of shelters closed as a result of the pandemic, many LGBTQIA+ young people had no choice but to stay in hostile home environments—where they were more at risk of being misgendered or deadnamed—becoming less affirmed in their identity and experiencing violence hinged on their sexuality and gender.

The challenges faced by homeless youth are extensive, but there are supportive housing agencies across the country that are passionate about protecting the young minds, bodies, and hearts of our future like Covenant House, True Colors United, Ali Forney Center, the Ruth Ellis Center, New Alternatives, SMYAL, Thrive Youth Center, Homeless Youth Alliance, the National Coalition for the Homeless, and many LGBT centers. These organizations, and the activists and donors who support them, understand the specific challenges endured when facing homelessness at a young age, giving our youth the safety, housing, financial, and emotional support they need to thrive.

IAFAB

▼ *adjective*

An acronym for "intersex assigned female at birth." This term is used by some intersex people as a way to communicate to others the gender assigned to them at birth (based solely on their sexual anatomy). This term can be used to describe an intersex individual's experience, but not solely considered a person's identity. The term "forcibly assigned female at birth" or acronym "FAFAB" can also be used.

SEE ALSO

INTERSEX

66 *Sometimes babies are born with bodies that are unique—not strictly a girl or a boy—and doctors and parents make a choice to call them a girl. So the baby is IAFAB."*

 WANT MORE INFO? *THINK:* **BORN WITH A UNIQUE SEXUAL ANATOMY THAT IS A COMBINATION OF MALE AND FEMALE BUT ASSIGNED TO THE FEMALE GENDER.**

USAGE NOTE: This term is commonly used in the intersex community. The use of this term relies on an individual's preference. Do not assume that an individual wants to be identified by this term. Please ask for and use a person's chosen name and pronouns.

IAMAB

▼ *adjective*

An acronym for "intersex assigned male at birth." This term is used by some intersex people as a way to communicate to others the gender assigned to them at birth (based solely on their sexual anatomy). This term can be used to describe an intersex individual's experience, but not solely considered a person's identity. The term "forcibly assigned male at birth" or acronym "FAMAB" can also be used.

SEE ALSO
INTERSEX

❝ *Hi, I am Brody and I'm intersex. My parents decided not to change my body. I didn't do gender-normalizing surgery when I was a baby, even though the doctor said I should be a boy, or IAMAB."*

 WANT MORE INFO? *THINK:* BORN WITH A UNIQUE SEXUAL ANATOMY THAT IS A COMBINATION OF MALE AND FEMALE BUT ASSIGNED TO THE MALE GENDER.

USAGE NOTE: This term is commonly used in the intersex community. The use of this term relies on an individual's preference. Do not assume that an individual wants to be identified by this term. Please ask for and use a person's chosen name and pronouns.

I CAN'T OR I CANNOT

▼ idiom

A phrase commonly used as a response of disbelief, disapproval, or annoyance. The phrase "I can't deal" can also be used.

❝All these bugs flying around! I hate camping. I can't!"

Ice Cream ▲

WANT MORE INFO?
THINK: ABSOLUTELY OVER IT.

I Can't ▲

ICE CREAM

▼ noun

A person who exhibits the qualities of being sweet and desirable.

❝OMG gorg! Look at her, over there by the ticket counter. I scream, you scream, we all scream for ice cream!"

 WANT MORE INFO?
THINK: SOMEONE YOU HAVE A CRUSH ON.

ICON

▼ *noun*

A highly respected and influential individual who is deemed worthy of praise and reverence.

RELATED
ICONIC *adjective*

SEE ALSO
BICON, DYKON

❝ *Class, this Pride Month we will learn about a few historic LGBTQIA+ icons like Sally Ride, Frank Kameny, Christine Jorgensen, and Sylvester James, who broke down gender and racial barriers and stood the test of time.*❞

 WANT MORE INFO? THINK: A DEITY OF SORTS, A GODDESS, A SUPERSTAR.

In ballroom culture, this is usually a person who has over twenty years of ballroom experience and has won numerous ball competitions; an icon is one step above a legend.

SEE ALSO
LEGENDARY

❝ *This is the one that has slayed. Yolanda, my daughter, where are you, girl? The icon!*❞ —SINIA EBONY, HOUSE OF EBONY

 WANT MORE INFO? THINK: ANGIE XTRAVAGANZA, DORIAN COREY, AVIS PENDAVIS, AND PEPPER LABEIJA.

IDENTITY

▼ *noun*

The characteristics that define who or what a person is; a person's character, personality, individuality, self-expression, and core being.

SEE ALSO
GENDER IDENTITY

❝ *The younger generation has a better understanding*

IDENTITY POLITICS

of what diversity, equity, and inclusion look like. They have little bias and are oftentimes not attached to stigmas older generations have formed. Parents and grandparents, let's take a back seat and let them lead this important conversation around identity."

 WANT MORE INFO? *THINK:* "TO ANYBODY WHO HAS EVER QUESTIONED YOUR IDENTITY . . . I PROMISE YOU THIS: THERE IS . . . A PLACE FOR US." —ARIANA DEBOSE

Identity ▲

▼ *noun*

The tendency for people of similar backgrounds/ identities to form politically focused groups, with the goal of pushing a particular agenda forward.

 We rely on identity politics because in today's world, the LGBTQIA+ community is still fighting for acceptance, understanding, equality, and respect."

WANT MORE INFO? *THINK:* POLITICAL ACTION ROOTED IN IDENTITY LIKE MARRIAGE EQUALITY, TRANSGENDER RIGHTS, BLACK LIVES MATTER, AND IMMIGRATION REFORM.

I DON'T HAVE YOU UP

▼ *idiom*

A phrase used to indicate something is unclear and could possibly be dismissed.

❝*I don't have you up. You're speaking nonsense . . . gibberish!*❞

 WANT MORE INFO? *THINK:* **"I DON'T GET WHAT YOU ARE SAYING, AND I HAVE LITTLE PATIENCE."**

USAGE NOTE: This term is commonly used in the Black gay and queer community.

I DON'T SEE YOU OR I DON'T SEE HER

▼ *idiom*

A phrase used to intentionally disregard a person, place, or thing.

❝*Not answering my call, huh? Well, two can play this game. You're now invisible, dust, and BLOCKED. I don't see you!*❞

 WANT MORE INFO? *THINK:* **"I'M IGNORING YOU."**

USAGE NOTE: This term is commonly used in ballroom culture and the larger queer and trans people of color (QTPOC) community.

I'M IN CHARGE OF THE GIRLS

▼ *idiom*

In ballroom culture, this phrase is used by a competitor at the top of the game to indicate their status. It may also turn into a competitive group chant initiated by the commentator at a ball competition.

❝*Who's in charge of the girls?! I'm in charge of the girls!*❞

 WANT MORE INFO? *THINK:* **"I'M THE BOSS."**

I'M INTO IT

▼ *idiom*

An expression indicating interest and support.

"

Chrissy: I'm thinking about asking Counselor Akins to help us start a GSA club at our school. Some fifth and sixth graders have been talking about wanting one here. What you think?

Ashanti: I'm into it! Actually, I'm all the way into it. I want to plan the Pride Month parade at the end of the school year!

 WANT MORE INFO? *THINK:* **"I LIKE THAT IDEA."**

USAGE NOTE: This term is commonly used in the Black gay community and the larger queer and trans people of color (QTPOC) community.

I'M SLEEP

▼ *idiom*

A deliberate dismissal; uninterested. The phrase "I'm sleep though" can also be used.

"

Jacey: Did you like the talent show? I liked the comedy act Candace and Lee did with the puppets! That was funny. But other than that . . .

Joshua: Yeah, I'm sleep. I was playing on my Nintendo Switch the whole time.
Jacey: Dang! Was it that boring?

 WANT MORE INFO? *THINK:* **AN INDICATION OF BOREDOM.**

USAGE NOTE: This term originated in Black American culture and is commonly used in the Black gay and queer community.

233

INTERSECTIONALITY

▼ noun

The complex way in which varied forms of discrimination overlap or intersect; the importance of focusing on the presence of all marginalized communities within the larger framework of society.

RELATED
INTERSECTIONAL *adjective*

  ❝ *[Kimberlé] Crenshaw introduced the theory of intersectionality, the idea that when it comes to thinking about how inequalities persist, categories like gender, race, and class are best understood as overlapping and mutually constitutive rather than isolated and distinct."* **–ADIA HARVEY WINGFIELD**

 **WANT MORE INFO?**
THINK: LOOKING

AT EQUALITY WITH EVERYONE'S UNIQUE EXPERIENCES IN MIND.

INTERSEX

▼ adjective

Born with variations on sex characteristics that would traditionally assign a child male or female. Variations may involve genital ambiguity and/or combinations of the chromosomal genotype and sexual phenotypes other than XY-male and XX-female.

SEE ALSO
COERCIVE SURGICAL GENDER REASSIGNMENT, GENDER NONCONFORMING, "The Genderbread Person," p. 73

  ❝ *Being intersex is a naturally occurring variation of being human; it isn't a medical problem. Just* because I may appear female on the outside but have male-typical anatomy on the inside doesn't mean I'm abnormal."

🤔 **WANT MORE INFO?**
THINK: NOT AMAB OR AFAB BUT BORN WITH WHAT DOCTORS CONSIDER "ATYPICAL" SEX CHARACTERISTICS (I.E., A GIRL BORN WITH A LARGE CLITORIS OR A BOY BORN WITH A DIVIDED SCROTUM THAT LOOKS LIKE A LABIA).

DID YOU KNOW Many intersex children are given coercive surgery to firmly place them in a traditionally male or female body. Some parents and doctors think that existing in a body that does not fit into the gender binary is too difficult for a child, so they have to "choose" one sex or the other. Because of intersex activists and resources like Hanne Gaby Odiele, Pidgeon Pagonis, Mari Wrobi, the Intersex Justice Project, and many others, the cultural conversation around gender is evolving, giving voice to the intersex experience and making positive change in the medical treatment of intersex people. In 2018, the state of Colorado was the first state to issue an intersex birth certificate.

@jessvosa_art

IN THE LIFE

▼ *idiom*

Involved in or part of the LGBTQIA+ community.

SEE ALSO

"History Lesson: The Harlem Renaissance," *p. 000*

❝ *Back in the day, Studio 54 was a place to be in the life. Famous people like Cher, Michael Jackson, Elizabeth Taylor, and Liza Minnelli would always come to New York City and dance the night away.* ❞

 WANT MORE INFO? *THINK:* **IMMERSED IN QUEER CULTURE.**

CHLOE O. DAVIS

DID YOU KNOW This term is a century old, with historical roots tracing back to the Black gay slang used in Harlem, New York, during the early 1920s. It is still used in the Black gay community and has since been appropriated by the LGBTQIA+ community and mainstream culture.

INVISIBILITY

▼ *noun*

The cultural dismissal of a particular identity or group of people due to a lack of understanding, acceptance, or representation.

SEE ALSO
ERASURE

❝ *LGBTQIA . . . where is my letter? I am a ten-year-old genderqueer kid that always experiences invisibility.* ❞

 WANT MORE INFO? *THINK:* **IGNORING PEOPLE WHO DON'T FIT NEATLY INTO BOXES.**

-IQUE

▼ *suffix*

A suffix used to make something extravagant and/or extra.

❝

BILLY: *Merritt was angelic at the Hendersons' dinner party* last night. I'm so proud of our baby boy. He is growing up!

MAURICE: *I think you mean angel-ique. He runs this fam and he knows it! Plus, I gave him extra video game time before we left if he promised to be on his best behavior!*

WANT MORE INFO? THINK: QUEERING AN ADJECTIVE BY MAKING IT FANCY AND CHIQUE!

-Ique ▲

IRON CLOSET

▼ *noun*

The superlative form of "closet"—refers to an individual who is extremely uncomfortable with being gay, bisexual, transgender, intersex, or otherwise queer, so much so that the individual is reluctant to publicly display any signs of their queer identity.

SEE ALSO

CLOSET, COME OUT, DISCREET, OUT, "Coming Out 101," *p. 101*

❝ *So many of us have difficulty admitting we are gay. It's not that we don't want to come out, it's just that we don't want to be made fun of or bullied. No one wants to be in the iron closet, but it's just the safest place for me right now."*

 WANT MORE INFO? THINK: THE CLOSET, BUT WITH A PADLOCK AND NO KEY.

I SEE YOU

▼ *idiom*

A compliment given to someone, or a term that acknowledges someone's accomplishment.

❝ *I see you! I was screaming my face off when you slid to home base and won the game for the team!*❞

 WANT MORE INFO? *THINK:* **A WHOLEHEARTED AFFIRMATION.**

USAGE NOTE: This term is commonly used in the Black gay community and the larger queer and trans people of color (QTPOC) community.

I WON'T

▼ *idiom*

An expressive, dramatic way to say no.

SEE ALSO
I CAN'T

❝ *How many times do I have to say it? How many ways do I have to show it? I can't and I won't. And that is final.*❞

 WANT MORE INFO? *THINK:* **"ABSOLUTELY NOT."**

JACKIE

▼ *noun*

A person who seems deceptive or pretentious.

❝*He is such a Jackie. I am warning you! Don't tell him anything because the whole world will know in less than two minutes . . . such a blabbermouth!*❞

 WANT MORE INFO? THINK: AN UNTRUSTWORTHY PERSON.

JOCK

▼ *noun*

A label for a gay, bisexual, or queer person—often a boy or a man—who has an athletic body type.

> **SEE ALSO**
>
> **"Help! What Type of Gay Am I?," p. 203**

❝*Byron, Xander, and Noah are like the cool jocks at our school. They started a student-run workout club and got one of the local health food stores to sponsor energy bars.*❞

 WANT MORE INFO? THINK: TWEENS THAT HAVE ABS AND BICEPS.

J-SETTING

▼ *noun*

A style of dance that uses highly energized, rhythmic movement and structured group formations. The dancers are often in a V-shape formation, with a leader initiating movement. The phrase "eight count girls" can also be used.

❝ *J-Setting Troupes roll call! Let me hear you, let me see you 'Salt and Pepper' and 'Strut'!"*

 WANT MORE INFO? *THINK:* **"AN UNDERGROUND DANCE FORM THAT GIVES LGBTQIA+ PEOPLE AN OPPORTUNITY TO STAND OUT WITH CONFIDENCE, POISE, AND ELEGANCE."** **—LELAND THORPE**

 USAGE NOTE: This term originated in Black American culture and is commonly used in the Black gay and queer community.

DID YOU KNOW J-Setting dates back to the 1970s with the Prancing J-Settes, an all-female dance team from Jackson State University. Gay male dancers from several Historically Black Colleges and Universities (HBCUs) adopted the style, creating competitive dance groups and bringing the dance to nightclubs, particularly in Southern states like Mississippi, Georgia, Texas, and Louisiana.

JUDY

▼ *noun*

In the gay male community, this term is used to acknowledge a good friend; usually refers to a gay man. The phrases "good Judy" or "my Judy" can also be used.

SEE ALSO
FRIEND OF DOROTHY, MARY

❝ *Headed out with my Judy. Thursday is pizza and movie night!"*

 WANT MORE INFO? *THINK:* **BESTIES.**

This term originated in the gay male community.

DID YOU KNOW Actress Judy Garland has been a gay icon since her rise to fame in the 1940s. Some scholars have even called her the quintessential gay icon. Garland died on June 22, 1969, just six days before the Stonewall riots. In the years following her death, Judy's elder daughter, Liza Minnelli, followed in her footsteps, becoming a gay icon herself.

JUGS

▼ *noun*

SEE **BOOBS**

JUST BE YOURSELF

Inclusivity in the **LGBTQIA+** Community

SOCIETY HAS BEEN conditioned to understand gender and sexuality in a binary way. Male and female, masculine and feminine, heterosexual and homosexual, cisgender and transgender—it's all very black and white. However, binaries are limiting and are an unrealistic representation of human expression. Gender and sexuality are vast and extend beyond binary boundaries. The LGBTQIA+ community represents the dynamic idea that our gender, sexuality, and outward expression are layered and complex. The intersectionality of your identity—inclusive of race, ethnicity, and culture—is also beautiful and unique. Be proud of who you are! Take a look and consider the layers of your own identity.

> **Every part of your identity is valid and should be celebrated!**

QPOC	Indigenous	Girl	Aromanti
QTPOC	European	Androgynous	Femm
QWOC	American	Gay	Butch
WOC	Mixed-race	Lesbian	Mas
MOC	Multiracial	Homo	Futch
POC	Immigrant	Hetero	Gayby
BlaQueer	First-generation	Flexible	Babyquee
Gaysian	Second-generation	Fluid	Monogamou
Asian	Disabled	Flux	Nonmonogamou
Asian and ific Islander	Able-bodied	Straight	Polyamorous
Native Hawaiian	Genderqueer	Asexual	
Latinx	No label	Bisexual	
Latine	Null gender	Pansexual	
Latina	Agender	Polysexual	
Latino	Gender nonconforming	Homosexual	
African	Transgender	Heterosexual	
Hispanic	Trans boy	Homoromantic	
ewish	Transmasculine	Heteroromantic	
White	Trans girl	Biromantic	
Black	Transfeminine	Panromantic	
Native American	Boy	Polyromantic	

WHO ARE YOU?

Kk

KIDS, THE

▼ *noun*

The Black and Latinx gay and trans community, particularly the youth and young adults.

The young queer community.

SEE ALSO

CHILDREN, THE

"❝ The kids are everywhere! I love DC Pride Weekend!"

 WANT MORE INFO? *THINK:* "YOUNG AND BLACK AND FINE AND GAY." —AUDRE LORDE

USAGE NOTE: This term originated in ballroom culture. It has been appropriated by the larger LGBTQIA+ community and mainstream culture.

The Kids ▼

KIDS OF TRANS (KOT)

▼ *noun*

SEE **PEOPLE WITH TRANS PARENTS (PTP)**

KIKI

▼ *noun*

A social gathering of like-minded friends. A kiki is marked by intimate, fun-filled conversations and hot gossip.

An onomatopoeia for the sound of laughter.

❝ *We had a good kiki last night after band rehearsal, laughing about how everyone might look when they get old. Dante said Jay Jay was gonna be toothless still tryna play the trumpet!"*

 WANT MORE INFO? *THINK:* "LET'S HAVE A KIKI" BY SCISSOR SISTERS.

 USAGE NOTE: This term originated in ballroom culture. It has been appropriated by the larger LGBTQIA+ community and mainstream culture.

▼ *adjective*

A dated term for a queer woman who does not identify as butch or femme, nor does she have a preference for a butch or femme partner. This term was considered derogatory when it originated in the 1940s because "kiki girls" did not fit into the butch/femme binary and were often mocked by others. Can also be seen as "ki ki."

❝ *Hilary is a kiki girl. She's cool with dating any type of woman."*

 WANT MORE INFO? *THINK:* **LESBIAN WHO DOESN'T DISCRIMINATE BASED ON THE BUTCH/ FEMME SPECTRUM.**

 USAGE NOTE: This term originated in the lesbian community.

Kiki ▲

> 66 *The kiki scene is a space for youth development, where everyone's unique. And the kiki scene is a place for everyone to explore that uniqueness."*

—GIA MARIE LOVE

 WANT MORE INFO? *THINK: KIKI*, THE DOCUMENTARY FEATURING TWIGGY PUCCI GARÇON.

KIKI SCENE

▼ *noun*

In ballroom culture, this is a subcommunity for young queer and trans people of color (QTPOC) competitors, with ages ranging from twelve to twenty-four. The kiki scene mirrors the mainstream ballroom scene in many ways and has similar structures, including kiki houses, kiki ball competitions, and freedom to explore and express identity and sexuality.

DID YOU KNOW The kiki scene emerged in New York City in the early 2000s, providing young QTPOC with an outlet to deal with the challenges of homelessness, racial inequality, disease, and lack of acceptance. Young competitors would often be found practicing their routines inside local LGBTQIA+ wellness centers because they were safe spaces to hang out. Eventually, the centers began to sponsor the kiki community, hosting competitions and raising money for their balls.

KWEEN OR KWANE

▼ *noun*

SEE **QUEEN**

LABEL

▼ *noun*

An individual's gender, sexuality, appearance, and/ or other expression.

❝ *Labels are very personal. People can share the same label but interpret it differently. There is no right or wrong expression of a label.*❞

 WANT MORE INFO? *THINK:* **A PERSON'S UNIQUE IDENTITY AND ATTRACTION LAYERS.**

LADY

▼ *noun*

A person (regardless of gender) who is mannerly and poised.

❝ *Look at Devin eating his lunch with his legs crossed and napkin in his lap. He is such a mannerly little lady.*❞

 WANT MORE INFO? *THINK:* **A PRIM AND PROPER FEMME.**

LAID OR LAYED

▼ *adjective*

Looking exceptionally stylish.

SEE ALSO
DONE

❝ *Girl, your hair is laid! You look like a million bucks!"*

WANT MORE INFO?
THINK: **LOOKING SO FRESH AND SO CLEAN.**

USAGE NOTE: This term originated in Black American culture and is commonly used in the Black gay and trans community. It has been appropriated by the larger LGBTQIA+ community.

LALA

▼ *adjective*

SEE **LESBIAN**

LATE

▼ *adjective*

Not up-to-date on the current trends, events, or fashions.

❝ *You are still playing a 2DS? Ugh, late. I know what I'm getting you for Xmas."*

WANT MORE INFO?
THINK: **LIVING UNDER A ROCK.**

USAGE NOTE: This term is commonly used in the Black gay community and the larger queer and trans people of color (QTPOC) community.

LATINE

▼ *adjective*

SEE **LATINX**

LATINX

▼ *adjective*

A gender-neutral, inclusive alternative to Latino or Latina, identifying people of Latin American descent. The term LATINE can also be used.

MR. GONZALEZ: *What is this here? Creo que escribió la palabra "Latino" incorrectamente en su document. (I think you misspelled the word "Latino" in your document).*

MATEO: *No, deber de ser "Latinx" (No, it should be Latinx). Changing the o or a to x makes it more inclusive to all gender expressions. Inclusión es importante. (Inclusion is important).*

 WANT MORE INFO?
THINK: **AN EMPOWERING TERM FOR ALL PEOPLE OF LATIN AMERICAN DESCENT.**

USAGE NOTE: This term is pronounced \luh-TEE-neks\. An umbrella term for people of Latin American descent. This term originated in Latin American culture and has been adopted by mainstream culture. The use of this term relies on an individual's preference.

DID YOU KNOW There have been many Latinx queer icons who have made substantial changes in both the Latinx and LGBTQIA+ communities. Venezuelan and Puerto Rican trans woman Sylvia Rivera is known as the "Mother of the Movement" for her leadership in the Stonewall Riots; Colombian-American José Julio Sarria, founder of the charitable Imperial Court System, was the first openly gay American to run for office; Dennis deLeon, a former New York City human rights commissioner and president of the Latino Commission on AIDS, was one of the first officials to disclose his HIV status in 1993 and worked tirelessly to support gay equality in his community.

Latinx ▼

LAVENDER

▼ *noun*

A pale purple color often used to represent the LGBTQIA+ community.

66 *The color lavender is a symbol for empowerment and resistance in the gay community.*"

 WANT MORE INFO? *THINK:* **A COLOR FOR EQUALITY.**

In the 1950s, around the same time as the anticommunist movement known as McCarthyism, a series of mass firings of gay and lesbian government officials occurred, known as the Lavender Scare, claiming queer employees were both security risks and communist sympathizers. The color has since been reclaimed by the lesbian radical feminist group Lavender Menace and the larger LGBTQIA+ community. Decades later, on June 15, 2020, the Supreme Court ruled that LGBTQIA+ individuals are protected under the Civil Rights Act of 1964, meaning they cannot be discriminated against in employment.

LAVENDER LINGUISTICS

▼ *noun*

The study of jargon, expressions, and colloquial language used within the LGBTQIA+ community.

 Lavender linguistics celebrates our language, our vernacular, our story!"

WANT MORE INFO?
THINK: **QUEER LANGUAGE AND THE HISTORICAL MEANING OF WORDS.**

LAVENDER MARRIAGE

▼ *noun*

A marriage between a man and a woman used to conceal the sexual orientation of one or both partners.

 The most famous lavender marriage I know is Rock Hudson and his wife, Phyllis Gates."

WANT MORE INFO?
THINK: **CLOSETED MARRIED COUPLE.**

DID YOU KNOW Lavender marriages were popular in Old Hollywood because of an indecency code enforced by the Motion Picture Association of America (MPAA) between the 1930s and 1960s. The Hays Code prohibited homosexuality on film; the MPAA censored all studios' scripts and put "morals clauses" into many actors' and directors' contracts. Big names like Marlene Dietrich, Randolph Scott, Barbara Stanwyck, and Rudolph Valentino were pushed to participate in publicized lavender marriages.

LAWD

▼ *idiom*

A nonreligious and non-blasphemous spelling of the word "Lord."

66 *Lawd, no! She did not just say that!"*

 WANT MORE INFO?
THINK: "OH MY GOD!"

USAGE NOTE: This term originated in Black American culture and is commonly used in the Black gay and queer community. It has been appropriated by mainstream culture.

Leather Community ▼

LEATHER COMMUNITY

▼ *noun*

A community dedicated to a particular lifestyle denoted by leather garments and power dynamics in relationships. Traditional themes seen within the community are hypermasculinity, motorcycles, and leather enthusiasts; however, the community's evolution has embraced elements of family, safety, and empowering femininity.

RELATED
LEATHER *adjective*

66 *There are two popular schools within the leather community: Old Guard and New Guard. Old Guard is regimented, based on militaristic traditions, and prioritizes leather in one's uniform. New Guard is more flexible in power dynamics* and uses various textiles in addition to leather, like latex, neoprene, and rubber."

 WANT MORE INFO?
THINK: LEATHER FOLKS UNITED BY IDENTITY, RELATIONSHIP STRUCTURE, AND SEXUAL EXPRESSION.

DID YOU KNOW The leather community in the United States originated in the 1940s and 1950s as an extension of post–World War II biker culture. Thousands of gay servicemen were given blue discharges, and they began to build leather and biker communities in port cities like San Francisco and New York City. The first American leather bar, the Gold Coast, was established in Chicago, Illinois, making the city one of the pioneers of leather culture. In 1964, the leather community gained widespread recognition when *Life* magazine published an article called "Homosexuality in America," and mentioned San Francisco's gay and leather scene. This was one of the first mainstream publications to acknowledge gay culture.

LEGENDARY

▼ *adjective*

Honored and remembered for displaying the highest degree of fierceness. In ballroom culture, this describes a person who has had five to ten years of ballroom experience and has won countless competitions.

RELATED
LEGEND *noun*

SEE ALSO
ICON

❝ *Rick is legendary in the ballroom scene. He shows the girls exactly how to destroy the runway, winning the Legends Ball year after year!*"

 WANT MORE INFO?
THINK: RENOWNED FIERCENESS.

LESBIAN

▼ *adjective*

As a woman (or girl), having an attraction toward woman (or girls). This term has also evolved to include transgender, genderqueer, and nonbinary people who are attracted to women.

▼ *noun*

A lesbian women or nonbinary person.

RELATED
LESBIANISM noun

SEE ALSO
"The Lesbian Spectrum," *p. 255*

SEE ALSO "The Lesbian Spectrum," p. 255

❝ *Falling in love with a lesbian was the best thing that ever happened to me."*

 WANT MORE INFO?
THINK: HIP HOP HOORAY FOR OUR HISTORY-MAKING LESBIAN GOVERNORS, MAURA HEALEY AND TINA KOTEK!

USAGE NOTE: This term can be associated with females, girls, women, and feminine-identifying people.

DID YOU KNOW The word "lesbian" is derived from the Greek island of Lesbos, where poet Sappho lived in the sixth century BC. Much of her poetry focused on her admiration of and romances with women.

▶ Lesbian

The Lesbian Spectrum

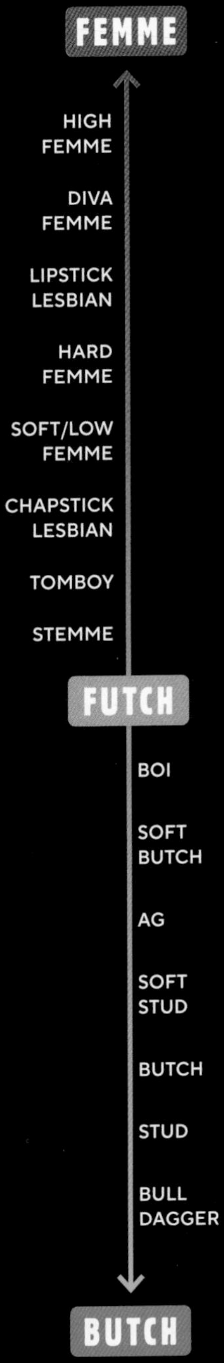

FEMME

HIGH FEMME

DIVA FEMME

LIPSTICK LESBIAN

HARD FEMME

SOFT/LOW FEMME

CHAPSTICK LESBIAN

TOMBOY

STEMME

FUTCH

BOI

SOFT BUTCH

AG

SOFT STUD

BUTCH

STUD

BULL DAGGER

BUTCH

AS EARLY AS the 1940s, when women were first allowed to go out to bars without the company of men, lesbian women began to establish their own community, finding visibility and acceptance in speakeasies and dive bars. Some queer women preferred stereotypically feminine garb, while others dressed in starched shirts and trousers; thus, the butch/femme binary was born. Over time, the binary evolved into a myriad of identities along the butch/femme spectrum. While some of the commonly used identifiers are shown below, there are countless ways for queer women to express their identity.

Like a lot of language in *The Queens' English*, the interpretation of the Lesbian Spectrum can be totally fluid. Have fun rearranging the label order. That's the best part!

LESBIAN DAD

▼ *noun*

In a lesbian relationship with the presence of children, this is the partner who establishes the parental role that most closely resembles the social and heteronormative stereotypes of a father.

❝*I am absolutely Brett and Connor's lesbian dad. I feel like I can't really embrace parenthood if I have to be a conventionally feminine mother. I offer my boys balance and love in a different way—ya know?*❞

 WANT MORE INFO? *THINK:* **LESBIAN PARENT WHO IDENTIFIES WITH THE TRADITIONAL ROLE OF A FATHER.**

LESBIAN SEPARATIST

▼ *noun*

A gay woman who chooses not to associate with males.

SEE ALSO

SEPARATISM, TERF

❝*There is a well-established lesbian separatist community in Alabama. It is a male-free world.*❞

 WANT MORE INFO? *THINK:* **WOMYN WHO WON'T EVEN BRING THEIR YOUNG SONS TO ALL-FEMALE MUSIC FESTIVALS.**

LESBIFLEXIBLE

▼ *adjective*

Describing a person who identifies as predominantly lesbian but is open to experiencing queer relationships with other genders. This person is not likely to identify as bisexual.

SEE ALSO

HETEROFLEXIBLE, HOMOFLEXIBLE

❝*Lesbiflexible, similar to homoflexible and heteroflexible, is the ability* to have flexibility in how you are attracted to others. You can identify as a lesbian and still have attraction to other genders."

 WANT MORE INFO?
THINK: **LESBIAN, BUT OCCASIONALLY ATTRACTED TO SOMEONE OF A DIFFERENT GENDER.**

USAGE NOTE: The term can be associated with females, girls, women, and feminine-identifying people. The use of this term relies on an individual's preference. Do not assume that an individual wants to be identified by this term.

LESBIHONEST OR LEZ BE HONEST

▼ *idiom*

A play on "let's be honest," typically used in a lesbian context.

❝ *Lez be honest, lesbians are simply the best!"*

WANT MORE INFO?
THINK: **LET'S BE REAL. (REAL GAY.)**

LESBOPHOBIA

▼ *noun*

Aversion, fear, or hatred toward female homosexuality and queerness.

RELATED
LESBOPHOBIC *adjective*
LESBOPHOBE *noun*

SEE ALSO
ACEPHOBIA, BIPHOBIA, FEMMEPHOBIA, HOMOPHOBIA, QUEERPHOBIA, TRANSPHOBIA

❝ *The student body is launching a campaign against lesbophobia during Women's History Month. Each day, we are going to highlight the accomplishments of queer women in history to show our support for the lesbian community."*

 WANT MORE INFO?
THINK: **DISLIKE OF OR PREJUDICE AGAINST LESBIANS.**

LET THEM HAVE IT

▼ *idiom*

To reprimand someone strongly.

" *I am about to let her have it if something else negative comes out her mouth again. She's killing my vibe!"*

 WANT MORE INFO? *THINK:* **TO PUT SOMEONE IN CHECK.**

To overwhelm with fierceness and power.

" *OMG! That last contestant just let them have it! She is going to win* The Voice *this season, for sure!"*

 WANT MORE INFO? *THINK:* **I WILL OUTDO AND BE MORE SUCCESSFUL THAN YOU!**

USAGE NOTE: This term is commonly used in the Black gay community and the larger queer and trans people of color (QTPOC) community.

LEWK

▼ *noun*

Another spelling for the word "look," for having fashionable attire.

" *Ooh wee! She is in a lewk, honey! Yas, queen!"*

 WANT MORE INFO? *THINK:* **A FIERCE LOOK!**

LGB

▼ *noun*

An acronym for "lesbian, gay, and bisexual."

" *In the eighties, the use of LGB replaced the word 'gay' because it wasn't considered inclusive. A decade later, LGBT was introduced as the more inclusive term for the queer community."*

 WANT MORE INFO? *THINK:* **THE OLD QUEER CODE (AND NOT THE LONG BEACH AIRPORT CODE).**

LGBTQ(IA+)

▼ *noun*

An acronym for the lesbian, gay, bisexual, transgender, queer, and/or questioning community and an umbrella term for all nonheteronormative identities. The acronym GLBT is also used, where "gay" leads the grouping. LGBTQIA includes the intersex, asexual, agender, and aromantic communities. LGBTQIA+ is an inclusive acronym for all gender identities and sexualities.

❝

GRAND MARSHAL: *LGBTQIA+ roll call! Lesbian, gay, gender nonconforming, bisexual, biromantic, transgender, queer, questioning, intersex, asexual, aromantic, agender, androgynous, flexible, fluid, poly, pan, no label, and every other beautiful human riding on the rainbow we call life?*
US: *Heeeeeere!!*

 WANT MORE INFO? *THINK:* AN INCLUSIVE ACRONYM FOR THE ENTIRE QUEER COMMUNITY.

DID YOU KNOW Around 1988, activists started a movement for equal rights for lesbian, gay, bisexual, and transgender people. The acronym LGBT was created because simply saying gay or lesbian did not accurately describe the entire community. In 2016, GLAAD created the tenth edition of their media reference guide and included Q—for queer or questioning folks—in the commonly used acronym, forming the initials LGBTQ.

LIBRARY

▼ *noun*

A snarky extension of a read; a form of insult commonly used and referred to within the QTPOC community. Often used in the phrase "the library is open" or "opened up the library."

SEE ALSO
READ

 ❝ *The library is open, and the kids are reading. The clapback is in full effect!"*

 WANT MORE INFO?
THINK: **A COLLECTION OF SASSY, DISPARAGING REMARKS.**

USAGE NOTE: This term originated in ballroom culture. It has been appropriated by the larger LGBTQIA+ community and mainstream culture.

DID YOU KNOW The library was introduced to mainstream culture in the documentary *Paris Is Burning*. This iconic film provided an intimate look into the ballroom scene of

1980s New York City. Director Jennie Livingston highlighted family values, the support of house culture, an exploration of gender expression and sexuality, the creative movement of vogue dance, and the magical language of a marginalized and powerful community of Black and Latinx queens.

LIES AND FAIRYTALES!

▼ *exclamation*

An exclamation used to signal dishonesty and deception.

 ❝ *Lies and fairytales! You did not say that. I have proof because I recorded our conversation."*

 WANT MORE INFO?
THINK: **DECEIT! DRAMA! FABRICATIONS!**

USAGE NOTE: This term originated in ballroom culture.

CHLOE O. DAVIS

LIGHT IN THE LOAFERS

▼ *idiom*

A dated expression to refer to a gay boy or man.

❝ *You know, Mary's son Kirk is light in the loafers. I saw him kissing a man at the docks.*❞

 WANT MORE INFO?
THINK: GAAAAAAAAAY AS THE DAY IS LONG.

LIMP WRIST

▼ *noun*

A behavioral indicator of an effeminate, gay boy or man.

❝ *A limp wrist is a stupid gay stereotype. People were teasing this guy in class because he always had limp wrists but he's straight! Anything someone does that 'seems' effeminate, people always say, 'That's so gay.' This needs to stop!*❞

 WANT MORE INFO?
THINK: WHEN HE DROPS HIS WRIST AND SAYS, "HEY, GIRL!"

USAGE NOTE: This term originated as a derogatory slur for gay men but has been reclaimed by some members of the larger LGBTQIA+ community. It may still have negative connotations for some people.

LIPSTICK LESBIAN

▼ *noun*

A super-feminine lesbian. The term "lipstick" can also be used.

SEE ALSO
CHAPSTICK LESBIAN, "The Lesbian Spectrum," *p. 255*

❝ *I kissed a lipstick and my heart exploded!*❞

 WANT MORE INFO?
THINK: LESBIAN GIRLS WHO ARE INTO MAKEUP AND TRADITIONALLY "GIRLY" OUTFITS.

261

LIPSTICK MAFIA

▼ *noun*

A group of lesbian, bisexual, or queer women who identify as femme or lipstick lesbians.

" *Watch out, Tony Soprano. The lipstick mafia is in town.*"

 WANT MORE INFO? *THINK:* **HIGH FEMME GAY GIRL SQUAD.**

USAGE NOTE: This term originated in the lesbian community and can be associated with females, girls, woman, and feminine-identifying people.

LIVE FOR HER

▼ *idiom*

An expression of appreciation toward someone or something.

" *Raja Gemini? Oh, I live for her! The face always slays.*"

 WANT MORE INFO? *THINK:* **TO ABSOLUTELY ADORE.**

USAGE NOTE: This term originated in the Black gay community. It has been appropriated by the larger LGBTQIA+ community.

LIVING

▼ *verb*

Completely enjoying and embracing one's current experience.

" *I am living for this vacation. The sand, the sun, the music, the people . . . nothing beats a family getaway to Cancun.*"

 WANT MORE INFO? *THINK:* **LIVING, LAUGHING, AND LOVING; THE ULTIMATE STATE OF HAPPINESS.**

USAGE NOTE: This term originated in the Black gay community and is commonly used by the larger queer and trans people of color (QTPOC) community. It has been appropriated by mainstream culture.

LP

▼ *noun*

An acronym for "lesbian potential": a girl or woman who could possibly be a lesbian based on appearance and demeanor.

66 *Piper is giving me major LP. I wonder if she is questioning?"*

 WANT MORE INFO? *THINK:* **"ARE YOU POSSIBLY A LESBIAN?"**

 USAGE NOTE: This term may be considered a stereotype or derogatory.

LUG

▼ *noun*

An acronym for "lesbian until graduation," stereotypically used at liberal arts or all-girls schools. Refers to a girl who is a lesbian in school but straight after graduation. The terms BUG (bisexual until graduation) and GUG (gay until graduation) can also be used.

66 *Alison and Lee are total LUGs. I give them each a week after graduation to find a boyfriend."*

 WANT MORE INFO? *THINK:* **EXPLORING ONE'S QUEER SEXUALITY WITH THEIR PEERS.**

USAGE NOTE: This term assumes sexuality cannot be fluid and enforces hetero- and mono-normativity.

LURK

▼ *verb*

To be behind in rhythm or a request.

66 *Dakota, you are a count behind on the choreography! You are lurking! Stay on the beat."*

 WANT MORE INFO? *THINK:* **FALLING BEHIND.**

History Lesson:
The Harlem Renaissance

THE HARLEM RENAISSANCE birthed some of America's most extraordinary intellects, writers, and entertainers, during an era that was, according to some scholars, just as gay as it was Black.

In 1920s Harlem, New York, a community of queer Black artists, writers, musicians, and performers made their mark on history. Drag balls at the Savoy Ballroom and the Hamilton Lodge were called "spectacles of color," where gays and lesbians would dress in drag, and over three thousand spectators would marvel at the elegant fashion and new styles of song and dance. Queer Black women reigned onstage at venues like the Ubangi Club and the Clam House, where singers Gladys Bentley and Ethel Waters both performed in men's clothing, and famous blues singer Ma Rainey wrote lyrics expressing her love for women:

I went out last night with a crowd of my friends,
It must've been women, 'cause I don't like no men.
Wear my clothes just like a fan,
Talk to the girls just like any old man.

—"Prove It on Me Blues," Ma Rainey, 1928

The Harlem Renaissance brought us the Black queer brilliant minds like scholar Alain Locke, performer Josephine Baker, poet Angelina Weld Grimké, and writers Countee Cullen, Alice Dunbar-Nelson, Langston Hughes, Claude McKay, Zora Neale Hurston, Wallace Thurman, and James Weldon Johnson.

Harlem was known for its jazz and blues, speakeasies, and extravagant parties, but it was also known for the vibrant, coded language that emerged to represent the gay Harlem lifestyle. Some of the terms we recognize today (including "bull dagger," "daddy," "hype," "in the life," "in the closet," and "scram") came from this dynamic celebration of art, queerness, and Black community.

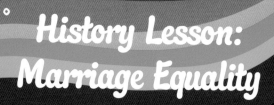

History Lesson: Marriage Equality

MARRIAGE EQUALITY IS the recognition of equal marriage rights granted to partners of any and every sexual orientation. Formerly referred to as the right to same-sex marriage (before our understanding of sex and gender had become what it is today—see "The Genderbread Person," p. 73), activists began fighting for the cause as early as the 1970s, when homosexuality was still largely criminalized in the United States.

In September 1996, the Defense of Marriage Act (DOMA) legally defined marriage as the union of a man and a woman and banned federal recognition of same-sex unions. This act denied many LGBTQIA+ couples from the benefits granted to heterosexual couples and gave power to the states to refuse the acknowledgment of same-sex marriages.

Massachusetts became the first state to legalize gay marriage, in 2004. Cities in California, Oregon, and New Mexico began issuing marriage licenses to same-sex couples shortly thereafter, and over the course of the next ten years, gay marriage was legalized in thirty-seven states.

The fight for federal recognition of marriage equality would continue until June 26, 2015, when the United States Supreme Court ruled in favor of gay marriage, stating that the fundamental right to marry should extend to same-sex couples. This ruling legalized same-sex marriage in every state in the country. That night, the White House was lit up with the colors of the rainbow, celebrating the victory for marriage equality and love everywhere. History was made again, on December 13, 2022, when DOMA was repealed and the Respect for Marriage Act (RFMA) was signed into law—a bill that protects the rights of both LGBTQIA+ and interracial couples in America. #loveislove

MAJOR

▼ *adjective*

Describing someone or something impressive.

66

NIKITA: *Okay, best female rapper. Pick one. Cardi B, Nicki Minaj, or Megan Thee Stallion?*
JUNE: *Does it matter? They are all major!*

 WANT MORE INFO? THINK: AMAZING.

 USAGE NOTE: This term is commonly used in the Black gay community and the larger queer and trans people of color (QTPOC) community.

MALE

▼ *adjective*

A biological sex or identity expression often associated with the display of masculine physicality, demeanor, and behavior.

▼ *noun*

A male-identifying person.

> **SEE ALSO**
>
> **"The Genderbread Person,"** *p. 73*

66 *The term 'male' is inclusive. Just because someone who identifies as a man has a uterus or vagina,*

doesn't mean they aren't male."

 WANT MORE INFO? *THINK:* ASSOCIATED WITH BOYS AND MEN.

MALE PRIVILEGE

▼ *noun*

The inherent rights and immunities granted to boys and men.

SEE ALSO
PRIVILEGE, CISGENDER PRIVILEGE, STRAIGHT PRIVILEGE, WHITE PRIVILEGE

❝*I see how male privilege is demonstrated at my school. I rarely learn about any women in history class. Why aren't we learning about Mary Tape, Emilia Casanova de Villaverde, or Maggie Lena Walker? We existed back then and did great things, too!*"

 WANT MORE INFO? *THINK:* THE ENTITLEMENT OF BOYS AND MEN.

MALE-TO-FEMALE

▼ *noun*

A person who is assigned male at birth but has transitioned or is in the process of transitioning to female. The term is often abbreviated as "MTF" or "M2F."

SEE ALSO
AMAB, FEMALE-TO-MALE, FEMALE-TO-NONBINARY/ GENDER NEUTRAL/ NEUTROIS, MALE-TO- NONBINARY/GENDER NEUTRAL/NEUTROIS, TRANSFEMININE

▼ *adjective*

Describing a person who has undergone MTF transition.

❝*Hi, my name is Camila, I'm thirteen, I live in Texas, and I identity as MTF.*"

WANT MORE INFO?
THINK: A TRANS GIRL OR TRANS WOMAN.

USAGE NOTE: This term may be considered outdated by some members of the LGBTQIA+ community. The use of "AMAB," or "assigned male at birth," is widely accepted because it does not imply an individual's gender identity has changed, instead acknowledging the binding nature of being assigned a specific gender at birth. The use of this term relies on an individual's preference. Please ask for a person's chosen name and pronouns.

MALE-TO-NONBINARY/ GENDER NEUTRAL/ NEUTROIS

▼ *noun*

A person who was gendered male at birth who has since adopted the identity of nonbinary, gender neutral, or neutrois. The term is often abbreviated as "MTN."

▼ *adjective*

Describing a person who has undergone an MTN transition.

> **SEE ALSO**
>
> **AMAB, FEMALE-TO-MALE, FEMALE-TO-NONBINARY/ GENDER NEUTRAL/ NEUTROIS, MALE-TO-FEMALE**

 I took my foster mom to my MTN youth group, and afterward she told me that she understands who I am now."

WANT MORE INFO?
THINK: BORN AMAB AND PART OF THE GENDER-EXPANSIVE COMMUNITY.

USAGE NOTE: This term may be considered outdated by some members of the LGBTQIA+ community. The use of "AMAB," or "assigned male at birth," is widely accepted because it does not imply an individual's gender identity has changed, instead acknowledging the binding nature of being assigned a specific gender at birth. The use of this term relies on an individual's preference. Please ask for a person's chosen name and pronouns.

MAMA

▼ *noun*

A term of endearment, especially in the drag community.

❝ *Mama dear, will you go to the thrift store with me today? Need your advice on creating a fierce lewk that gives vintage glamour and sass for my next show.*"

 WANT MORE INFO?
THINK: LOVED ONE.

MAMA AND PAPA RELATIONSHIP

▼ *noun*

A lesbian relationship where one partner identifies as feminine and the other as masculine.

SEE ALSO
BUTCH/FEMME RELATIONSHIP

❝

EVE: *I went to the Schomburg Center yesterday to do some research on Black queer culture. Did you know that mama and papa relationships came from the Black lesbian community in the 1920s, right here in Harlem?*
IMANI: *Yeah, I did know that! The Harlem Renaissance was everything.*

 WANT MORE INFO?
THINK: A BUTCH/FEMME LESBIAN COUPLE.

DID YOU KNOW This term is a century old, with historical reference to Black gay slang used in Harlem, New York, during the early 1920s. It is still used in the Black lesbian community and has since been appropriated by the larger LGBTQIA+ community.

MARGINALIZE

▼ verb

To treat as insignificant or less than within the social system and give less access to resources and power than the majority.

RELATED
MARGINALIZATION *noun*

❝ Queer youth of color—gay, trans, and nonbinary kids—and kids who are disabled are often marginalized and discriminated against in school. Every child deserves their fair chance at success.❝

 WANT MORE INFO? *THINK:* **TO DEEM PERIPHERAL, UNIMPORTANT, OR POWERLESS.**

MARRIAGE EQUALITY

▼ noun

The concept of recognizing same-sex and queer marriage as equal to cisgender heterosexual marriage. The terms GAY MARRIAGE or SAME-SEX MARRIAGE can also be used.

SEE ALSO
"History Lesson: Marriage Equality," *p. 266*

❝ We fought hard and we fought long for marriage equality!❝

 WANT MORE INFO? *THINK:* **THE EQUAL TREATMENT OF LGBTQIA+ PEOPLE WITHIN THE INSTITUTION OF MARRIAGE.**

DID YOU KNOW Gay marriage was not legal in the United States until 2004, when Massachusetts became the first state to legally recognize same-sex unions. Since then, the movement has taken on a more inclusive term—marriage equality—and on June 26, 2015, the United States Supreme Court ruled that same-sex and queer couples are allowed to marry on the same terms and conditions as opposite-sex couples, with all the accompanying rights and responsibilities. The Respect for Marriage Act (RFMA)

was signed into law on December 13, 2022, requiring all US states, territories, and the federal government to legally recognize LGBTQIA+ marriage, as well as interracial marriage.

MARY

▼ noun

A name used to greet and identify other gay people, typically within the gay male community. The term BETTY, BLANCHE, ROSE, and SALLY can also be used.

SEE ALSO
JUDY

❝ *Oh, Mary, Rose, Betty! It's time for popcorn and binge-watching* Game of Thrones *again!"*

 WANT MORE INFO?
THINK: **PAL, BUDDY, CUTIE, FRIEND.**

 USAGE NOTE: This term originated in the gay male community.

MASC

▼ adjective

Abbreviation of masculine, referring to the physical and personality characteristics stereotypically associated with boys or men.

❝ *The three of us identify as masc. I'm a boi, Maxwell is a transman of experience, and Tasha is a butch lesbian."*

 WANT MORE INFO?
THINK: **THE OPPOSITE OF FEMME.**

 USAGE NOTE: This term is commonly used in the transgender, nonbinary, and gender nonconforming communities.

MASC FOR MASC

▼ *idiom*

Expression referring to a relationship between two queer masc-of-center people. This also can be referred to as "masc on masc" or abbreviated as "M4M."

SEE ALSO
FEMME FOR FEMME

❝M4M is for masc for masc, just like F4F is for femme for femme or T4T is for trans for trans. Being attracted to energy that is similar to you is A-OKAY!"

 WANT MORE INFO? *THINK:* **DESCRIBING A BUTCH COUPLE.**

USAGE NOTE: This term may be considered exclusionary.

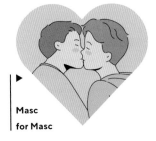

▶ **Masc for Masc**

MASC-OF-CENTER

▼ *adjective*

Referring to gender identities that lean toward masculinity.

SEE ALSO
FEMME-OF-CENTER

❝

NOSHI: *You heard of the Brown Boi Project in Oakland?*

CASEY: *No, what's that?*

NOSHI: *A group of mad-conscious masc-of-center womyn, trans, queer, and two-spirited folks who work to dismantle the stigma of gender in communities of color. I'm going to take you to their next event!*

 WANT MORE INFO? *THINK:* **MASCULINE-LEANING.**

USAGE NOTE: This term is commonly used in the transgender, nonbinary, and gender nonconforming communities.

Masculine-Presenting ▼

MASCULINE-PRESENTING

▼ *adjective*

Describing a gender expression—outward expression, behavior, style, or physical look—that is masculine.

SEE ALSO

MASC, MASC-OF-CENTER

❝ *I'm agender, but more masculine-presenting. That doesn't mean I want to identify as male or any gender, actually. I just prefer to dress more masculine.*

 WANT MORE INFO?
THINK: APPEARING MASCULINE.

MASCULINIZING HORMONE THERAPY

▼ *noun*

A process in which hormones are altered and leveled to produce physiological changes within the body to exhibit secondary male sex characteristics. Often abbreviated as MHT. The term HORMONE REPLACEMENT THERAPY can also be used.

SEE ALSO
FEMINIZING HORMONE THERAPY

❝ *The doctor said that once I start MHT and take testosterone, my period may stop.* ❞

 WANT MORE INFO? *THINK*: MEDICAL THERAPY USED FOR GENDER AFFIRMATION.

DID YOU KNOW Some transgender, nonbinary, and genderqueer youth use pubertal blockers to temporarily suppress their current puberty process. This allows them to achieve a physical body that is more aligned with their gender identity. If a TGNC adolescent decides to continue their transitional process, hormone replacement therapy and other medical procedures can usually start around the age of sixteen.

MASTURBATION

▼ *noun*

To physically stimulate one's genitals or private parts.

❝ *Don't be embarrassed by masturbation. It is a normal thing for adolescents to explore their own bodies.* ❞

 WANT MORE INFO? *THINK*: SELF-STIMULATION.

 USAGE NOTE: This term can be considered mature.

MATILDA

▼ *noun*

SEE **BLUE BOYS**

MEG

▼ *noun*

SEE **BLUE BOYS**

MESSY

▼ *adjective*

Being inappropriate or intentionally disturbing the peace by creating chaos.

❝ Bronx is so messy. He is always getting into fights and causing trouble. I swear he is in detention more than he is in class!"

 WANT MORE INFO? *THINK:* ON THE HOT MESS EXPRESS.

USAGE NOTE: This term originated in Black American culture and is commonly used in the Black gay and queer community. It has been appropriated by mainstream culture.

METOIDIOPLASTY

▼ *noun*

SEE **BOTTOM SURGERY**

METROSEXUAL

▼ *noun*

A label for a heterosexual male who has a keen sense of style and takes great pride in his grooming and appearance. A portmanteau of "metropolitan" and "heterosexual."

❝ People think I'm gay just because I am beautiful and love fashion. I'm not gay, I'm just metrosexual."

 WANT MORE INFO? *THINK:* STRAIGHT GUY SO METICULOUS ABOUT HIS LOOKS, YOU MIGHT MISTAKE HIM FOR GAY.

MHT

▼ *noun*

SEE **MASCULINIZING HORMONE THERAPY**

MINIBALL OR MINI-BALL

▼ *noun*

In ballroom culture, this is a small competition for ball walkers. This type of ball promotes skillful competitors, but the guidelines are less formal, and the competition usually has fewer categories and/or rules.

❝ *I heard you lost last night. Girl, you better pull up and get her back at the next mini-ball. We are legendary, you better represent! Juicy!"*

 WANT MORE INFO? *THINK:* PERFORMANCE COMPETITION THAT IS SMALLER THAN A TRADITIONAL BALL.

MISAPPROPRIATE

▼ *noun*

To appropriate wrongly.

RELATED
MISAPPROPRIATION *noun*

SEE ALSO
APPROPRIATE, REAPPROPRIATE

❝ *Honestly, cultural appropriation should be renamed 'cultural misappropriation' because it's the theft of thousands of years of cultural history."*

 WANT MORE INFO? *THINK:* TO STEAL.

MISGENDER

▼ *verb*

To incorrectly use a gendered term or pronoun for someone.

SEE ALSO
"Common Pronouns 101," *p. 101*

"It is so important to be aware of misgendering people—it is hurtful and can make a person feel both unseen and unsafe. When you aren't sure of the person's pronouns, it's best to just use their name."

WANT MORE INFO? THINK: TO USE THE WRONG GENDER IDENTIFIER.

USAGE NOTE: Misgendering is problematic. Please use language that respects and affirms someone's identity. Gender is a journey of exploration and someone's identity can change over time. Their identity is still valid.

DID YOU KNOW Generation Z youth are at the forefront of the conversation around gender identity. They understand gender diversity at a much earlier stage in life than older generations. Some studies show that one out of every ten students identity as transgender, nonbinary, or genderqueer, while many other students are exploring other non-cisgender identities to see what feels right for them. Pronouns like she, he, they, zie, sie, ey, fae,

and ve are important identifiers that affirm gender identity. International Transgender Day of Visibility, International Nonbinary People's Day, and International Pronouns Day are some annual events that celebrate and raise awareness to the spectrum of gender identity.

Misgender ▲

MISOGYNY

▼ *noun*

An extreme dislike, contempt, and/or ingrained prejudice against females, girls, women, and the overall feminine expression. Not limited to cisgender women, misogyny is often directed at trans and/or intersex women as well as effeminate men and other groups.

SEE ALSO
FEMMEPHOBIA, TRANSMISOGYNY

❝ *I'm sick of the blatant sexism and misogyny in the media today. When will we, as a society, learn that it's not just a man's world anymore?"*

 WANT MORE INFO? *THINK:* **CULTURAL, SOCIETAL, SYSTEMIC HATRED TOWARD WOMEN.**

MISS CONGENIALITY

▼ *noun*

A person who tries desperately to be perfect, popular, and liked but is greatly disliked in spite of their efforts.

❝ *You are trying way too hard. Nobody likes when you act like Miss Congeniality!"*

 WANT MORE INFO? *THINK:* **MISS POPULAR, MISS PERFECT . . . NOT!**

MISS GIRL OR MISS GURL

▼ *idiom*

A term used to command attention or commend a show of sass. The phrase "Miss Ma'am" can also be used.

❝ *Miss Girl! You are talking too much! This is my favorite anime show and you are disturbing my experience."*

WANT MORE INFO?
THINK: A LIVELY AND SPIRITED ONE.

 USAGE NOTE: This term originated in the Black gay community and is commonly used in the larger queer and trans people of color (QTPOC) community. It has been appropriated by mainstream culture.

MISS THING OR MISS THANG

▼ *idiom*

A sarcastic way of referring to a self-important person by not calling them by their given name.

❝ *Ugh, Miss Thing thinks she is all that.*❞

 WANT MORE INFO?
THINK: A DIVA.

 USAGE NOTE: This term originated in Black American culture and is commonly used in the Black gay and trans community. It has been appropriated by the larger LGBTQIA+ community and mainstream culture.

MIXED ORIENTATION

▼ *noun*

SEE **CROSS ORIENTATION**

MLM

▼ *noun*

An abbreviation for "men loving men."

SEE ALSO
GAY, SAME-GENDER LOVING

❝ *I just bought a cool MLM pride flag button to put on my bookbag.*❞

 WANT MORE INFO?
THINK: SHADES OF BLUE.

MOC

▼ *noun*

An abbreviation for man/men of color, referring to a person who identifies as such.

SEE **POC, QPOC, QWOC**

❝*I signed up for the youth MOC mentorship program. It focuses on exploring issues we young Black, Asian, and Latinx teens face in both academic and social settings.*❞

 WANT MORE INFO? THINK: TITUSS BURGESS, NICO SANTOS, WILSON CRUZ—A NONWHITE MALE.

DID YOU KNOW
Men of color, particularly Black and Latinx people, face extreme racial discrimination in accessing equal opportunity in employment, housing, education, and other public benefits. Statistics show that boys and men of color are punished, policed, and incarcerated at disproportionately higher rates than their white male counterparts. Leading organizations like NAACP, Black Lives Matter, Color of Change, and 100 Black Men of America are working tirelessly to change this narrative.

MOMMI

▼ *noun*

A mature woman—regardless of sexuality—who oozes personality, confidence, and feminine dominance; the femme counterpart to DADDY or ZADDY.

A femme-of-center person who practices the role of provider and protector in a queer relationship. Typically, this partner exhibits an alluring, confident attitude and is the dominant one in the partnership.

❝*Mommi = Oversized Sunglasses + Sassiness + Fun.*❞

WANT MORE INFO?
THINK: SARAH PAULSON,
RUBY ROSE, AND RAVEN-
SYMONÉ.

MONOGAMY

▼ *noun*

The custom of having only
one partner in a physical
and/or romantic relationship
at a time.

RELATED
MONOGAMOUS *adjective*

SEE ALSO
POLYAMORY

66 *Monogamous people
decide that they are going
to exclusively be with each
other. On the other hand,
polyamorous people are
not exclusive; they are open
to emotionally connecting
with multiple partners at the
same time.*"

 WANT MORE INFO?
THINK: THE *ONLY*
PERSON THAT GETS MY

TIME AND ENERGY IN A
RELATIONSHIP.

MONONORMATIVITY

▼ *noun*

A belief that physical and
romantic relationships can
or should only exist between
two monogamous partners.

RELATED
MONONORMATIVE
adjective

SEE ALSO
HETERONORMATIVITY

66 *Why is mononormativity
considered our culture's
'normal' way to love? Love
has huge power that doesn't
always have to be confined
only between two people.*"

 WANT MORE INFO?
THINK: A VIEW ON
RELATIONSHIPS THAT
EXCLUDES POLYAMORY.

283

MONOSEXISM

▼ *noun*

The belief that monosexuality is superior to bisexuality and other non-monosexual orientations.

SEE ALSO

MONOSEXUAL

"

Interviewer: Are you familiar with bisexuality, asexuality, pansexuality, and polysexuality?
Monosexism: I'm sorry, I don't understand. Who are they?

 WANT MORE INFO?
THINK: **STRICTLY HOMOSEXUAL OR HETEROSEXUAL, NOTHING IN BETWEEN.**

MONOSEXUAL

▼ *adjective*

A person who has a physical and romantic preference for only one gender.

SEE ALSO

NON-MONOSEXUAL

"*A gay person and a straight person are both considered monosexual.***"**

 WANT MORE INFO?
THINK: **WOULD YOU LIKE AN APPLE AND AN ORANGE? NAH, JUST THE ORANGE, PLEASE.**

MOTHER or MOTHA

▼ *noun*

The symbolic matriarch of a social group and/or a respected mentor. The term may also be spelled "mutha" or "muva."

SEE ALSO
DRAG MOTHER, HOUSE MOTHER, MAMA

❝ *Oh, that's Motha right there in the mink coat. She is the most popular drag queen here in Cincinnati!* ❞

 WANT MORE INFO? *THINK:* **THE HEAD HONCHO.**

 USAGE NOTE: This term is commonly used in the Black gay and trans community.

MOTHER OF THE HOUSE

▼ *noun*

SEE **HOUSE MOTHER**

MOTHER SUPERIOR

▼ *noun*

An older and wiser gay man.

SEE ALSO
AUNTIE

❝ *Mother Superior holds the truth! The stories he told me about being openly gay in the 1970s are wild. I have so much respect for him.* ❞

 WANT MORE INFO? *THINK:* **A GAY ROLE MODEL.**

 USAGE NOTE: This term is commonly used in the gay male community.

MTF

▼ *noun*

SEE **MALE-TO-FEMALE**

MTN

▼ *noun*

SEE **MALE-TO-NONBINARY/ GENDER NEUTRAL/ NEUTROIS**

MUSCLE MARY

▼ *noun*

SEE **GYM BUNNY**

MX.

▼ *noun*

A gender-neutral title used before the surname or full name of a person. Similar to Ms., Mrs., and Mr., Mx. is often the title used by those who do not identify with a particular gender.

66 *The title Mx. was created in the 1970s as an honorific that does not indicate a gender. Many nonbinary, agender, genderqueer, and even no-label individuals use this title."*

WANT MORE INFO?
THINK: **MX. MADDY SIMS OR MX. SIMS.**

 USAGE NOTE: Pronounced \MIKS\, this term is commonly used by the transgender, nonbinary, and gender nonconforming communities.

Navigating Safe Spaces for Us!

Let's create safe spaces to **UNPACK** our true feelings.

IT IS NOT always easy to deal with the uncomfortable feelings that may come up because of who you are and how you identify. Being LGBTQIA+ is powerful, unique, and liberating, but sometimes we have moments when we feel uneasy, isolated, and lost.

Many queer tweens and teens are exploring to find their truest selves but are often faced with the challenge of being pressured to conform into labels that may not feel completely right. Even when queer youth embrace an identity that feels right, they may not always feel comfortable speaking about their attraction or gender identity in public. Some LGBTQIA+ youth experience body dysphoria and do not feel that the physical body they are born into fits their identity. Other times, queer youth may feel unseen, misunderstood, and not accepted because of the intersectionality of their gender, sexual orientation, race, ethnicity, spirituality, and disability.

Feeling the negativities of queerphobia, ableism, bullying, shaming, and other prejudices is hard to navigate, and a mental health check-in helps to ease this stress and refocus the mind. Remember that mental health is an important part of your overall health. Your feelings deserve a safe place, so let's think of check-ins as a self-care MUST DO!

It's okay to have a mental health check-in with someone you trust. Queer youth and those who are still questioning their identity need an affirming space to figure out the complexities of life. It is not uncommon to feel anxiety, fear, confusion, and even depression when navigating your identity. These feelings are honest and they come from a place of needing acceptance, support, and care.

When we start to feel uneasy, it is always a good idea to reach out for help. Sometimes we just need a trusted and safe space to tackle the issues that are concerning us or seek the guidance needed to grow into our best selves. A safe space can be with a family member, friend, counselor, therapist, LGBTQIA+ peer, queer mentor, or simply an environment that feels trusting and affirming. There are several organizations across the country like the LGBT National Youth Hotline, the Trevor Project, It Gets Better, GLSEN, GSA, the National Runaway Safeline, National Suicide Prevention Lifeline, Q Chat Space, and Love Is Respect that aim to provide queer youth the outlet they need to talk confidentially about their identity, personal challenges, traumas, or crisis. Mental health is imperative. Never feel embarrassed to seek out help when you feel uncomfortable.

When we prioritize
more welcoming and inclusive
environments for everyone to
thrive in, we are investing in a
more promising future.

We all want to learn,
feel valued, be encouraged,
and experience success.

Create affirming and
safe spaces where EVERY BODY,
EVERY MIND, and EVERY HEART
is empowered.

Nn

NAIL IT

▼ verb

To achieve total perfection.

❝ Lena Waithe nailed it in her rainbow pride cape at the Met Gala. She will go down in fashion history, right next to Björk's swan dress and anybody who's ever worn Alexander McQueen. ❞

 WANT MORE INFO? *THINK:* TO ACCOMPLISH GREATNESS.

NANCY BOY

▼ noun

An outdated term used to refer to an effeminate, gay boy or man. Often shortened to "Nancy" or "Nance."

SEE ALSO
LIGHT IN THE LOAFERS, LIMP WRIST, NELLY

❝ Nancy boy, light in the loafers, nelly, and flit are back-in-the-day, postwar words used to speak about gay men. ❞

 WANT MORE INFO? *THINK:* AN OLD-FASHIONED, SEXIST WAY TO DISPARAGE A MAN'S MASCULINITY.

USAGE NOTE: This may be considered a stereotype or derogatory.

NASTY

▼ *adjective*

SEE **FIRE**

NAVY CAKE

▼ *idiom*

A gay man who serves in the United States Navy. Often used in the phrase "a piece of navy cake."

SEE ALSO
ANGEL FOOD

66 *Did you know that Harvey Milk has a ship named after him? He was a gay rights leader, and he served in the US Navy. Talk about a piece of navy cake!"*

 WANT MORE INFO?
THINK: **AN AMERICAN NAVY GAY.**

USAGE NOTE: This term originated in the gay male community.

Navy Cake ▲

NEG

▼ *adjective*

An abbreviation for the word "negative," usually referring to negative HIV test results but may also refer to other STDs.

SEE ALSO
POZ

❝ *Sexual health education and safe sex practices are important educational components. Being proactive about learning healthy romantic relations and having access to protection and testing will result in youth feeling empowered to explore healthy physical relationships and neg statuses!* ❞

 WANT MORE INFO?
THINK: STD-FREE.

NELLY

▼ *adjective*

Extremely effeminate, usually referring to a gay boy or man. The terms NANCY BOY and PERCY can also be used.

SEE ALSO
PANSY

❝ *Charles is too nelly for my taste. I prefer the manlier type.* ❞

 WANT MORE INFO?
THINK: ULTRAGAY.

 USAGE NOTE: This term may be considered a stereotype and derogatory.

NEOPRONOUN

▼ *noun*

A grammatical way to refer to someone without expressing a gender identity. Neopronouns go beyond the traditional binary gender and allow a person to engage with a concept of identity that feels most authentic. Common neopronouns may include xe/xem/xers, ze/hir/hirs, e/em/eirs, and ve/ver/vers, among others. The term NOUN-SELF PRONOUN—gender-neutral pronouns that use nouns as self-identifiers, like sun/sunself or bloom/bloomself—can also be used.

66 Neopronouns are fun and empower me to explore deeper into my identity! I feel stuck when I just use conventional pronouns and labels. They just don't fit me."

 WANT MORE INFO?
THINK: **NEW PRONOUNS USED BY AGENDER, NONBINARY, AND GENDERQUEER PEOPLE.**

DID YOU KNOW Some of the first neopronouns ever recorded were "ou" dating back to 1789, "thon" meaning "that one" created in 1858, and "ze" dating back to 1854. Today, pronouns are still continuing to evolve, and the use of new neopronouns and even noun-self pronouns are creating positive change in affirming nonbinary, agender, genderqueer, and other genderfluid identities.

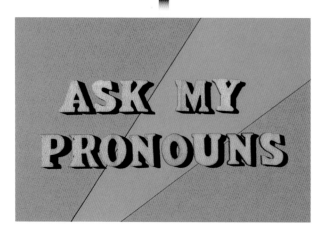

NEURODIVERGENT

▼ *noun*

A person with various degrees of mental abilities and challenges—causing one's brain to work differently from what is considered typical. Some conditions can include autism spectrum disorder, high IQ or advanced learning abilities, attention deficit/hyperactivity disorder, and other learning disabilities, medical disorders, or conditions that have not been diagnosed. This term is a nonmedical descriptor for people who are differently able.

RELATED
NEURODIVERSE

66 *The documentary,* How To Dance in Ohio—*about how teenagers who are neurodiverse are navigating being a part of a social skills therapy program, which may include having a big dance to help them feel more comfortable with social integration—is now a Broadway Musical! I can't wait to see it!"*

 WANT MORE INFO?
THINK: OPPOSITE OF
NEUROTYPICAL.

> **DID YOU KNOW**
> In 1998, sociologist Judy Singer coined the word "neurodiversity" to explain how each person's brain is unique and no two brains are alike; thus, there is no true definition of a normal brain.

NEUTROIS

▼ *noun*

A gender identity that does not conform to the gender binary and is typically thought of as gender neutral. There is no one definition for neutrois; people who identify as neutrois may also identify with the terms AGENDER, GENDERLESS, and/or NONGENDER, among others. The term NULL GENDER can also be used.

SEE ALSO

GENDERQUEER, NONBINARY, GENDER NONCONFORMING

❝ *Identifying as neutrois has allowed me to be part of the nonbinary and trans community. No boundaries, no rules. Gender is what you make of it.* ❞

 WANT MORE INFO?
THINK: **GENDERLESS.**

USAGE NOTE: Pronounced \neu-troys\, \nuh-twah\, or \nu-trwah\; there are many variations. This term is commonly used in the transgender, nonbinary, and gender nonconforming communities.

DID YOU KNOW This term was coined in the 1995 by H. A. Burnham to refer to herself as a gender identity that was neither male or female, but a neutral gender or absence of gender. Neutrois in French can be derived as "neutre" meaning "neutral" and "trois" meaning "third." There are many ways to experience being neutrois and not all people who identity with this label use neopronouns like ze, hir, or xe. Some may use traditional pronouns like he or she.

NEW WAY (VOGUING)

▼ *noun*

The modern technique of vogue house dance established after 1990. This technique is known for its sharpness, flexibility, limb contortions, hand and wrist illusions, and stylized, geometric movement.

SEE ALSO

OLD WAY (VOGUING), VOGUE FEMME

❝ *These up-and-coming children are slaying the new way. Walk for me!* ❞

 WANT MORE INFO?
THINK: **TUTTING AND LOCKING TO "THE HA DANCE" BY MASTERS AT WORK.**

USAGE NOTE: This term originated in ballroom culture.

NIBLING

▼ *noun*

A gender-neutral term for niece or nephew.

66 *My oldest nibling is thirteen years old and my youngest nephew is five years old."*

 WANT MORE INFO?
THINK: **A SIBLING'S NONBINARY CHILD.**

USAGE NOTE: The term is commonly used in the transgender, nonbinary, and gender nonconforming communities. The use of this term relies on an individual's preference. Do not assume that an individual wants to be identified as such.

DID YOU KNOW The term "nibling" was coined by Samuel Elmo Martin, a linguist professor, in 1951. The word means the child of one's sibling and is derived from the "n" in niece and nephew and "ibling" from sibling.

NO BLACKS, NO ASIANS

▼ *idiom*

An exclusionary, racist phrase used in dating profiles and relationship apps to indicate a person's prejudice against people of color. The phrase "No Asians, No Blacks, No Hispanics" is also used.

66 *His profile says, 'No Blacks, No Asians!' Just because it's online doesn't make your blatant racism invisible."*

SEE ALSO

NO FATS, NO FEMMES

 WANT MORE INFO?
THINK: **PREJUDICE AGAINST DATING QTPOC.**

USAGE NOTE: The term originated in gay dating apps. It is an exclusionary phrase that much of the gay community is trying to extricate from its vocabulary. Please be aware that this term can be considered mature.

NO FATS, NO FEMMES

▼ *idiom*

An exclusionary, body-shaming phrase used in dating profiles and relationship apps to indicate a distaste for specific types of people who are considered full-bodied and/or femme.

SEE ALSO
NO BLACKS, NO ASIANS

❝ *Identity shaming is an absolute no-no. 'No Fats, No Femmes' is stigmatizing language."*

 WANT MORE INFO? *THINK*: A BIGOTED PHRASE USED ON GAY DATING APPS.

USAGE NOTE: The term originated in gay dating apps. It is an exclusionary phrase that much of the gay community is trying to extricate from its vocabulary. Please be aware that this term can be considered mature.

NO LABEL

▼ *adjective*

Describing a person who does not identify with any gender or sexuality labels.

❝ *I don't want to be in a box . . . no label. I want to feel and experience my own way."*

 WANT MORE INFO? *THINK*: "IT'S BECOMING MORE ACCEPTABLE NOT TO LABEL YOUR SEXUALITY, TO NOT SAY I ONLY LIKE BOYS, OR I ONLY LIKE GIRLS." —LILY-ROSE DEPP

THE QUEENS' ENGLISH

NONBINARY OR NON-BINARY

▼ *adjective*

A gender identity that is open to a full spectrum of gender expressions, not limited by masculinity and femininity. Nonbinary people may express a combination of masculinity and femininity, or neither.

SEE ALSO

ENBY, GENDER NONCONFORMING, GENDERQUEER

66 *When I was five years old, I used to feel like a boy and a girl. I liked to wear dresses and liked to get my hair cut short. Now that I'm eleven, I know now that I'm not a girl or a boy, I'm nonbinary."*

WANT MORE INFO?
THINK: **AN INCLUSIVE TERM FOR GENDER IDENTITIES THAT ARE NOT CISGENDER.**

DID YOU KNOW
The New York City, Boston, and London marathons have a nonbinary gender option for their racing applicants, giving nonbinary runners the ability to compete without registering for the women's or men's division. In 2022, Jake Caswell was the first person to win prize money in the nonbinary division of the New York City Marathon.

NONGENDER

▼ *adjective*

SEE **AGENDER**

NON-MONOSEXUAL

▼ *adjective*

Having physical and romantic attraction to more than one gender.

SEE ALSO
MONOSEXUAL

66 *Bisexual and pansexual people are considered non-monosexual because they are attracted to more than one expression of gender.*"

 WANT MORE INFO?
THINK: **PEOPLE WHO IDENTIFY AS ANYTHING OTHER THAN STRICTLY STRAIGHT OR GAY.**

NON-MONOGAMY

▼ *noun*

The practice of having multiple interpersonal relationships that are not physically or romantically exclusive. People may be open or private about this lifestyle choice and have multiple partners and/or romantic relationships.

RELATED
NON-MONOGAMOUS
adjective

SEE ALSO
POLYAMORY

66 *I really don't believe humans are supposed to be with just one person romantically. Non-monogamy is natural to us. It's primal.*"

 WANT MORE INFO?
THINK: **ENTERTAINING MORE THAN ONE INTIMATE RELATIONSHIP.**

THE QUEENS' ENGLISH

NO SHADE

▼ *idiom*

Saying something directly without the intent of being offensive. However, people often use "no shade" with a snide tone, intending to criticize. The phrase NO T, NO SHADE is also used.

SEE ALSO
SHADE

❝ *No shade, but you need to put on deodorant after PE class. I can smell you.*"

 WANT MORE INFO? *THINK:* "NO OFFENSE, BUT . . ."

 USAGE NOTE: This term originated in ballroom culture. It has been appropriated by the larger LGBTQIA+ community and mainstream culture.

NO T, NO SHADE

▼ *idiom*

A phrase meaning, "No disrespect, but . . ."—an evolution of the phrase "all T, no shade," meaning "here's the entire truth, but I meant no shade." Can also be seen as "no tea, no shade."

❝ *No T, no shade, but I don't want another snow day. I prefer NOT to be sitting in this hot school through the month of June!*"

 WANT MORE INFO? *THINK:* NO OFFENSE.

 USAGE NOTE: The term originated in ballroom culture. It has been appropriated by the larger LGBTQIA+ community and mainstream culture.

NOT ABOUT THIS LIFE

▼ *idiom*

Completely uninterested in a particular situation, thing, or person.

❝ *Nope, no way, never. I will not be going to the circus. Clowns freak me out. I am not about that life.*"

WANT MORE INFO?
THINK: **DON'T WANT TO BE INVOLVED.**

USAGE NOTE: This term originated in Black American culture and is commonly used in the Black gay and queer community. It has been appropriated by mainstream culture.

NOT FEATURING

▼ *idiom*

Not amused by; uninterested in.

SEE ALSO
FEATURE

❝ *Sage and Talli cannot sit with us. You know I am not featuring those divas today.*❞

 WANT MORE INFO?
THINK: **NOT FOND OF.**

USAGE NOTE: This term originated in ballroom culture and is commonly used in the larger queer and trans people of color (QTPOC) community.

NOT YOUR MINISTRY

▼ *idiom*

A phrase highlighting a person's notable lack of skill or talent in a particular area.

❝ *Please stop singing. Not your ministry, boo boo.*❞

 WANT MORE INFO?
THINK: **"THAT IS NOT IN YOUR WHEELHOUSE...."**

USAGE NOTE: This term originated in Black American culture and is commonly used in the Black gay and queer community.

NOUN-SELF PRONOUN

▼ *noun*

SEE **NEOPRONOUN**

NULL GENDER

▼ *adjective*

SEE **NEUTROIS**

OH, NO YOU DIDN'T

▼ *idiom*

A phrase used to express irritation, distaste, or disbelief at someone's actions.

❝ *Oh, no she didn't! She just ate off my plate without asking. Do I look like a buffet station?*❞

 WANT MORE INFO? *THINK:* **"CAN YOU BELIEVE?"**

USAGE NOTE: This term originated in Black American culture and is commonly used in the Black gay and queer community. It has been appropriated by mainstream culture.

DID YOU KNOW Black American women coined the phrase, "Oh, no you didn't!" in response to an unfavorable action. The idiom gained mainstream exposure when comedian Martin Lawrence, dressed in drag as the character Sheneneh Jenkins, would say her signature line, "Oh, no you didn't!"

OLD WAY (VOGUING)

▼ *noun*

The technique of vogue house dance established prior to 1990. This technique is known for its symmetry, precision, and stylized movements based on Egyptian hieroglyphs and high-fashion poses. In a ball competition, the movement is often used in a dance duel; the winner must trap the other competitor, rendering them unable to execute another move.

SEE ALSO

NEW WAY (VOGUING), VOGUE, VOGUE FEMME

❝ The terms 'Old Way' and 'New Way' are generational. Earlier generations called the style of voguing that was practiced by generations before them 'Old Way.' Voguers, therefore, reuse these terms to refer to the evolutionary changes of the dance that are observable almost every ten years."

—ALEXANDRA STEPANOVA

 WANT MORE INFO?
THINK: **WILLI NINJA, THE GODFATHER OF VOGUING.**

 USAGE NOTE: This term originated in ballroom culture.

OMNIGENDER

▼ adjective

Treating all genders as one, without distinguishing from or discriminating against one or the others.

❝ It's time to implement omnigender bathrooms in AAAALLLLLL public places. Why the gendered divide?"

 WANT MORE INFO?
THINK: **ALL FOR ONE AND ONE FOR ALL.**

Omnigender ▲

OMNISEXUAL

▼ *adjective*

A sexual orientation where a person is attracted to all types of humans equally and has no distinct preferences based on sexuality or gender, though there is an awareness of gender.

RELATED
OMNISEXUALITY *noun*

SEE ALSO
BISEXUAL, PANSEXUAL

❝ *Omnisexuals desire people for who they are and don't let sexuality or gender get in the way of their attraction.*❞

 WANT MORE INFO?
THINK: **ATTRACTION NOT LIMITED TO A SPECIFIC GROUP OF PEOPLE.**

OOP

▼ *exclamation*

A sound made when you are shocked. It is usually accompanied with a retraction of the neck. The length, tone, and pitch of the sound determines the severity.

❝ *Oop! Did she just fart and not say excuse me? Rude.*❞

 WANT MORE INFO?
THINK: **WHOA.**

USAGE NOTE: This term originated in Black American culture and is commonly used in the Black gay and queer community.

Oop   ▼

OTTER

Orphan ▼

ORPHAN

▼ *noun*

A person who hangs around couples looking for attention and intimacy. An orphan is often newly single and in need of company.

❝ *Please, I am just asking you and Justin to come over and watch* American Horror Story *and maybe cuddle a little? I can't help that I'm an orphan right now.*"

 WANT MORE INFO?
THINK: **A PERSON IN NEED OF EXTRA TLC.**

 USAGE NOTE: This term may be considered mature.

▼ *noun*

A body label for a gay, bisexual, or queer man who has excessive amounts of body hair and a lean body type.

 SEE ALSO

"Help! What Type of Gay Am I?," p. 203

❝ *Well, look at that otter splashing in the swimming pool.*"

 WANT MORE INFO?
THINK: **GAY GUY WHO IS ATHLETIC AND HAIRY WHO PROBABLY GOES TO THE GYM FOUR TIMES A WEEK.**

USAGE NOTE: This term originated in the white gay male community.

OUT

▼ *adjective*

Openly LGBTQIA+.

"

LONDON: *Are you out to your family and friends?*

TESSA: *Absolutely, I am out and PROUD!*

 WANT MORE INFO?
THINK: **OPEN ABOUT BEING ON THE LGBTQIA+ SPECTRUM.**

▼ *verb*

To make someone's sexual identity public knowledge—either with or without the person's consent. Often used in the phrase "come out," referring to the metaphor of coming out of the closet.

SEE ALSO
COME OUT, CLOSET

" *You outed that boy and now he is being bullied at school! I am so disappointed in you."*

 WANT MORE INFO?
THINK: **TO REVEAL AN INDIVIDUAL'S QUEERNESS.**

DID YOU KNOW In 2022, under the regulations of the "Don't Say Gay" bill, the Sarasota County School District and other school districts in Florida incorporated a new policy requiring teachers and administration to notify parents or guardians if a child comes out to them as LGBTQIA+ or requests to use a chosen name and/or pronouns different from the school records. If the guardian does not consent to the child's sexuality or gender identity, then the school will not support the student. However, if the guardian does consent, the student would be required to participate in a "Gender Support Plan," and fill out a form that must be signed by the guardian.

OVAH

▼ *adjective*

Exquisite.

" *When I saw* Hamilton *on Disney+, I was at a loss for words. It's so ovah!"*

WANT MORE INFO?
THINK: INCREDIBLE.

USAGE NOTE: This term originated in ballroom culture.

OVER IT OR OVER THIS

▼ *idiom*

Annoyed, fatigued, "done" with something or someone.

66 *I am so over this snow! I have been shoveling our driveway for over an hour. My arms hurt!"*

WANT MORE INFO? *THINK*: "I HAVE MOVED ON."

OVERLIVING

▼ *adjective*

Totally happy; overjoyed. The superlative form of LIVING.

66 *Go-kart paintball, Dave & Buster's, PlayStation VR headset, plus a sleepover*

with thirteen of my friends! I was overliving for my thirteenth birthday weekend. It was the best!"

WANT MORE INFO?
THINK: EUPHORIC.

USAGE NOTE: This term originated in the Black gay community.

OWL

▼ *noun*

An acronym for "older wiser lesbian."

66 *Have you seen the INTO video called 'The Old Lesbians'? Belita, Phyllis, and Sabel are the cutest OWLs I have even seen!"*

WANT MORE INFO?
THINK: HERSTORY MAKERS—EDIE WINDSOR AND THEA SPYER.

USAGE NOTE: This term originated in the lesbian community.

History Lesson: The Ballroom Scene

DECADES AFTER THE cultural revolution known as the Harlem Renaissance, an even more fluid, more diverse group of artists took to the very same streets to create a safe space for LGBTQIA+ self-expression in the midst of intense political, racial, and homophobic strife.

By the late 1970s, the extravagant gay drag balls of 1920s Harlem had evolved into a full-fledged underground queer community. The ballroom scene—as captured in the highly acclaimed 1990 documentary *Paris Is Burning*—became home for Black and Latinx gay and trans people in Harlem and other New York City neighborhoods.

During this time, drag emerged as more than just an idea—it was a way of life. A powerful new lexicon exploded from the ballroom scene. Highly energetic balls featured a variety of categories in which queer and trans people of color (QTPOC)

A house typically consists of a house mother and/or house father and the family members are called "the children." Among the first houses created were the House of LaBeija, House of Corey, House of Wong, House of Dupree, House of Christian, House of Plenty, House of Ebony, House of Pendavis, House of Princess, and House of Omni (Ultra Omni). Some houses no longer exist but should be credited as trailblazers to ballroom culture.

of all gender expressions—butch queens, femme queens, trans men, drag queens, butches, and women—could walk for trophies and cash prizes. A commentator with a legendary reputation would act as emcee, freestyling, chanting, and pumping up the crowd while reading and throwing shade at the kids. Walkers competed in categories like Face, Runway, Vogue, Realness, and Realness with a Twist, hoping for "TENS ACROSS THE BOARD!" or else they'd be chopped.

Along with the feisty language that would eventually trickle into mainstream culture—fierce, slay, read, fiyah, shade, work, and more—the ballroom scene embraced the values of family, self-expression through movement and identity, and the art of confidence, fierceness, and attitude. For queer people who experienced trauma, abuse, or neglect from their biological families, the social houses in ballroom culture became family. These families were built to provide support networks for QTPOC to live freely and embrace their true identity.

In our modern world, LGBTQIA+ culture is finally being celebrated after years of being forced underground. The ballroom scene has seen the most support in mainstream pop culture. RuPaul's Drag Race is a pillar of reality television. FX's groundbreaking Pose had the largest cast of trans actors in TV history. HBO Max's Legendary celebrates the underground ballroom houses and voguing. Ballroom choreography has influenced pop and R&B greats like Madonna, Beyoncé, Teyana Taylor, and Lady Gaga, and the music has inspired new forms of house and queer hip-hop. Ballroom culture and houses have expanded into major cities across the nation, and balls have been held in international cities like London, Paris, Hong Kong, Auckland, and St. Petersburg, providing people all over the world with the opportunity to express themselves, strike a pose, and vogue.

Pp

PACKING

▼ *verb*

Wearing padding or a phallic object, called a packer, to create a non-flesh penis.

❝ *I like to use an adhesive when I am packing. That way I can wear boxers.*"

 WANT MORE INFO?
THINK: PROSTHETIC PHALLUS TO SUPPORT MASC GENDER EXPRESSION.

 USAGE NOTE: This term is commonly used in the transgender, nonbinary, gender nonconforming, and drag communities.

PADDING

▼ *verb*

Using special undergarments that enhance the figure of the body to look more feminine. Garments such as padded panties, bras, and breast and buttocks forms are often used.

❝ *Drag queens usually use padding to create the feminine look they desire.*"

 WANT MORE INFO?
THINK: SHAPING THE BODY TO HAVE BREASTS, BUTT, AND HIPS.

USAGE NOTE: This term is commonly used in the transgender, gender nonconforming, and drag communities.

PAID IT

▼ *verb*

Purposely ignored.

66 *She paid it. She just walked past and didn't even say hello."*

 WANT MORE INFO? *THINK:* **MARSHA P. JOHNSON. THE "P" STANDS FOR "PAY IT NO MIND."**

USAGE NOTE: This term originated in ballroom culture.

PAINTED

▼ *adjective*

Beautifully adorned with makeup.

SEE ALSO
BEAT

66 *Okay, your face is painted! Who taught you*

how to do makeup like that? I want to learn!"

 WANT MORE INFO? *THINK:* **EXQUISITELY MADE UP.**

USAGE NOTE: This term originated in ballroom culture and is commonly used in the drag community.

PANGENDER

▼ *adjective*

A person who identifies with all—"pan" meaning "all"—genders, without distinguishing one from another.

SEE ALSO
BIGENDER, POLYGENDER, GENDERFLUID, GENDERFLUX, NONBINARY

66 *Many gender-expansive identities like pangender, bigender, polygender, and even genderfluid are becoming more recognized in our society."*

WANT MORE INFO?
THINK: **A PROUD MEMBER OF ALL GENDERS.**

PANSEXUAL

▼ *adjective*

A sexual orientation where a person is attracted to people of all—"pan" meaning "all"—genders and sexualities.

▼ *noun*

A pansexual person.

RELATED
PANSEXUALITY *noun*

SEE ALSO
OMNISEXUAL

❝ *I identify as both non-binary and pansexual, which are two very fancy ways of saying I don't care."*
—LACHLAN WATSON

 WANT MORE INFO?
THINK: **JANELLE MONÁE, BRENDON URIE, AND ASIA KATE DILLON BELIEVE LOVE KNOWS NO GENDER!**

PANSY

▼ *adjective*

Effeminate or girly.

▼ *Noun*

A sissy.

SEE ALSO
NELLY

❝ *Don't be such a pansy, Mo. Go talk to him!"*

 WANT MORE INFO?
THINK: **DELICATE.**

USAGE NOTE: This term originated as a derogatory slur for gay males but has been reclaimed by some members of the LGBTQIA+ community. It may still have negative connotations for some people.

DID YOU KNOW In the early 1930s, during the era of Prohibition and a thriving underground bohemian life, drag culture experienced a surge in popularity in big American cities like New York, San Francisco, and Los Angeles. At the time, drag queens were called "pansy performers," and this celebration of queer culture was called the Pansy Craze.

PASSING

▼ **verb**

Describing a transgender individual who is perceived as cisgender.

RELATED
PASS verb

SEE ALSO
CLOCK, STEALTH

❝ Passing feels like when people are blind to my transness.❞

 WANT MORE INFO?
THINK: WHEN A TRANS PERSON "PASSES" THE TEST OF ADHERING TO A TRADITIONAL GENDER EXPRESSION.

USAGE NOTE: This term is controversial within the transgender community. Not all trans and gender-expansive people feel the need to "pass" as cisgender, and many are comfortable shaking up gender norms. In the broader queer community, passing can be linked to other societal privileges—like being cisgender, straight, white, able-bodied, etc.

❝ Being straight-passing comes with its privileges for sure. I don't get bullied or anything, but I also sometimes don't feel accepted by my peers who are queer. It's complicated.❞

 WANT MORE INFO?
THINK: APPEARING "NORMAL" WITHIN A MAJORITY COMMUNITY.

PASSION FRUIT

▼ **noun**

A dated term used to refer to a gay boy or man who was not easily identified as gay due to an outwardly masculine, straight-passing appearance.

❝ Actor Rock Hudson gave serious passion fruit back in the 1960s. That's why fans were so shocked when they found out he had a boyfriend.❞

WANT MORE INFO?
THINK: A MASCULINE GUY WHO DOESN'T "LOOK" GAY.

PEOPLE WITH TRANS PARENTS (PTP)

▼ *noun*

Describing a person with a transgender, nonbinary, or genderqueer parent or guardian. The term KIDS OF TRANS (KOT) can also be used.

❝ *Growing up I thought I was the only PTP/KOT on earth! But I'm not! Being a part of COLAGE opened up a supportive community of friends who share and understand my unique experience."*

 WANT MORE INFO?
THINK: A KID WITH A TRANS PARENT.

People with Trans Parents (PTP) ▶

PEP

▼ *noun*

An antiretroviral medication used to prevent human immunodeficiency virus (HIV) infection after potential exposure. PEP stands for post-exposure prophylaxis.

SEE ALSO
PrEP

❝ *PEP is an emergency medication that must be taken within three days of potentially being exposed to HIV. A doctor or the nearest hospital can give you a prescription."*

 WANT MORE INFO?
THINK: EMERGENCY PILLS TO HELP STOP HIV FROM SPREADING.

PERCHED

▼ *adjective*

Sitting or posing in a confident and/or elegant manner.

❝ *Lillie's cat Puma is always so sassy and perched! She needs to be a cat model.*❞

 WANT MORE INFO? *THINK:* REGAL LIKE A KWEEN!

USAGE NOTE: This term originated in ballroom culture and is commonly used in the larger queer and trans people of color (QTPOC) community.

PERCY

▼ *adjective*

SEE **NELLY**

PGP OR PREFERRED GENDER PRONOUN

▼ *noun*

SEE **PRONOUN**

PHALLOPLASTY

▼ *noun*

SEE **BOTTOM SURGERY**

Pibling ▼

PIBLING

▼ *noun*

A gender-neutral term for aunt or uncle. The word is a blend of "parent" and "sibling."

A term used to refer to a nonbinary, genderqueer, agender, or otherwise gender-expansive sibling to a parent.

❝ *My pibling and I always hang out at Venice Beach Skatepark on Sundays.*❞

WANT MORE INFO?

THINK: REFERRING TO YOUR NONBINARY FAMILY.

> **USAGE NOTE:** This term is commonly used by the transgender, nonbinary, and gender nonconforming communities. The use of this term relies on an individual's preference. Please do not assume an individual wants to be identified as such.

PINK TRIANGLE

▼ *noun*

A symbol adopted by the LGBTQIA+ community to show pride in being gay and resistance against discrimination.

SEE ALSO
BLACK TRIANGLE

❝ *The pink triangle is not just a symbol of gay resistance—it's a symbol of the power we have as a community to reappropriate symbols and words that were historically used to hurt us.*❞

WANT MORE INFO?

THINK: A SYMBOL OF GAY LIBERATION.

> **DID YOU KNOW** The pink triangle was first used in Nazi concentration camps to mark male prisoners who were gay. During the AIDS crisis in the late 1980s, there was public discussion of putting gay men diagnosed with HIV/AIDS in concentration camps to keep the AIDS epidemic from spreading. One of the first organizations to bring public awareness to the AIDS epidemic was ACT UP, created by key member Larry Kramer and other founding members. Their slogan, Silence=Death, was one of the many ways the pink triangle has been reclaimed by the gay community as a symbol for pride, equality, and justice.

Pink Triangle ▼

PLEASE AND THANK YOU

▼ *idiom*

A sassy request for someone to do something immediately.

**" ** *Can you stop being so loud? Please and thank you!"*

 WANT MORE INFO?
THINK: "DO AS I SAY."

PLEASE OR PUH-LEASE

▼ *exclamation*

An expression of disagreement or disbelief.

**" ** *Oh child, puh-lease. That woman did not lose fifteen pounds in a week! Infomercials are so fake, fake, fake!"*

 WANT MORE INFO?
THINK: "COME ON!"

USAGE NOTE: This term originated in Black American culture and is commonly used in the Black gay and queer community.

POC OR **BIPOC**

▼ *noun*

An acronym for "people of color" or "person of color"—an inclusive term for supporting people within a community who face marginalization and erasure because of race or ethnicity. BIPOC, "Black, Indigenous, and people of color" may also be used.

SEE ALSO
MOC, QPOC or QTPOC, QWOC or QTWOC, WOC

"

JUNIPER: *Hey, I'm looking for any organizations for gay POC. Are there any represented here?*

FALLON: *Yes! Through these double doors, you'll see tables for the Trikone, Keshet, Gay Men of African Descent, the Trans Masculine Advocacy Network, and a ton of other social and political groups for LGBTQ POC.*

WANT MORE INFO?
THINK: NOT CAUCASIAN.

POLY

▼ *adjective*

A Greek prefix used to identify something that has "many" or "several" parts.

❝ I celebrate all the ways I am poly! I'm polysexual, polygender, and just plain polyamazing!"

WANT A LITTLE MORE?
THINK: MORE THAN ONE AND MORE THAN TWO.

Poly ▲

POLYAMOROUS

▼ *adjective*

Having or desiring multiple partners and/or romantic relationships at one time. The term is often abbreviated as "poly" and "polyam."

❝ People think being poly is complicated, and sure, it can be, but it's all about setting ground rules and communicating effectively with your partners. The more love you receive, the more you are capable of giving."

WANT MORE INFO?
THINK: MAINTAINING DIFFERENT TYPES OF INTIMATE RELATIONSHIPS WITH DIFFERENT PEOPLE.

USAGE NOTE: Please note that the abbreviation "poly" is also a shortened version for Polynesian and many polyamorous people prefer using "polyam" out of respect.

POLYAMORY

▼ noun

The practice of having multiple romantic and/or physical relationships at once, with consent of all individuals involved.

RELATED
POLYAMORIST noun

SEE ALSO
MONOGAMY

❝ My parents came out that they are now practicing polyamory. They said they still love each other and that will never change but they want to hang out and connect with other partners.❞

 WANT MORE INFO? THINK: A MUTUAL AGREEMENT TO HAVE PARTNERS OUTSIDE OF A PRIMARY RELATIONSHIP.

POLYGENDER

▼ adjective

A person who identifies

with many—"poly" meaning "many"—genders, without distinguishing one from another.

SEE ALSO
BIGENDER, PANGENDER, GENDERFLUID, GENDERFLUX, NONBINARY

❝ My gender expression is vast and always changing. I identify as polygender and genderflux.❞

 WANT MORE INFO? THINK: IDENTIFYING AS MULTIPLE GENDERS EITHER SIMULTANEOUSLY OR VARYING BETWEEN THEM.

POLYSEXUAL

▼ adjective

Physically attracted to people of several genders and sexualities, with "poly" meaning "many." A polysexual person's sexual attraction is not limited to a specific gender identity. However, polysexuality does not indicate an attraction to *all* genders, but a specific set of gender expressions that are particular to each individual.

▼ *noun*

A polysexual person.

" *Joey is attracted to masc-of-center folks who may identify as male, nonbinary, genderqueer, or boyflux. He's polysexual.*"

 WANT MORE INFO? *THINK:* **ATTRACTION IS BOUNTIFUL, BUT SPECIFIC.**

POST-OP

▼ *noun*

A shortened word for postoperative. Describing when a person has undergone gender affirmation surgery or other medical procedures that

changes the body to align with a specific gender.

SEE ALSO
GENDER AFFIRMATION SURGERY

" *Many states allow queer youth to get gender affirmation surgery as early as sixteen, but only with the support of a parent or guardian. A great amount of medical, mental, and physical aftercare is needed post-op.*"

 WANT MORE INFO? *THINK:* **HAVING UNDERGONE SURGERY THAT AFFIRMS ONE'S GENDER.**

USAGE NOTE: Some transgender, nonbinary, and genderqueer people get gender affirmation surgery and some do not. There are many ways to express gender-expansive identities and they are all valid.

POWER LESBIAN

▼ *noun*

An influential lesbian with a commanding presence.

66 *My role model is Rachel Maddow. She is always showing those men in suits who's boss. She is such a power lesbian.*"

WANT MORE INFO? *THINK:* **A LESBIAN POWERHOUSE!**

POZ

▼ *adjective*

HIV-positive.

SEE ALSO
NEG

66 *To my younger queer peers who are exploring their bodies with other people, be safe! Testing poz is no joke!*"

WANT MORE INFO? *THINK:* **FIGHTING HIV/AIDS.**

DID YOU KNOW HIV was originally called GRID, meaning gay-related immune deficiency. It was also colloquially known as "gay cancer" before the disease was understood. The *New York Times* was the first to mention GRID, in an article written on May 11, 1982, along with A.I.D., which meant acquired immunodeficiency disease.

PRE-OP

▼ *noun*

A shortened word for preoperative. Describing when a person has not undergone gender affirmation surgery or other medical procedures that changes the body to align with a specific gender, but may be considering it or in the preparation phrase.

SEE ALSO
GENDER AFFIRMATION SURGERY

66 *Just because a trans person is pre-op doesn't mean they are not trans. You are who you are and you don't always need a surgery to affirm that.*"

WANT MORE INFO? *THINK:* **THE PERIOD BEFORE GENDER AFFIRMATION SURGERY.**

USAGE NOTE: Some transgender, nonbinary, and genderqueer people get gender affirmation surgery and some do not. There are many ways to express gender-expansive identities and they are all valid.

PrEP

▼ *noun*

Medication used to reduce the risk of contracting the human immunodeficiency virus (HIV) in people who have not been previously exposed and/or at risk. PrEP stands for pre-exposure prophylaxis; it is a highly effective way to prevent HIV infection, if taken as prescribed.

SEE ALSO
PEP

"

KAILEY: *What are all these ads about Truvada?*
TERRANCE: *Oh, that's PrEP. You don't remember learning about it in health class last month? You only take it to prevent getting HIV.*

 WANT MORE INFO? *THINK:* **GROUNDBREAKING MEDICATION USED TO PREVENT HIV INFECTION.**

DID YOU KNOW Gilead Sciences established a medication assistance program to help individuals at risk of HIV gain proper medical access to treatments. Truvada for PrEP Medication Assistance Program (MAP) assists eligible HIV-negative people who are uninsured or need financial assistance.

PRESSED

▼ *adjective*
Overly eager.

" *I was so pressed to get Frank Ocean's autograph that when I finally saw him, I almost peed my pants!"*

 WANT MORE INFO? *THINK:* **IMPATIENT, SUPER-EXCITED.**

USAGE NOTE: This term originated in Black American culture and is commonly used in the Black gay and queer community.

PRIDE

▼ *noun*

Confidence in one's identity as a lesbian, gay, bisexual, transgender, queer, intersex, asexual, nonbinary, or otherwise nonheteronormative person.

A movement that promotes equal rights and social justice for all members of the LGBTQIA+ community.

SEE ALSO
RAINBOW

❝ *Gay pride is such a big part of my identity. I'm obsessed with gay culture, gay neighborhoods, gay clubs and institutions, gay TV, films, artists, musicians—I am so proud to be a part of a community that remains strong and united in the face of hate.*❞

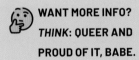

WANT MORE INFO?
THINK: **QUEER AND PROUD OF IT, BABE.**

DID YOU KNOW

In the United States, Gay Pride—or simply, Pride—is celebrated during the month of June in honor of a series of violent demonstrations that occurred at the Stonewall Inn, a New York City gay bar, on June 28, 1969. The Stonewall riots are largely credited for starting the cultural conversation around gay rights and continue to be celebrated as a symbol of gay liberation.

PRISSY

▼ *noun*

SEE **PANSY**

PRIVILEGE

▼ *noun*

A special right or immunity granted to a particular group of people.

SEE ALSO
CISGENDER PRIVILEGE, MALE PRIVILEGE, STRAIGHT PRIVILEGE, WHITE PRIVILEGE

▼ *verb*

To grant a privilege to.

66 *A lot of straight people don't understand the privilege they have to simply love the person they love. Love is love—it is our right! We need society to respect all of us!"*

 WANT MORE INFO?
THINK: THE INVISIBLE WAYS IN WHICH CERTAIN GROUPS OF PEOPLE HAVE FREEDOM BASED ON THEIR IDENTITY.

PROCESSING

▼ *verb*

In ballroom culture, this refers to a skilled competitor eliminating all others from the competition.

66 *That queen was processing the girls in Vogue Femme, taking them out one by one, hand by hand."*

 WANT MORE INFO?
THINK: LEAVING OTHER COMPETITORS IN THE DUST.

USAGE NOTE: This term originated in ballroom culture.

PRONOUN

▼ *noun*

A grammatical way to refer to someone without naming them, according to gender identity. As our cultural

SHE/HER HE/HIM THEY/THEM HE/THEY ZE/ZIR XE/XEM

understanding of gender has expanded, pronouns, too, have expanded from the traditional use of she/her/hers and he/him/his to include nonbinary and genderqueer identities, such as they/them/theirs, ze/hir/hirs, and ey/em/eirs, and others.

SEE ALSO

NEOPRONOUN, "The Genderbread Person," *p. 73,* **"Common Pronouns 101,"** *p. 101*

"

JAMEELAH: *Let's introduce ourselves by sharing our name and pronouns. I'll start! I'm Jameelah and I use she/her/hers or they/them/theirs.*

JURGEN: *I'm Jurgen and I use ze/hir/hirs.*

IZZY: *I'm Izzy and I prefer they/them but also respond to he/him.*

KIYOKO: *I'm Kiyoko and I use she/her pronouns.*

 WANT MORE INFO? *THINK:* **PERSONAL IDENTIFIER THAT REFLECTS ONE'S GENDER EXPRESSION.**

USAGE NOTE: Pronouns are important identifiers in the transgender, nonbinary, and gender nonconforming communities, as they validate and support a person's gender identity. It is important to respect and properly use a person's pronouns and/or chosen name.

327

DID YOU KNOW International Pronouns Day was first celebrated October 17, 2018 in twenty-five countries to acknowledge the many ways gender expression is represented in our queer community. It is annually observed on the third Wednesday of October.

PRO-SEX(UALITY)

▼ *adjective*

SEE **SEX POSITIVE**

PULLED

▼ *adjective*

Sophisticated and proper.

❝ *Yaaaasssssssss, you look pulled and ready to slay!"*

 WANT MORE INFO?
THINK: COSMOPOLITAN.

> **USAGE NOTE:** This term originated in ballroom culture.

PULL UP

▼ *verb*

To look and act one's best.

❝ *Girl, pull up and stop acting nervous. You can do this!"*

 WANT MORE INFO?
THINK: PUT ON YOUR SUNDAY CLOTHES AND ACT YOUR SUNDAY BEST.

> **USAGE NOTE:** This term is commonly used in ballroom culture.

PUMP

▼ *verb*

To walk with a display of confidence, often mimicking a woman's walk on a high-fashion runway.

❝ *You betta pump down that street, diva!"*

 WANT MORE INFO?
THINK: STRUT WITH PRIDE!

▼ *noun*

A long distance.

❝ *It's a pump to get to the top of the mountain. But when you see your dreams come true, it's priceless."*

 WANT MORE INFO?
THINK: A TREK.

> **USAGE NOTE:** This term originated in Black American culture. It has been appropriated by the larger LGBTQIA+ community and mainstream culture.

PUP

▼ *noun*

A young gay or queer male.

SEE ALSO
TWINK, TWUNK

❝ *He is just a pup with a lot to learn about being gay.*❞

 WANT MORE INFO?
THINK: A GAY MALE IN HIS TWEENS AND TEENS (AND EVEN EARLY TWENTIES).

PURPLE

▼ *adjective*

SEE **LAVENDER**

PUSH THROUGH

▼ *idiom*

To command and take charge of a space or task.

 Push through, choir! Y'all betta sing. The spirit of the Lord was here this morning!❞

 WANT MORE INFO?
THINK: GET THE JOB DONE.

USAGE NOTE: This term is commonly used in the Black gay community.

Queer Parents and the Family Dynamic

"It's time to celebrate! Oh yeah! #LGBTQFAMILIESDAY!"

MANY LGBTQIA+ COUPLES who want to grow their love for each other into a family have children. Some queer people may choose to raise a child in a loving single-parent household. LGBTQIA+ adults have several options on how to build their home. When starting a family, it is important to acknowledge that there are unique needs for LGBTQIA+ parents and their kids.

Many couples or single parents may choose to use sperm donation or have a surrogate, which is called assisted reproduction. A child may come from a previous relationship. Many people adopt or foster children. Some also choose to co-parent with other LGBTQIA+ people. All of these choices are valid and respected in our LGBTQIA+ community. Establishing good values, proper communication, and unconditional love and finding a community that offers long-lasting support allow queer parents to build a strong and thriving family dynamic.

The opportunity for a child to have two moms, two dads, or a combination of queer parents is a unique experience and should be celebrated. However, there are some challenges LGBTQIA+ parents and their children may face, such as children not being socially accepted by their peers, judgment from other parents, and lack of support from immediate family, friends, and/or the children's school. In addition, some queer parents face long adoption wait times because of bias or prejudice and complications with legal guardianship.

Laws vary from state to state and are constantly evolving when it comes to recognizing queer parents and their families. On June 26, 2017, the Supreme Court reversed an Arkansas Supreme Court ruling, ordering all states to treat same-sex couples equally to opposite-sex couples in the issuance of birth certificates. This was a big win for our LGBTQIA+ families and the foundation for more wins to come. PFLAG, Family Equality, COLAGE, *Gay Parent* magazine, the Family Acceptance Project, and Family Week in Provincetown are examples of groups, publications, and events that provide support and resources to queer parents and their families.

"Any age where it's appropriate to talk about a kid's mom and dad, then it should be appropriate to talk about a kid's mom and mom or dad and dad or whatever family structure we live with. That's part of what it means to be pro-family, is to be pro-every family." —PETE BUTTIGIEG

QPOC OR QTPOC

▼ noun

An inclusive acronym for queer people/person of color or queer trans people/person of color, diverse people who have traditionally been marginalized because of race, sex, and gender. This community centers the experiences of its members and provides spaces and language for empowerment.

SEE ALSO

MOC, POC, QWOC, WOC

❝ Being a queer person of color (QPOC) often feels like being on the front lines of the fight for equality in two groups, with both treating you as an 'other.' For me, the challenge has been dealing with racism and colorism in the gay community and homophobia and transphobia in the Black community. . . . The majority of my friends are QPOC because they understand what it's like to be the rainbow sheep in your Black family, and the Black sheep in a white world."

—KAYLA INMAN

 WANT MORE INFO?
THINK: AN ACRONYM THAT CREATES SPACE

AND EMPOWERMENT FOR MARGINALIZED GENDERS, SEXUALITIES, AND RACES WITHIN THE LGBTQIA+ COMMUNITY.

USAGE NOTE: Other iterations of this acronym exist, one of the most popular being QTBIPOC: queer, trans, Black, Indigenous, and people/person of color.

DID YOU KNOW Due to the adversity queer and trans people of color face—because of racism, queerphobia, and transphobia—many QTPOC, youth especially, find themselves at high risk for homelessness, poverty, and violence. As a result, activist groups have formed to serve and protect QTPOC youth and the community at large, such as the National Black Justice Coalition, Audre Lorde Project, QLatinx, and Fabulous Independent Educated Radicals for Community Empowerment (FIERCE).

Q/T APA OR Q/T AAPI

▼ *noun*

An inclusive acronym for queer and trans Asian Pacific American or queer and trans Asian American and Pacific Islander, members of a group of diverse Asian ethnicities who have traditionally been marginalized because of race, sex, and gender. This community centers the experiences of its members and provides spaces and language for empowerment.

SEE ALSO
AAPI

❝*Amplify Q/T AAPI voices! Celebrate the distinct cultural nuances of the many Asian queer and trans communities.*❞

 WANT MORE INFO? *THINK:* HIGHLIGHTING THE EXPERIENCE AND STORIES OF THE LGBTQIA+ ASIAN AMERICAN COMMUNITY.

DID YOU KNOW Asian American and Pacific Islander Heritage Month is annually celebrated during the month of May to highlight the achievements, histories, and cultures of Asian Americans, Native Hawaiians, and Pacific Islanders in America. The month of May commemorates important historical advancements in the AANHPI community—when the first Japanese immigrant came to America on May 7, 1843, and when the transcontinental railroad was successfully completed, largely due to Chinese immigrants, on May 10, 1869—and honors the many Asian ethnic communities standing together in solidarity.

QUEEN

▼ *noun*

A gay, bisexual, or queer man, usually flamboyant in nature. Femininity is often celebrated and glorified in the gay male community, so there are many labels using the word "queen." Alternate spellings include QWEEN, KWEEN, and KWANE.

RELATED

QUEENY *adjective*

A term of endearment for a friend (of any gender and/or sexuality).

In ballroom and drag culture, "queen" is a term used to unite all LGBTQIA+ people, blurring the line between genders and celebrating queerness.

SEE ALSO

BUTCH QUEEN, FAUX QUEEN, FEMME QUEEN, DRAG QUEEN

❝ *['Queen' is] the line between us. The unity. Because we are family. We are queens—but he's a guy queen, and I'm a girl queen.*"
—NICOLE BOWLES

 WANT MORE INFO? *THINK:* **A GAY, A BFF, AND/ OR A MEMBER OF THE BALLROOM COMMUNITY.**

QUEENAGER

▼ noun

A teenage queen. The term QUEER TEEN can also be used.

❝

ARROW: *Let me give you the cafeteria tour. The lacrosse and dance teams sit over by the east doors. The speech club sits here. . . .*

LUNA: *That's fine, but where do the queenagers sit?*

ARROW: *I thought you would never ask! We all sit over there, by the big windows.*

 WANT MORE INFO? *THINK:* **ADOLESCENT QUEER.**

DID YOU KNOW

In 2010, gay activists Dan Savage and Terry Miller created the It Gets Better Project in direct response to the increasing rates of suicide among LGBTQIA+ youth. In an effort to build a supportive community around those struggling with bullying and mental health issues related to gender, identity, and sexuality, Savage and Miller created a video-sharing platform to empower and uplift the youth and connect them with adults who could affirm that life does indeed get better. Since its inception, the It Gets Better Project has collected over seventy thousand video entries from people all around the world, reminding LGBTQIA+ youth that hope is out there, and it does get better.

QUEENING OUT

▼ idiom

Heightened emotional behavior or fits.

❝ *He was queening out just because he saw a rat! It's New York! Get over it."*

 WANT MORE INFO? *THINK:* **ACTING MELODRAMATIC.**

The act of a queer male exaggerating femininity.

❝ *I am ready to queen out for Troy's birthday! The theme is chic, fun, and fabulous, darling!"*

 WANT MORE INFO? *THINK:* **FEMME-ING IT UP.**

QUEER

▼ *adjective*

An umbrella term describing anyone who identifies as something other than heterosexual and/or cisgender.

▼ *noun*

A queer person.

"

Eric: I have something to tell you, but I am sacred you are not going to like it. I . . . I feel like I'm queer.

Mom: Hey, kiddo. It's okay to be queer! Explore and find your most authentic self and know Mommy will love and accept you no matter how you identify.

 WANT MORE INFO?
THINK: ANYONE ON THE LGBTQIA+ SPECTRUM.

▼ *verb*

To make something queer; to analyze, deconstruct, and challenge thoughts or ideas rooted in heteronormativity.

" *The queering of literary classics brings diversity to young readers. I can't wait to share Ash, the queer version of 'Cinderella,' with my class!"*

 WANT MORE INFO?
THINK: THE ACTS OF GENDERBENDING, CHALLENGING SEXUAL NORMS, AND QUESTIONING MASCULINE AND FEMININE IDEALS.

USAGE NOTE: Once derogatory, the term has been reappropriated by much of the LGBTQIA+ community to be an inclusive identifier for anyone within the community. However, not all members of the LGBTQIA+ community are comfortable with this term and some refrain from using it.

DID YOU KNOW

The word "queer" came into popular use in the gay community in the early 1900s after being used for hundreds of years to mean strange or peculiar. For many years, the term was used in a derogatory way to describe people who identified as homosexual, gay, or same-gender loving, until the 1980s, when activists reclaimed the word as a politically provocative way to take ownership of their identities.

Over time, "queer" has become an all-encompassing umbrella term for anyone who identifies as something other than cisgender and/or heterosexual. Many people not only proudly label themselves as queer, but also embody the word to promote social and political change. "Queer existence is resistance" is a popular saying created by the LGBTQIA+ community to both empower and advocate for queer people, identity, culture, history, and our future.

▼ Queer Geek ☆

QUEER GEEK

▼ *noun*

A queer enthusiast of technology, comics, video games, or any other specified topic of interest.

"

IVY: *I'm rallying up the queer geek squad to volunteer for Flame Con next month. Sai and Astrid are in!*

EMILE: *Amazing! Lacie and Shanita are too! #flamies #GeeksOUT #geeksjustwannahavefun*

WANT MORE INFO?
THINK: **A COOL, NERDY, AND FORWARD-THINKING LGBTQIA+ PERSON.**

DID YOU KNOW
The nonprofit organization Geeks OUT was formed in 2010 to provide a space for queer geeks. The organization produces positive queer geek events, advocacy campaigns, and podcasts, and created the world's largest LGBTQIA+ comics and pop culture convention called Flame Con.

QUEER PARENT(S)

▼ *noun*

A queer person or couple raising a child. For couples who identify as "same-sex," the term SAME-SEX PARENT(S) can also be used.

RELATED
QUEER PARENTING *verb*

SEE ALSO
"Queer Parents and the Family Dynamic," *p. 330*

> **66** *Groups for gay, lesbian, bisexual, transgender, and queer parents build community power and are valuable resources for the family equality movement. Moreover, they're a great place to share ideas, discuss parenting tips, and to find support."*

—FAMILY EQUALITY

 WANT MORE INFO? *THINK:* LGBTQIA+ PARENTS WHO DO BEDTIME STORIES, PARENT/TEACHER CONFERENCES, AND TIKTOK DANCES FOR THEIR KIDS.

QUEERPHOBIA

▼ *noun*

Aversion, fear, or hatred toward queerness.

RELATED
QUEERPHOBIC *adjective*
QUEERPHOBE *noun*

SEE ALSO
ACEPHOBIA, BIPHOBIA, FEMMEPHOBIA, HOMOPHOBIA, LESBOPHOBIA, TRANSPHOBIA

> **66** *Our state representative's queerphobic rhetoric is problematic not only for political reasons, but for the safety of the LGBTQIA+ community."*

 WANT MORE INFO? *THINK:* DISCRIMINATION TOWARD QUEER PEOPLE.

◄ **Queer Parent(s)**

QUEERPLATONIC PARTNER

▼ *noun*

A partner in a queerplatonic relationship. The terms SQUISH or ZUCCHINI can also be used. The term may be abbreviated as "QP" or "QPP."

SEE ALSO
QUEERPLATONIC RELATIONSHIP

❝ *Victoria and I have been in the same class since kindergarten. We are like the same person. She knows exactly what I am thinking and sometimes we finish each other's sentences. We support and love each other as queerplatonic partners.* ❞

 WANT MORE INFO? THINK: A LOVING, NONROMANTIC, NONSEXUAL BESTIE AND PARTNER.

 USAGE NOTE: This term originated in the asexual and aromantic communities. It has been appropriated by some members of the larger LGBTQIA+ community.

QUEERPLATONIC RELATIONSHIP

▼ *noun*

An extremely close, passionate attachment between two friends that has a strong emotional connection that may extend beyond the boundary of a "normal" friendship. These relationships do not develop into a romantic partnership. A person in a queerplatonic relationship can be called a QUEERPLATONIC PARTNER, SQUISH, or ZUCCHINI.

❝ *Your aura is beautiful, and you affirm me with such goodness. We've developed the most*

extraordinary queerplatonic
relationship, and I've never
felt safer."

WANT MORE INFO?
THINK: **A LOVING
BOND BETWEEN TWO
PEOPLE THAT DOES
NOT FIT THE MODEL
OF A TRADITIONAL
FRIENDSHIP OR SEXUAL
RELATIONSHIP.**

USAGE NOTE: This term originated
in the asexual and
aromantic communities.
It has been appropriated by some
members of the larger LGBTQIA+
community.

▲ **Queerplatonic Relationship**

QUEERSPAWN

▼ *noun*

A person who has one or
more LGBTQIA+ parents
or guardians. The term
COLAGEr can also be used
by those in the COLAGE
community.

❝ *Some queerspawn are
adopted into queer families
that are of a different
race and/or nationality.
It's called transcultural
adoption. I have a dad that
is white and a dad that is
Cuban-American and I
am Guatemalan. We call
ourselves the rainbow
tribe!"*

WANT MORE INFO?
THINK: **CHILDREN OF
LGBTQIA+ PEOPLE.**

USAGE NOTE: Not all queerspawn
identity as queer;
many queerspawn are
heterosexual. Please do not label
someone's gender identity or sexual
orientation based on assumptions or
stereotypes.

Queer
Teen

QUEER TEEN

▼ *noun*

Youth, usually between the ages of twelve and nineteen, who identify as queer or LGBTQIA+.

SEE ALSO
QUEENAGER

66 *To all the queer teens who continue to stand up for yourselves, for others, and what you believe in, the LGBTQIA+ community thanks you! We commend you for your passion to change the world in a more positive way."*

 **WANT MORE INFO?**
THINK: **LGBTQIA+ YOUTH.**

DID YOU KNOW Media representation of queer tweens and teens has encouraged and supported LGBTQIA+ youth in a dynamic way. Films like *The Half of It*; *Love, Simon*; and *Strange World*, and television shows like *Raven's Home*; *Steven Universe*; *Dead End: Paranormal Park*; *She-Ra and the Princesses of Power*; *Sailor Moon Crystal*; and many others all had groundbreaking moments in showing positive LGBTQIA+ representation. Films, TV shows, YouTube channels, music, and social media have provided important outlets for queer tweens and teens to connect on social issues, organize grassroots projects, create peer groups, and inspire each other. Some noted influencers who use their social media platforms to empower the young queer community are Jazz Jennings, Hayley Kiyoko, Tyler Oakley, Amandla Stenberg, JoJo Siwa, Aaron Philip, Ella Briggs, and Schuyler Bailar.

QUEER THEORY

▼ *noun*

A field of critical theory that grew out of women's and gender studies; a form of critical thinking that dismantles traditional assumptions about sex, sexuality, and gender as they relate to the social environment.

❝ *The work of so many philosophers, writers, and great thinkers paved the way for queer theory. My favorites are Simone de Beauvoir and Adrienne Rich.*"

 WANT MORE INFO?
THINK: LOOKING AT ALL EXPRESSIONS OF HUMANITY THROUGH A CRITICAL, QUEER LENS.

QUESTIONING

▼ *adjective*

An identifier for an individual who is curious about or exploring their gender identity or sexual orientation.

SEE ALSO
"Finding My Identity: 'Who Am I,'" *p. 136*

❝ *To tell you the truth, I'm still questioning my sexuality. When I find new labels I connect with, I get curious. There is such liberation in self-discovery and I'm going to take my time exploring.*"

 WANT MORE INFO?
THINK: EXPLORING ONE'S IDENTITY.

QWEEN

▼ *noun*

SEE **QUEEN**

QWOC OR QTWOC

▼ *noun*

An inclusive acronym for queer women/woman of color or queer and transgender women/ woman of color, members of a group of diverse women who have traditionally been marginalized because of race, sex, and gender. This community centers the experiences of its members and provides spaces and language for empowerment.

SEE ALSO

MOC, POC, QPOC or QTPOC, WOC

" *QTWOC will not be overlooked anymore! Femininity, queerness, and melanin are our superpowers and we are a force to be reckoned with."*

 WANT MORE INFO? *THINK:* **AN ACRONYM THAT AMPLIFIES THE VOICES OF MARGINALIZED WOMEN/ FEMMES, SEXUALITIES, AND RACES WITHIN THE LGBTQIA+ COMMUNITY.**

QWOC
or
QTWOC

Rr

RAINBOW

▼ *noun*

A symbol of colors associated with the diversity and empowerment of the LGBTQIA+ community.

SEE ALSO
FULL-SPECTRUM, PRIDE

▼ *adjective*

Bearing the colors of the rainbow.

❝ *The rainbow flag and the rainbow itself are symbols that remind us love is love, no matter what size, shape, or color it comes in.*❞

 WANT MORE INFO?
THINK: PRIDE.

DID YOU KNOW The rainbow flag was created in 1978. Politician Harvey Milk challenged an artist named Gilbert Baker to create an image that promoted hope for the gay community amid the progressive movement toward gay liberation in the late seventies. The original flag consisted of eight colors: hot pink for sexuality, red for life, orange for healing, yellow for the sun, green for nature, turquoise for art, indigo for harmony, and violet for spirit. In 2017, the Philadelphia Office of LGBT Affairs debuted a new pride flag that added black and brown stripes to celebrate people of color within the LGBTQIA+ community. In 2018, Daniel Quasar designed the Progress Flag, incorporating the colors of the transgender pride flag into the rainbow flag. This flag was redesigned by Valentino Vecchietti in 2021, celebrating intersex identity by adding a purple circle superimposed over a yellow triangle.

REACHING

REACHING

▼ verb

An attempt to make something work but not quite achieving the desired result.

❝ *Baby, you are reaching with that bright blue! Who dyed your hair? Papa Smurf?"*

 WANT MORE INFO? *THINK:* **TRYING, BUT . . . D+.**

 USAGE NOTE: This term is commonly used in the Black gay community.

READ

▼ noun

A skillful insult, piece of criticism, or mocking observation, usually rooted in some truth.

SEE ALSO

LIBRARY, READ FOR FILTH

▼ verb

To insult or disrespect.

❝ *Shade comes from reading. Reading came first. Reading is the real art form of insults. You get in a smart crack and everyone laughs and kikis because you found a flaw and exaggerated it . . . then you've got a good read going."*

—DORIAN COREY

 WANT MORE INFO? *THINK:* **READING IS FUNDAMENTAL!**

 USAGE NOTE: This term originated in ballroom culture. It has been appropriated by the larger LGBTQIA+ community and mainstream culture.

READ FOR FILTH

▼ idiom

A harsh, merciless attack on someone's character.

SEE ALSO

LIBRARY, READ

❝ *Oh, no! Who spilled ketchup all over my new*

bookbag? I am going to be read for filth!"

 WANT MORE INFO?
THINK: REPRIMANDED.

 USAGE NOTE: This term originated in ballroom culture.

READ SOMEONE THEIR RIGHTS

▼ *idiom*

To publicly point out someone's flaws. The attack can be mild, earnest, and honest, or it can be spiteful with major intent to hurt.

" *Miss Thing thought she was going to read someone their rights with her finger all in Kiara's face. But I gave her the nastiest stare-down and she knew not to try us!"*

 WANT MORE INFO?
THINK: TO OPENLY CRITICIZE OR HUMILIATE.

 USAGE NOTE: This term originated in ballroom culture. It has been appropriated by the larger LGBTQIA+ community and mainstream culture.

REALLY GIRL

▼ *idiom*

Questioning a statement or action.

 Really girl? You just gonna jump the line? We have all been patiently standing here. You can kindly find your way to the back!"

 WANT MORE INFO?
THINK: "ARE YOU SERIOUS?"

USAGE NOTE: This term originated in Black American culture and is commonly used in the Black gay and queer community. It has been appropriated by the larger LGBTQIA+ community and mainstream culture.

REALNESS

▼ *noun*

A quality someone possesses when they have the ability to copy and bring to life a specific look or behavior. The term is often used in succession with another adjective or noun.

❝ *To be able to blend, that's what realness is. If you can pass the untrained eye, or even the trained eye, and not give away the fact that you are gay, that's when it's realness."* —DORIAN COREY

 WANT MORE INFO? *THINK:* **"IF YOU DON'T RECOGNIZE THE REALNESS, SHADE ON YOU!"** —SUGUR SHANE, **"BUDDAH VS SUGUR"**

In gay ballroom culture, this is a category in a ball competition where a competitor is judged on their ability to embody a particular look or persona in an authentic, realistic way. Popular subcategories include Femme Queen Realness, Schoolboy Realness, Executive Realness, and Thug Realness.

❝ *The Prodigy boys are in Armani from head to toe. We are snatching the realness category tonight!"*

 WANT MORE INFO? *THINK:* **A COMPETITION CATEGORY JUDGING HOW REAL YOU LOOK.**

USAGE NOTE: This term originated in ballroom culture. It has been appropriated by mainstream culture.

REAPPROPRIATE

▼ *verb*

To reclaim a word or expression that was once derogatory and give it positive meaning.

RELATED
REAPPROPRIATION *noun*

SEE ALSO

APPROPRIATE, MISAPPROPRIATE

❝ *The LGBTQIA+ community has reappropriated so many terms, like queer, sissy, fag, and dyke, and we're prouder than ever to use these former slurs to radically celebrate our queerness! Yes, we are queer, we are dykes, we are faggots, we are nellies and sissies and pansies, and we are proud!"*

 WANT MORE INFO?
THINK: **TO TAKE BACK WHAT WAS TAKEN AND MAKE IT *WERK*.**

USAGE NOTE: There are many people in the LGBTQIA+ who have reappropriated terms like queer, dyke, faggot, sissy, among others and use them in a positive way. There are some members of the community who choose not to use them at all. Please respect each person's preference. These terms should never be used toward others in a negative manner, and people outside the LGBTQIA+ community should not use them, expect if a person self-identifies as such.

RING OF KEYS

▼ *idiom*

A symbol representing lesbian identity and visibility. This phrase comes from a song in the Broadway musical *Fun Home*, when a young girl sees a butch woman and, for the first time, a living embodiment of her own identity. Often used in the phrase "ring of keys moment."

SEE ALSO

BECHDEL TEST, THE

❝ *I listened to the Nancy podcast episode about 'ring of keys' moments yesterday, and it made my heart just melt into a puddle of lesbian love."*

 WANT MORE INFO?
THINK: **THAT MOMENT WHEN REPRESENTATION MATTERS MOST.**

RING OF
KEYS
CONT.

DID YOU KNOW Ring of Keys is an artist organization formed by Andrea Prestinario and Royer Bockus in 2018 to foster LGBTQIA+ visibility and representation in the theater industry, with a particular focus on queer women and the TGNC community.

ROMANTIC ORIENTATION

▼ *noun*

Similar to sexual orientation, this term allows people to identify who they are romantically attracted to. The term "affectional orientation" is also used.

❝ *There are several ways you can experience attraction. Your romantic orientation is how you desire to emotionally* connect with someone that does not have to include physical touch. Physical intimacy is only part of a relationship's dynamic." ❞

 WANT MORE INFO?
THINK: **SEXUAL ORIENTATION IS WHO YOU ARE PHYSICALLY ATTRACTED TO. ROMANTIC ORIENTATION IS WHO YOU ARE EMOTIONALLY ATTRACTED TO.**

USAGE NOTE: This term is commonly used in the asexual community.

Romantic Orientation ▼

ROOT

▼ *noun*

A person, piece of media, or situation that may have been an early sign of being LGBTQIA+.

"

JOON: *My root was definitely either playing with my sisters' Barbies or—weirdly—Captain Hook in the cartoon version of* Peter Pan? *I love a fancy queen.*

CLAIRE: *That's not weird at all. My root was She-Ra, Rainmaker, Batwoman . . . well, I have many.*

 WANT MORE INFO?
THINK: THE "REASON" YOU'RE QUEER.

ROSE

▼ *noun*

SEE **MARY**

History Lesson: Religion and LGBTQIA+ Believers

LGBTQIA+ and Religion Can **SHARE** the Same World.

THERE ARE MANY LGBTQIA+ people who identify as religious. We center our lives around our faith and the teachings of a higher power. However, many gay and queer people who choose to live in faith often face harsh discrimination from religious institutions, spiritual leaders, and even family members because our sexual orientation or gender identity is deemed incongruous with the practices of a particular faith.

Faith-based spaces for the queer community are important, and several religious and spiritual institutions have welcomed diversity, promoting compassion and love for all people in their spiritual teachings. Noted religious communities include the Metropolitan Community Church founded by Troy Perry, the Buddhist Fellowship, the Institute for Judaism and Sexual Orientation, the Naming Project, Many Voices, and Muslims for Progressive Values.

History Lesson: Stonewall

"It was a rebellion, it was an uprising, it was a civil rights disobedience—it wasn't no [dang] riot."

—STORMÉ DELARVER E

ON JUNE 28, 1969, a series of intense demonstrations by gay and transgender protesters began at the Stonewall Inn, a gay club in New York City. That night, police raided the club and arrested several patrons and employees. This was not the first time a bar or club in Greenwich Village—a well-known gayborhood—was raided. For years, the police and the New York State Liquor Authority would target and antagonize gay establishments in the city.

Rioting followed for days after the first punch was

thrown (allegedly by Black lesbian and drag performer Storme DeLarverie), continuing up and down Christopher Street and throughout the neighborhood. These demonstrations eventually propelled the organization of the gay rights movement which regarded Stonewall as the catalyst for social and political change.

> "If you want gay power, then you're going to have to fight for it. And you're going to have to fight until you win." —SYLVIA RIVERA

Prominent drag queens and trans activists like Sylvia Rivera and Marsha P. Johnson were instrumental figures in spearheading the fight for resistance and equality and advocating for gay and transgender rights after the Stonewall events. Together they founded Street Transvestite Action Revolutionaries (STAR) and the Gay Liberation Front. These organizations paved the way for others to follow, and Rivera and Johnson, both trans women of color, are now considered two of the most revered icons in LGBTQIA+ history.

SAFE SPACE

▼ *noun*

An environment where a person feels supported, protected, and affirmed. This could be a physical space, a community, or a person.

> SEE ALSO
>
> **"Navigating Safe Spaces for Us!"** *p. 287*

❝ *Safe spaces are places and people that make you feel confident and loved. You know when you go there you are special and important to them."*

 WANT MORE INFO? *THINK:* **NONTHREATENING, NO-NEGATIVITY-ALLOWED ENVIRONMENTS.**

SAGA

▼ *noun*

An acronym standing for "Sexuality and Gender Acceptance."

❝ *Should the community use SAGA instead of LGBT, I mean LGBTQ, I mean, LGBTQIA+. I mean . . . never mind."*

 WANT MORE INFO? *THINK:* **AN INCLUSIVE CATCHALL TERM FOR QUEER EQUALITY.**

SALLY

▼ *noun*

SEE **MARY**

SAME-GENDER LOVING

▼ *noun*

Having an attraction to people of the same gender. Can be abbreviated as SGL.

❝Same-gender loving ain't different from any other type of loving. Love is love, man.❞

 WANT MORE INFO? **THINK: AN INCLUSIVE TERM FOR SAME-SEX ATTRACTION.**

USAGE NOTE: This term originated in the Black gay and queer community. It has been appropriated by the larger LGBTQIA+ community.

DID YOU KNOW The expression "same-gender loving" was popularized in the African American community in the early 1990s when activist

Cleo Manago used it to refer to homosexuality and bisexuality as a means of empowering Black queers.

SAME-SEX ATTRACTION

▼ *noun*

An interest in connecting romantically, physically, or platonically with people of the same sex. Some people who experience same-sex attraction may not identify with being gay or queer.

❝A group of my friends were talking about same-sex attraction at Starbucks yesterday and Molly said she knew she was a lesbian by the third grade. But Jasper said that he is attracted to boys but doesn't think he is gay. The word 'gay' just doesn't feel right to him. I kinda feel like Jasper, too.❞

WANT MORE INFO? *THINK:* THE MILLIONS OF PEOPLE WHO NATURALLY HAVE AN ATTRACTION TO SOMEONE OF THE SAME SEX.

SAME-SEX MARRIAGE

▼ *noun*

SEE **MARRIAGE EQUALITY**

SAME-SEX PARENTS

▼ *noun*

SEE **QUEER PARENT(S)**

SAPPHIC

▼ *adjective*

Of or relating to lesbianism; derived from the lesbian Greek poet Sappho, of the island of Lesbos. The term WOMAN LOVING WOMAN (WLW) can also be used.

RELATED
SAPPHISTRY *noun*

66 My Sapphic beauty, my Princess Charming, oh how I love thee!"

 WANT MORE INFO? *THINK:* LADY-LOVIN'.

Sapphic ▲

SAPPHO DADDY-O

▼ *noun*

A straight boy or man who enjoys friendships and hanging out with lesbians.

66 Grayson is our crew's Sappho daddy-o. He is the girls' soccer team mascot and comes to every GSA meeting."

 WANT MORE INFO? *THINK:* ONE OF THE GIRLS.

357

THE QUEENS' ENGLISH

SASHAY

▼ *verb*

To walk with swagger; to show off with exaggerated movements of the hips and shoulders.

SEE ALSO

SHANTAY

" *I love you, darling, and keep your head up high, but it is time for you to sashay away. You have been eliminated from the competition!"*

 WANT MORE INFO?
THINK: A CONFIDENT, FEMININE GAIT.

USAGE NOTE: This term was coined by American drag queen and entertainer RuPaul Charles and is commonly used in the drag community. It has been appropriated by mainstream culture.

Sashay ▼

SATURDAY NIGHT LESBIAN

▼ noun

A dated term for a girl or woman who does not openly display her affection toward other females, limiting her exploration with same-sex attraction to weekend social engagements that are not too public.

❝ *She is only gay at the weekend slumber parties. A true Saturday night lesbian."*

 WANT MORE INFO? *THINK*: **A COVERT LEZ.**

The Scene **▼**

SCENE, THE

▼ noun

The atmosphere or current social location.

❝

DEVIN: *I'll be there soon—five minutes away. What's the scene giving?*

LLOYD: *Everything you can dream and more. Girl, hurry up!*

 WANT MORE INFO? *THINK*: **A PLACE TO MEET UP AND SOCIALIZE.**

USAGE NOTE: This term is commonly used in the Black gay community and the larger queer and trans people of color (QTPOC) community.

SCREAM

▼ *verb*

SEE **GAG**

SECOND GENERATION

▼ *noun*

A person who identifies as LGBTQIA+ and also has a parent or guardian who is LGBTQIA+. The spelling "2nd Gen" can also be used.

❝ *P-Town's Family Week is my favorite place to meet up with other second-generation queers like me.*❞

 WANT MORE INFO? THINK: QUEER PEOPLE WHO HAVE QUEER PARENTS.

SELLING

▼ *verb*

Displaying high levels of self-confidence, a fierce attitude, behavior, or style. Often used in the phrase "selling it." The term SERVING can also be used.

❝ *She was serving, she was selling, she was slaying! What a goddess!*❞

 WANT MORE INFO? THINK: SELLING AND SERVING CONFIDENCE IS HOW YOU MAKE YOUR ENEMIES EAT THEIR WORDS.

USAGE NOTE: This term originated in ballroom culture and is commonly used in the larger queer and trans people of color (QTPOC) community. It has been appropriated by mainstream culture.

SEMI-CLOSETED

▼ *adjective*

Open about one's sexuality with members of the queer community, but not publicly with the heterosexual community.

❝ *Please don't dismiss someone who is*

semi-closeted. Everyone
protects their sexuality
in different ways and for
different reasons. Be kind
and give them the time
they need to grow into
themselves."

 WANT MORE INFO?
THINK: **ONE FOOT IN THE
CLOSET, ONE FOOT OUT.**

SEPARATISM

▼ *noun*

A practice of separation of a
certain group of people from
the larger whole. Separatism
is often advocated for on
the basis of culture, gender,
government, religion, or
sexuality.

RELATED
SEPARATIST adjective, noun

SEE ALSO
IDENTITY POLITICS,
LESBIAN SEPARATIST, TERF

❝

Scott: What if all gay people

lived on one island? That's
my idea of utopia.
Titus: Well, sorry to burst
your utopian bubble, but
separatism isn't my idea of
fun. We have to learn to live
together and accept each
other's differences.

 WANT MORE INFO? *THINK:*
**MAKING CLIQUES AND
LEAVING PEOPLE OUT.**

SERVE FISH

▼ *idiom*

To deliver feminine realness.
This idiom was first used
in drag culture, referring
to queens who looked
convincingly female.

❝ Serve fish, honey! Give
me mahi-mahi and tuna in
that slinky little dress, thigh-
highs, and heels! I love when
you dress in drag."

 WANT MORE INFO? *THINK:*
**TO DISH OUT ULTRAFISHY
FEMININITY.**

SERVING

▼ *verb*

SEE **SELLING**

SEVERE

▼ *adjective*

Of epic proportion; larger than life.

❝ *OMG, all these artists are going on tour together? This concert is going to be severe and I must get tickets as soon as they go on sale!"*

 WANT MORE INFO?
THINK: **FIERCE.**

USAGE NOTE: This term is commonly used in the Black gay community and the larger queer and trans people of color (QTPOC) community.

SEX

▼ *noun*

A category of humans based on reproductive organs and functions.

SEE ALSO
"The Genderbread Person," *p. 73*

❝ *My sex is female, but my gender expression is more expansive. I identify as queer in every sense of the word. I'm a queerdo!"*

 WANT MORE INFO?
THINK: **MALE, FEMALE, OR INTERSEX.**

Sexual intercourse or intimacy. This act is considered mature.

❝

Student: I'm not ready to have sex yet. I want to wait till I get older. But I do like kissing other people. Is that okay?

Health Teacher: Absolutely, there are so many ways we can physically show our attraction to people without, you know, having intercourse.

 WANT MORE INFO?
THINK: **MAKING LOVE.**

SEX ASSIGNED AT BIRTH

▼ *noun*

SEE **CISGENDER**

SEX NEGATIVE

▼ *adjective*

Having an unfavorable attitude toward sex, sexuality, and sexual diversity. A sex negative person views sexual exploration as undisciplined, problematic, and risky.

❝ *Because of moral and cultural beliefs, many cultures around the world are sex negative and some laws even restrict any public display of affection.*❞

 WANT MORE INFO? *THINK:* **SHAMING THOSE WHO SHOW PHYSICAL ATTRACTION.**

USAGE NOTE: This term is commonly used to identify people who are sexually adverse or repulsed. This term can be considered mature.

SEX POSITIVE

▼ *adjective*

Having a progressive, open attitude toward sex, sexuality, and sexual diversity. A sex positive person views safe and consensual sexual activity as healthy and liberating. The term PRO-SEX can also be used.

❝ *Adequate education and resources are two key components that will assist in developing healthy sex positive mindsets. Let's continue to have informative conversation about sex, so everyone is properly informed about their attractions, bodies, and physical interactions.*❞

 WANT MORE INFO? *THINK:* **POSITIVELY EMBRACING SEXUALITY AND SEXUAL EXPRESSION.**

USAGE NOTE: This term is commonly used in the asexual and gray sexual communities. This term can be considered mature.

THE QUEENS' ENGLISH

SEXUALITY

▼ *noun*

A complex identity based on a person's sexual orientation, feelings, preferences, and practices.

SEE ALSO

"The Genderbread Person," *p. 73*

"

LUCAS: *My sexuality is this basket of chili cheese fries!*
ZADIE: *Come on, it's more complicated than that.*
LUCAS: *All right, all right. I identify as a pansexual, homoromantic, femme-of-center queer. Happy?*

 WANT MORE INFO?
THINK: **THE COMBINATION OF PREFERENCES THAT CONSTRUCTS YOUR SEXUAL IDENTITY.**

DID YOU KNOW In 1948, Alfred Kinsey created the Kinsey Scale to research the depths of a person's sexual orientation. He believed that sexuality is fluid and could range along the spectrum between homosexuality and heterosexuality. Kinsey published two books on his research, *Sexual Behavior in the Human Male* (1948) and *Sexual Behavior in the Human Female* (1953) and is recognized as "the father of the sexual revolution." Dr. Kinsey's research and the Kinsey Institute have been a critical source for sexuality, gender, love, and reproduction study and discussion.

SEXUALLY AVERSE

▼ *adjective*

Feeling uneasy or disgusted by the act of sexual intercourse.

SEE ALSO

ASEXUAL, SEX NEGATIVE

" *Hannah really doesn't want to fool around, because she is sexually averse. Just communicate with her, okay?"*

 WANT MORE INFO?
THINK: **DISLIKES SEX.**

USAGE NOTE: This term is commonly used in the asexual community. This term can be considered mature.

SEXUAL ORIENTATION

▼ *noun*

The physical, emotional, and romantic attraction a person has toward others.

SEE ALSO
"The Genderbread Person," *p. 73*

❝ *No person should be discriminated against because of sex, age, race, creed, or sexual orientation.*❞

 WANT MORE INFO?
THINK: INNER ATTRACTION COMPASS POINTS TOWARD GIRLS, BOYS, BOTH, NEITHER, ALL, OTHER.

DID YOU KNOW Politician Ron DeSantis signed a bill that limited the discussion on sexual orientation and gender identity in classrooms called the Parental Rights in Education Act—more commonly known as the "Don't Say Gay" bill by LGBTQIA+ activists and allies across the county. There was controversy over the bill potentially endangering the safety, both physically and mentally, of LGBTQIA+ children and adolescents. Banning queer books and resources hinders the proper instructional education on understanding the spectrum of identity, resulting in a path of erasure to most nonheteronormative identities. Other states like Alabama and South Dakota prohibited schools from using curriculum that discusses gender identity and sexual orientation. Students across the country are firmly standing in solidary and speaking out on this inequality.

SHADE

▼ *noun*

A statement or look filled with subtle criticism or a blunt insult.

RELATED
SHADY *adjective*

SEE ALSO
NO SHADE, THROW SHADE

▼ *verb*

To subtly insult or blatantly show contempt for.

66 *Shade is, 'I don't tell you you're ugly, but I don't have to tell you because you know you're ugly.' And that's shade."* –DORIAN COREY

 WANT MORE INFO? *THINK:* **SLANDER.**

 USAGE NOTE: This term originated in ballroom culture. It has been appropriated by the larger LGBTQIA+ community and mainstream culture.

CHLOE O. DAVIS

SHANTAY

▼ *verb*

Similar to sashay, this term was coined by famous drag queen and entertainer RuPaul, in the 1993 hit song "Supermodel (You Better Work)." RuPaul has said the term means "to weave a bewitching spell." The alternate spelling "shanté" can also be used.

SEE ALSO
SASHAY

66 *Shantay, you stay!"*

 WANT MORE INFO? *THINK:* **TO CAPTIVATE THE CROWD.**

DID YOU KNOW Internationally known drag queen, actor, singer, and producer RuPaul Andre Charles is considered one of the most influential queer people in entertainment today. In 1993, his debut single, "Supermodel (You Better Work)," skyrocketed him to mainstream fame. In 2009, RuPaul's popular reality television show, *RuPaul's Drag Race*, became the first of its kind, bringing viewers into the once intimate world of drag culture. Now there are several international versions of the drag show—including *Drag Race Thailand*, *Drag Race España*, *Drag Race France*, and *Drag Race Brazil*, to name a few—and the RuPaul's DragCon events in Los Angeles, New York, and London. RuPaul has starred in films like *The Brady Bunch Movie* and *But I'm a Cheerleader*, among others, and even guest starred in the popular animated sitcom *The Simpsons*, opening the door for other queens, like Bob the Drag Queen and Monét X Change, to also guest star on the show. RuPaul Andre Charles continues to be a visible activist for LGBTQIA+ rights and a beacon of hope for queer culture.

SHE/HER/HERS

▼ *pronouns*

A set of pronouns used for femme or female-identifying people.

SEE ALSO
"The Genderbread Person," *p. 73,* **"Common Pronouns 101,"** *p. 101*

> 66 *Share your pronouns! Mine are she/her/hers!"*

A pronoun that can reference anything that is animate or inanimate.

> 66 *Ugh, she has been sold out for a month, when am I going to get my new iPhone?"*

 WANT MORE INFO? THINK: FEMME IDENTIFIER.

DID YOU KNOW Feminine names and pronouns are commonly used as terms of endearment in the gay male community and also served as a form of protection in a time when being openly gay was dangerous. When gay men spoke about same-sex relationships in public or in letters, they would often use women's names (see MARY or JUDY, for example) or switch the pronouns of their lovers from "he" to "she." Many gay men continue to use feminine pronouns to refer to one another as a sign of friendship. While some consider it subversive, some consider it problematic, too.

SHOW QUEEN

▼ *noun*

A person who is a musical theater or drag show enthusiast.

❝*I can't wait until my spring break trip to New York! I am seeing* The Book of Mormon *on Thursday,* Hadestown *on Friday,* The Lion King *to celebrate #SNOB, and rounding the weekend off Sunday with, of course,* Wicked*!!!! Broadway, here I come!*❞

WANT MORE INFO? **THINK: SOMEONE WHO LISTENS TO BROADWAY CAST ALBUMS ALL DAY, EVERY DAY.**

SICKENING

▼ *idiom*

Astonishingly impressive.

❝*Oh my Gawd, that Chanel bag is sickening!*❞

WANT MORE INFO? *THINK:* **BREATHTAKING.**

USAGE NOTE: This term originated in ballroom culture. It has been appropriated by mainstream culture.

SIE/SIE/HIRS

SEE **"COMMON PRONOUNS 101,"** *p.101*

SIS

▼ *noun*

SEE **SISTER OR SISTA**

SISSY

▼ *noun*

An effeminate boy or man. This term typically implies weakness.

❝

MR. RUSSELL: *Your son looks like a sissy with that pink hat on.*

MRS. RUSSELL: *That's inappropriate, Ron. Stop that.*

WANT MORE INFO?

THINK: PANSY.

USAGE NOTE: This term originated as a slur for gay men, but it has been reclaimed by some members of the LGBTQIA+ community. It may still have negative connotations for some people.

SISSY THAT WALK

▼ *idiom*

A command used in drag and ballroom culture—to strut in the most feminine way possible.

 When she strutted down the runway, shouts of 'Sissy that walk!' proved that she had the audience in the palm of her hand."

WANT MORE INFO?

THINK: MAKE IT FEMME, MAKE IT FAB.

USAGE NOTE: This term is commonly used in the drag community and ballroom culture.

SISTER OR SISTA

▼ *noun*

A term of endearment used to acknowledge social kinship and/or friendship within a community of people. In the Black gay and QTPOC communities, the term "sis" can also be used. A friend.

 Sis, I'm always gonna have your back. I got you no matter what."

WANT MORE INFO?

THINK: A CLOSE FRIEND.

USAGE NOTE: This term originated in Black American culture and is commonly used in the larger queer and trans people of color (QTPOC) community. It has been appropriated by the larger LGBTQIA+ community and mainstream culture.

SITTING

▼ *adjective*

Looking polished and divine.

SEE ALSO
FAB

❝ *Diego is the queen of glam! They will have your face sitting after a makeover with them.*❞

 WANT MORE INFO?
THINK: **LIKE A MASTERPIECE.**

USAGE NOTE: This term originated in ballroom culture. It has been appropriated by the larger LGBTQIA+ community.

SLAY

▼ *verb*

To impress or amuse; to nail it.

❝ *Slay queen! YAAAAAAAAAASSSSS!!!*❞

 WANT MORE INFO?
THINK: **TO DOMINATE THE COMPETITION; TO KILL IT.**

USAGE NOTE: This term originated in ballroom culture. It has been appropriated by the larger LGBTQIA+ community and mainstream culture.

SLICE

▼ *verb*

To cut out.

❝ *If he tries to message me one more time, I am going to slice him. We are done!*❞

 WANT MORE INFO?
THINK: **TO REMOVE AND DELETE.**

USAGE NOTE: This term is commonly used in ballroom culture.

SNATCHED

▼ *adjective*

Extremely lean and toned, as it relates to physique.

❝ *Snatched means the body is together! You are lovely, lean, and shapely. And to be in this dance company, we have to be snatched for the gawds! So that means you have to eat air, drink hope, and take a wheatgrass shot for dessert.*"

 WANT MORE INFO? *THINK:* EXTREMELY FIT.

USAGE NOTE: The term "snatched" celebrates both fit bodies and physiques that are working toward being healthy, strong, and shapely. Always practice healthy eating habits and workout routines. It is best to consult with a doctor, nutritionist, and/or trainer when trying to change your body. Remember, good health practices will bring you the best results.

Small or inadequate.

❝ *I am about to die from thirst and you bring me this snatched cup of water?*"

 WANT MORE INFO? *THINK:* A LESS THAN AMPLE AMOUNT.

USAGE NOTE: This term originated in ballroom culture. It has been appropriated by the larger LGBTQIA+ community and mainstream culture.

▼ Snatched

SNATCHING WIGS

▼ *idiom*

Humiliating or exposing someone.

❝*She needs to keep it cute before I snatch her wig and embarrass her in front of our whole dressing room!*❞

 WANT MORE INFO?
THINK: **BLOWING UP SOMEONE'S SPOT.**

Stealing or earning a desired title or claim to fame, even (or especially) when someone already holds the position.

❝*She is snatching wigs, snatching crowns, and snatching trophies. She stole the whole competition.*❞

 WANT MORE INFO?
THINK: **SWEEPING THE COMPETITION.**

Someone doing something so incredible, shocking, or downright *good* that you metaphorically lose your hair.

❝*Beyoncé is always out there snatching wigs with her secret album drops and insane live performances. She is the reason I live!*❞

 WANT MORE INFO?
THINK: **BEING SUPER-DUPER FIERCE.**

USAGE NOTE: This term originated in the drag community. It has been appropriated by the larger LGBTQIA+ community and mainstream culture.

SOFT BUTCH

▼ *noun*

A lesbian who presents in a masculine or androgynous way, with some feminine touches and/or behaviors.

SEE ALSO
CHAPSTICK LESBIAN, FUTCH, STEMME, "The Lesbian Spectrum," *p. 255*

❝*OMG! I need this 'SOFT BUTCH' gray hoodie now, actually like yesterday!*❞

WANT MORE INFO? *THINK*: PINTEREST: SOFT BUTCHES. SUCH CUTIES!

USAGE NOTE: This term originated in the lesbian community.

SOFT MASC

▼ *noun*

A queer person whose appearance is mostly masculine but presents accents of femininity or feminine styles.

❝ *I think a lot of male rappers, models, and entertainers are soft masc. That's the trend now."*

 WANT MORE INFO? *THINK*: THE NEW MALE FASHION IS FLOWERS, FEATHERS, LACE, AND PASTELS.

SOFT STUD

▼ *noun*

A lesbian, bisexual, or queer female who leans toward a masculine or androgynous gender presentation with a sharp eye for style. This girl or woman tends to be softer-presenting or more feminine than a stud.

SEE ALSO
FUTCH, STEMME, STUD

❝

REMY: *Now, where do you think soft stud falls in the lesbian spectrum? Between femme and boi?*

DIAMOND: *Hmm, maybe? It's definitely close to futch and stemme.*

 WANT MORE INFO? *THINK*: LENA WAITHE.

USAGE NOTE: This term originated in the Black lesbian community. It has been appropriated by the larger lesbian community.

SPAGHETTI

▼ *idiom*

Someone who identifies as straight until they have a romantic attraction toward a queer person or person of the same gender.

"

Spaghetti and ragù sauce go hand in hand!"

 WANT MORE INFO?
THINK: A STRAIGHT PERSON EXPLORING QUEER ATTRACTION WHEN CURIOUS.

USAGE NOTE: This term originated in ballroom culture. It has been appropriated by the larger LGBTQIA+ community and mainstream culture.

SPILL THE T

▼ *idiom*

To deliver news or gossip. The *T* stands for "Truth."

" *Sis, spill the T! Tell me what's happening over there."*

 WANT MORE INFO?
THINK: "LET'S HAVE SOME TEA AND A KIKI."

SPOOKED

▼ *verb*

SEE **CLOCK**

SQUISH

▼ *noun*

SEE **QUEERPLATONIC PARTNER OR ZUCCHINI**

SRS

▼ *noun*

SEE **SEX REASSIGNMENT SURGERY**

STEALTH

▼ *adjective*

Describes a transgender person moving through daily life passing as cisgender. This individual makes a deliberate choice to not disclose to the public their trans identity.

> SEE ALSO
> **PASSING**

❝ *I am a trans boy, but I am stealth and don't ever talk about it. I transitioned when I was five years old.*❞

 WANT MORE INFO? *THINK:* **PASSING AS A CIS BOY OR GIRL WITHOUT BEING DISCOVERED AS TRANS.**

 USAGE NOTE: One should be sensitive or refrain from using these terms to identify a transgender person.

STEMME

▼ *noun*

A lesbian, bisexual, or queer female who either switches effortlessly between masculine and feminine looks or captures a fashionable combination of both. The word is a combination of STUD and FEMME. Alternate spellings include "stem."

❝ *A stemme can wear a dress and look bomb, and then all of a sudden go and sag her pants and look bomb. That's why it's so rare to be a stemme because you got to do both and do it right.*❞ –AMBER WHITTINGTON

 WANT MORE INFO? *THINK:* **SOMETIMES SHE SERVES A LITTLE TOM HOLLAND, SOMETIMES SHE SERVES ZENDAYA.**

 USAGE NOTE: This term originated in the Black lesbian community. It has been appropriated by the larger lesbian community.

STONE BUTCH

▼ noun

An extremely masculine lesbian or otherwise masculine person.

SEE ALSO
BUTCH, STUD

❝ Yes, I identity as a stone butch lesbian and yes, I am very masculine. But I never deny that I am female. Don't forget girls can be masculine, too."

 WANT MORE INFO? THINK: *STONE BUTCH BLUES* **BY LESLIE FEINBERG.**

USAGE NOTE: This term originated in the lesbian community. It has been appropriated by the larger LGBTQIA+ community.

STORM

▼ verb

Acting out of confidence about one's appearance or attitude.

❝ It's my birthday, and I am storming up in this school like a queen on her throne! Bow down!"

 WANT MORE INFO? THINK: "I GOT YOU (I FEEL GOOD)" BY JAMES BROWN.

USAGE NOTE: This term originated in the Black gay community.

STP

▼ noun

An abbreviation for "stand-to-pee," referring to a device that enables transgender or nonbinary AFAB people to urinate in public facilities in a standing position.

❝ I used to sit down to pee in public bathrooms and felt like I was being clocked. It made me feel paranoid. So now I use my STP."

WANT MORE INFO?
**THINK: FOR A MODEL
THAT FITS BEST VISIT
TRANSGUYSUPPLY.COM.**

STRAIGHT

▼ *adjective*

Heterosexual.

66 *My parents are gay and
I'm straight and everything's
great! Families come in all
types of ways."*

WANT MORE INFO?
**THINK: BOY MEETS GIRL
OR GIRL MEETS BOY.
EQUAL OPPORTUNITY.**

STRAIGHT
BOYFRIEND

▼ *noun*

A heterosexual male who
is a platonic companion to
a gay male. This friendship
places respect and value
on each person's sexual
orientation.

66

DANIEL: *Awww! What did my
straight boyfriend bring me
today?*

MUHAMMAD: *These are
flowers for Kate. We have
been dating for three
months now!*

DANIEL: *You are so sweet
to her. Can you please give
Jasper some pointers on
how to be more romantic?
We have been dating for
six months now. That's a big
deal!*

WANT MORE INFO?
**THINK: STRAIGHT BESTIE
TO A GAY GUY.**

STRAIGHT PRIVILEGE

▼ *noun*

The inherent rights and immunities granted to straight people.

SEE ALSO
PRIVILEGE, CISGENDER PRIVILEGE, MALE PRIVILEGE, WHITE PRIVILEGE

❝ *It must be nice to have straight privilege. I can imagine it would be so easy to not have to come out as straight. Or to be able to hold hands in public without getting glared at. Oh, right, and not to have to worry about getting teased constantly because of your queerness.*"

 WANT MORE INFO? *THINK:* **THE ENTITLEMENT OF STRAIGHT PEOPLE.**

STUD

▼ *noun*

A lesbian with a masculine demeanor and appearance. Other characteristics include having a great sense of style and confident swagger.

SEE ALSO
SOFT STUD

❝ *Some say there is nothing that a guy can do that a stud can't do better.*"

 WANT MORE INFO? THINK: A MASC LADY STUNNER.

 USAGE NOTE: This term originated in the Black lesbian community. It has been appropriated by the larger lesbian community.

STUD FOR STUD

▼ *adjective*

A romantic relationship between two masculine lesbians. The phrase "stud on stud" can also be used.

SEE ALSO

FEMME FOR FEMME

66 *Personally, I am into stud for stud relationships. My girlfriend and I are both masc and consider ourselves studs.*"

 WANT MORE INFO? *THINK:* **BUTCH FOR BUTCH, MASC FOR MASC.**

 USAGE NOTE: This term originated in the Black lesbian community. It has been appropriated by the larger lesbian community.

STUNT

▼ *idiom*

SEE **DOING SHOWS**

SWEET

▼ *adjective*

Describing an effeminate gay boy or man.

SEE ALSO

NELLY

66 *Child, you know he is sweet as a Georgia peach!*"

 WANT MORE INFO? *THINK:* ***SWEET TEA: BLACK GAY MEN OF THE SOUTH* BY E. PATRICK JOHNSON.**

 USAGE NOTE: This term originated in the Black gay community. It has been appropriated by the larger LGBTQIA+ community and mainstream culture.

▼ Sweet

SWITCH HITTER

▼ *noun*

A bisexual.

" *I'm ambidextrous and a switch hitter. My chances are 50/50!"*

 WANT MORE INFO?
THINK: LIKE IN BASEBALL, WHERE THE BATTER SWITCHES FROM THE LEFT TO THE RIGHT SIDE OF THE PLATE DEPENDING ON THE PITCHER'S DOMINANT HAND.

USAGE NOTE: This term may have negative connotations as it limits bisexuality to the gender binary. It is inappropriate to use this label if a person has not self-identified as such.

I ♥ BEING TRANS

WHETHER YOU IDENTIFY as transgender, demigender, agender, pangender, genderqueer, gender nonconforming, demi, nonbinary, or beyond, every aspect that encompasses your identity is yours and always will be. You deserve to be LOVED, **RESPECTED**, and **ACCEPTED** for who you are. One day the world will mature and understand that the spectrum of identity is complex, beautiful, and necessary. But until then, society must be educated and your queer queens will push to educate them! The TGNC communities still continue to face discrimination, inequality, hate crimes, and overall lack of support. This must change. Voices must be heard, bodies must be protected, and identities must be respected.

YOU ARE UNIQUE. The transgender, nonbinary, and genderqueer communities challenge society's narrow molds and teach the world an important lesson: One's assigned sex at birth does not determine one's gender identity. Only you have the power to assign yourself an identity. The transgender umbrella fosters an understanding of different expressions and ways of life, thus empowering the visibility of our great queer spectrum. The trans experience is a personal and unique journey. Surgeries, hormones, binding, and tucking can help some people affirm their gender but others may choose not to use these gender affirmation practices. And while it may be for some, passing is not always the goal for transgender people. We must acknowledge that all transgender identities (journeys and expressions!) are valid and should be respected.

Gender is fluid, it can exist or not, it can evolve or not. There are many identities to explore and it may take a few steps to find what feels comfortable. It is healthy to think about who you are and whether your current identity is the right one for you.

"I 🤍 Being Trans!" Let's say it again, "I 🤍 Being Trans!" You are beautiful, exceptional, unique, and deserving! Trans visibility and representation is HERE! As trans identities are becoming more well-known with public figures such as Laverne Cox, Elliot Paige, Sam Smith, Hunter Schafer, Zaya Wade, Ellie Desautels, Jazz Jennings, Michaela Jaé Rodriguez, Ser Anzoategui, LeA Robinson, Juliana Joel, Zach Barack, and even the Marvel superhero Escapade, the trans communities' visibility is present and empowered! International Transgender Day of Visibility, Trans Awareness Week, and Transgender Day of Remembrance, among other holidays, are promoting the necessary conversations around the spectrum of identity. Be authentic to you, be bold, have pride, and project the happiest version of yourself. We all see you and you are never alone. Every day you teach us what true courage and resilience looks like. Your community loves and supports you!

IDENTITY is the journey of seeking the fullest expression of yourself, because living in your truth is the ultimate **SELF-LOVE.**

T

▼ *noun*

Testosterone.

> ❝*A lot of body changes happen when you start taking T. I had no idea how much hair I'd grow and what insane acne I'd get. It was like going through puberty all over again.*❞

 WANT MORE INFO?
THINK: **HORMONES.**

USAGE NOTE: This term is commonly used in the transgender, nonbinary, and gender nonconforming communities.

T, THE

▼ *noun*

The truth.

SEE ALSO

SPILL THE T

> ❝*It's the 'T' not 'tea.' People always get it wrong. The 'T' stands for truth.*❞

 WANT MORE INFO?
THINK: **THE GOSSIP. THE 411.**

 USAGE NOTE: This term originated in ballroom culture. It has been appropriated by the larger LGBTQIA+ community and mainstream culture.

TENDER

▼ *adjective*
Used to describe a queer person who embraces vulnerability, in spite of society's gendered emotional expectations.

66 *I'm just your average city-dwelling tender queer, trying to make a living selling zines, teaching breath work, accepting my flaws, and organizing monthly volunteer trips to the local women's shelter."*

 WANT MORE INFO? *THINK:* **EMBRACING SOFTNESS AND EMOTIONS WHILE LISTENING TO TAYLOR HENDERSON, LOUIS THE CHILD, AND SAM SMITH.**

TENS

▼ *noun*
In ballroom culture, this refers to the preliminary round of competition, where walkers perform to receive a perfect score—a ten from each judge—moving them on to the main competition.

66 *Judges score? Tens, tens, tens! Tens across the board!"*

WANT MORE INFO? *THINK:* **SCORES NEEDED TO ELIMINATE THE COMPETITION AND TAKE THE GRAND PRIZE!**

 USAGE NOTE: This term originated in ballroom culture. It has been appropriated by mainstream culture.

TERF

▼ *noun*
An acronym for "trans-exclusionary radical feminist": a feminist who excludes trans women or trans girls from their brand of feminism.

SEE ALSO
LESBIAN SEPARATIST, SEPARATISM, TRANSMISOGNY, TRANSPHOBIA

"Get these TERFs spewing hateful, transphobic speech outta my timeline!"

WANT MORE INFO?
THINK: A PERSON WHO BELIEVES THAT IF ONE IS NOT BORN A CIS FEMALE, THEY DON'T MATTER.

DID YOU KNOW Viv Smythe, a trans-inclusive feminist writer and blogger, is credited with coining the term TERF as a shorthand phrase to identify feminists who consider themselves radical and refuse to recognize transgender females as women.

TGNC

▼ *adjective*

A commonly used acronym for the transgender and gender nonconforming communities.

SEE ALSO

GENDER NONCONFORMING, TRANSGENDER, GENDERQUEER

"The TGNC community empowers gender complexity. There are over seven billion people on this planet and many of us don't fit into the socially structured cishet model."

WANT A LITTLE MORE?
THINK: UMBRELLA TERM FOR TRANS, NONBINARY, AND GENDERQUEER FOLX.

DID YOU KNOW The transgender, nonbinary, and gender nonconforming communities have always challenged society's narrow molds, acknowledging that a person's assigned sex at birth does not have to determine a person's gender. In recent years, the emergence of public figures like Sam Zelaya, Ruby Rose, Lana and Lilly Wachowski, Alok Vaid-Menon, Lachlan Watson, Indya Moore, Jacob Tobia, Jill Soloway, Demi Lovato, Asia Kate Dillon, Jonathan Van Ness, and Janelle Monáe have provided unprecedented visibility of the TGNC community, encouraging people to think of gender as a personal journey of self-expression and fulfillment.

THE GAG IS

▼ *idiom*

A phrase meaning "the truth is" or "the funny thing is . . ."

❝ *I'm always watching Keke Palmer's YouTube channel. Her videos are so funny when she says, 'But the gag is!'"*

 WANT MORE INFO? *THINK:* **THE SHOCKING TRUTH.**

USAGE NOTE: This term originated in ballroom culture and is commonly used in the larger queer and trans people of color (QTPOC) community. It has been appropriated by mainstream culture.

THEY/THEM/THEIRS

▼ *pronouns*

A set of pronouns typically used by transgender, nonbinary, genderqueer people.

SEE ALSO

"The Genderbread Person," p. 73, **"Common Pronouns 101,"** p. 101

❝ *When I tell people that my pronouns are they/them/theirs, I usually get either a completely awkward and confused look or the supportive 'I don't know what that means, but good for you' look. I use the singular they because it works for me."*

 WANT MORE INFO? *THINK:* **IDENTIFIERS FOR GENDERQUEER AND NONBINARY PEOPLE.**

USAGE NOTE: This term is commonly used in the transgender, nonbinary, and gender nonconforming communities.

DID YOU KNOW The word "they" has been used as a singular pronoun since the fourteenth century, if not earlier. In addition, the *AP Stylebook* allows the usage of singular they in cases where a subject doesn't identify as male or female. In 2016, the singular they pronoun was announced the word of the year at the American Dialect Society's annual meeting.

THEYBIE

▼ *noun*

A child raised without gender whose parents or guardians use "they/them" pronouns to refer to their child.

❝ *We're raising little North here as genderqueer. We don't want to put the unnecessary pressure of conforming to gender roles on our precious little theybie.*"

 WANT MORE INFO?
THINK: PINK, BLUE, AND EVERY COLOR IN BETWEEN.

THROW SHADE

▼ *idiom*

To subtly insult or blatantly show contempt for. The terms "throwing shade" and "throws shade" can also be used.

❝ *If you're going to throw shade you better learn how to back it up, Miss Girl! Don't let me come for you because I have a PhD in cutthroat. Now, watch it!*"

 WANT MORE INFO?
THINK: TO SPREAD NEGATIVITY LIKE WILDFIRE.

 USAGE NOTE: This term originated in ballroom culture. It has been appropriated by the larger LGBTQIA+ community and mainstream culture.

TILAPIA

▼ *noun*

SEE **TUNA**

TOMBOY

▼ noun

A girl—regardless of sexuality—who is slightly masculine in behavior and appearance.

A gender expression of a queer female who is boyish or soft masculine.

 Uh, spare the makeup, it's not my vibe. My tomboy swag would prefer wearing funky high-top sneakers and snapbacks instead."

 WANT MORE INFO? THINK: SIMILAR TO SOFT BUTCH, CAN REFER TO YOUNGER LESBIANS.

USAGE NOTE: This term is commonly used in the lesbian community.

TONGUE POP

▼ noun

A sound or click made with the tongue, used for emphasis in a variety of situations.

 Don't come for me! You're just jealous because your tongue pop sucks. Go on YouTube and watch Alyssa Edwards's 101 class!"

 WANT MORE INFO? THINK: ONOMATOPOEIA USED PRIOR TO MAKING A POINT.

USAGE NOTE: The term originated in Black culture. It has been appropriated by the larger LGBTQIA+ community and mainstream culture.

DID YOU KNOW The tongue pop is very common to many traditional African languages and dialects. African Americans, especially women, continue to use the tongue pop to indicate disapproval. The sound has since been adopted by the gay and drag communities.

▲   **Tongue Pop**

TOO MUCH

▼ *idiom*

When a look or behavior becomes overdone.

SEE ALSO
EXTRA

❝ *He just does too much. Sequins, glitter, beads, and bells?*❞

 WANT MORE INFO? *THINK:* OVER-THE-TOP AND TACKY.

TOP SURGERY

▼ *noun*

Medical procedure for a person to change the physical appearance of their breasts or chest, often performed to better suit one's gender identity. Often shortened to "top."

❝ *Top surgery will differ depending on the individual. Some trans or nonbinary people may want tissue removed for a flatter chest, while others may want implants for a curvier shape.*❞

 WANT MORE INFO? *THINK:* SURGERY FOR GENDER AFFIRMATION.

USAGE NOTE: This term is commonly used in the transgender, nonbinary, and gender nonconforming communities.

TOXIC MASCULINITY

▼ *noun*

Expressions of masculinity that encourage boys or men to suppress emotions and maintain an aggressive and often prideful persona, hindering them from experiencing a healthy emotional balance.

❝ *Toxic masculinity is a cultural disease that views femmes—girls, gay guys, and femme queers—as inferior.*❞

THE QUEENS' ENGLISH

WANT MORE INFO?
THINK: MASCULINITY
AND MACHISMO THAT
NEGATIVELY AFFECT
MEN'S JUDGMENT AND
EMOTIONAL HEALTH.

TRANNY

▼ *noun*

An abbreviation for the
word "transsexual"; a person
assigned one sex at birth
who has used surgery and/or
medication to transition to
another sex.

SEE ALSO
TRANSSEXUAL

❝ *I don't like the word
'tranny.' Try trans or
transgender instead.*❞

 WANT MORE INFO?
THINK: DATED TERM FOR
A TRANS PERSON.

 USAGE NOTE: The use of this term
relies on an individual's
preference. Do not
assume that an individual wants to be
identified by the term. It is considered
a slur and highly derogatory.

TRANSAMOROUS

▼ *adjective*

Experiencing attraction
toward a transgender
person. Usually, a person
is exploring dating
and relationships with
transgender people. This
relation and/or connection
may sometimes be discreet.

❝ *I think I'm transamorous.
I just found out Sidney is
trans and that doesn't matter
to me. I still like him.*❞

 WANT MORE INFO?
THINK: ATTRACTED TO
TRANS PEOPLE.

TRANS ATTRACTED

▼ *adjective*

To be romantically attracted
to transgender people.

❝ *I'm trans attracted. I like
cis people as well as trans
people, but there's a lot of
stigmas associated with
being openly attracted to*

someone who is trans . . .
unfortunately."

WANT MORE INFO?
THINK: **ROMANTICALLY**
ATTRACTED TO
TRANSGENDER PEOPLE
FOR WHO THEY ARE.

TRANSFEMININE

▼ *adjective*

A term used to describe
a transgender, nonbinary,
or gender nonconforming
person who identifies
as feminine. The term
"transfemme" can also be
used.

❝ *There are some people*
in power who value the
leadership of transfeminine
people. Our collective
trans experience needs to
be heard in order to make
inclusive, powerful change."

WANT MORE INFO?
THINK: **IDENTIFYING**
AS BOTH TRANS AND
FEMME.

| **USAGE NOTE:** | This term is commonly used in the transgender, nonbinary, and gender |

nonconforming communities.

TRANSFEMINISM

▼ *noun*

A brand of feminism that
actively supports and
amplifies the needs and
equality of transgender
girls, transgender women,
and other queer-identifying
people.

❝ *This Women's March*
we will be heard loud and
clear, that we believe in
transfeminism. One day soon,
all women—ALL WOMEN—
will be treated fairly."

WANT MORE INFO?
THINK: **A BELIEF THAT**
TRANS LIBERATION IS A
FUNDAMENTAL PART OF
FEMINISM.

THE QUEENS' ENGLISH

TRANSGENDER

▼ *adjective*

Of, relating to, or being a person who identifies with a gender identity and/or expression that differs from their assigned sex at birth. The term is often shortened to "trans" or can be written as "trans*." In Latin, "trans" means on the other side.

66 *On this Transgender Day of Visibility, we honor transgender people who are fighting for freedom, equality, dignity, and respect.... We also celebrate parents, teachers, coaches, doctors, and other allies who affirm the identities of their transgender children and help young people reach their potential."*

—PRESIDENT JOE BIDEN

WANT MORE INFO?
THINK: **IDENTIFYING AS A GENDER THAT DOES NOT NECESSARILY MATCH UP WITH YOUR BIRTH CERTIFICATE.**

USAGE NOTE: A common misuse of the word "transgender" is to say a person is "transgendered." Transgender is explicitly not a noun. A person should not be called "a transgender."

DID YOU KNOW Transgender Day of Visibility (TDOV) was founded by trans activist Rachel Crandall-Crocker to celebrate the accomplishments and the substantial impact transgender people have made in building a more inclusive and equitable society. The term "transgender" acts as an umbrella term that includes trans boys or trans men, trans girls or trans women, and other people who do not identify with the gender they were assigned at birth; this may include people who are gender nonconforming, nonbinary, pangender, bigender, agender, genderqueer, and/or genderfluid.

TRANS BOY

▼ *noun*

A young transgender person who was assigned female at birth (AFAB) but whose gender identity is male and/or boy.

SEE ALSO
TRANSMASCULINE

66 *I feel proud telling people I'm a trans boy. When I share my story, I help other kids know that they can transition and be supported, too."*

 WANT MORE INFO?
THINK: **I AM A BOY AND I FEEL LIKE A BOY, EVEN THOUGH THE DOCTOR SAID I WAS A GIRL.**

TRANS GIRL

▼ *noun*

A transgender person who was assigned male at birth (AMAB) but whose gender identity is female and/or girl.

SEE ALSO
TRANSFEMININE

66 *Maybe I knew I was a trans girl around four when I started to put on my mom's high-heeled shoes and skirts. My parents thought it was a phase but every birthday I would ask for another dress and more Barbie dolls."*

 WANT MORE INFO?
THINK: **GENDER IDENTITY IS TRANS GIRL AND PRONOUNS ARE SHE/HER/HERS.**

393

TRANSGENDER HORMONE THERAPY

▼ *noun*

SEE **HORMONE REPLACEMENT THERAPY**

TRANSITION

▼ *noun*

The process of someone affirming their gender identity when it differs from the gender they were assigned at birth. This is not a process that "changes" someone from a girl or a woman to a boy or a man, or vice versa; it is the journey toward living a more authentic life—one that reflects a person's true gender identity and/or expression. Medical procedures may be pursued, or they may not.

▼ *verb*

To pursue affirming one's internal gender identity and external gender expression.

❝ *Making the decision to transition was the best thing I ever did for myself. I'm more me than I have ever been.*❞
—PERSEPHONE VALENTINE

 WANT MORE INFO? *THINK:* **COMING OUT AS TRANS.**

USAGE NOTE: Due to the sensitive and intimate nature of transitions, it is important to respect the way each individual speaks about their own transition. A transition should not be viewed as the ultimate achievement for a trans person. Each person's journey is unique and should be respected as such.

DID YOU KNOW Transitioning to a gender that feels more aligned with your truest self is a unique journey. Oftentimes a person will work with special doctors, therapists, and other health professionals to help support the transitional process. Hormone replacement therapy (HRT) is a medical treatment that helps support the development of secondary sexual characteristics. Other medical procedures like sex reassignment surgery (SRS)—more commonly known as gender affirmation surgery—and facial feminization surgery (FFS) may be pursued to physically alter the body to a look that feels affirming. Each person's transitional journey is unique and many transgender, nonbinary, and gender nonconforming people may not undergo any medical procedures, but still identify as transgender. There are many ways to socially, mentally, and physically transition and all transgender experiences should be respected.

TRANS KID OR TRANSGENDER KID

▼ *noun*

A young transgender person. The terms "trans youth" and "transgender children" can also be used.

❝ *Each summer, my family and I go to a camp for trans kids. It's the best week of the summer. Everybody is nice to me, and I don't feel different there. I feel cool!*❞

 WANT MORE INFO? *THINK:* **A CHILD WHO ASSERTS AND EXPRESSES THEIR TRANS IDENTITY.**

TRANS MAN OR TRANSMAN

▼ *noun*

A transgender person who was assigned female at birth (AFAB) but whose gender identity is male and/or man.

SEE ALSO
TRANSMASCULINE

❝ *Becoming a transman was a long but incredible journey. I started taking hormone blockers when I was eleven. By eighteen, I had started taking testosterone and had top surgery on my twenty-first birthday.*❞

 WANT MORE INFO? *THINK:* **CHAZ BONO, BRIAN MICHAEL SMITH, AND TOM PHELAN.**

TRANSMASCULINE

▼ adjective

Describing a transgender, nonbinary, or gender nonconforming person who identifies as masculine. The term "transmasc" can also be used.

❝ Now that I identify as transmasculine, I'm experiencing the effects of male-favored sexism firsthand. It's nuts!"

WANT MORE INFO?
THINK: **IDENTIFYING AS TRANS AND MASCULINE.**

USAGE NOTE: This term is commonly used in the transgender, nonbinary, and gender nonconforming communities.

TRANSMISOGYNY

▼ noun

A particular brand of misogyny that fosters an extreme dislike, contempt, and/or ingrained prejudice against trans girls and trans women.

SEE ALSO
MISOGYNY

❝ If our generation wants to eradicate misogyny, we must also demand that trans girls and trans women are included in the fight for equality. Transmisogyny is a blatantly hateful version of misogyny and should not be tolerated."

 WANT MORE INFO?
THINK: **AN OPPRESSIVE DOUBLE WHAMMY.**

TRANSPHOBIA

▼ noun

Aversion, fear, or hatred toward trans people.

RELATED
TRANSPHOBIC *adjective*
TRANSPHOBE *noun*

SEE ALSO

ACEPHOBIA, BIPHOBIA, FEMMEPHOBIA, HOMOPHOBIA, LESBOPHOBIA, QUEERPHOBIA

❝ *When government leaders in two of our most populated states, Texas and Florida, are denying trans youth their rights, what do you think they are displaying? TRANSPHOBIA!*❞

 WANT MORE INFO? *THINK:* **DISLIKE OF OR PREJUDICE AGAINST TRANSGENDER PEOPLE.**

TRANSSEXUAL

▼ *adjective*

Of, relating to, or being a person who identifies with a different sex than their assigned sex at birth.

❝ *My great-aunt Linda still identifies as a transsexual— she is proud of being a trans trailblazer, going through many challenges in the sixties and seventies, and coming out as the most amazing version of herself.*❞

 WANT MORE INFO? *THINK:* **A DATED, POTENTIALLY INSENSITIVE VERSION OF "TRANSGENDER."**

USAGE NOTE: The use of this term relies on an individual's preference. Do not assume that an individual wants to be identified as such, as it is considered derogatory by many.

 DID YOU KNOW While some transgender individuals still use "transsexual" as an identifier, it is largely considered a dated term. In 1965, psychiatrist John F. Oliven of Columbia University coined the term "transgenderism" to replace the then-popular "transsexualism." He posited that "transsexual" was misleading, because a person's decision to alter their gender expression was, in most cases, very much separate from their sexuality.

TRANSVESTITE

▼ noun

A dated term for a cross-dresser who is typically (but not always) a man.

SEE ALSO

CROSS-DRESSER

❝ *I was so embarrassed my grandmother asked my neighbor if he was a transvestite. But he was so nice and told her with a smile, 'Honey, I do love these lady clothes and I have a beautiful scarf that would look great on you!'* ❞

 WANT MORE INFO?
***THINK*: SOMEONE WHOSE DRESSING AS ANOTHER GENDER FULFILLS THEM.**

 USAGE NOTE: This term is often misused to refer to transgender people and/or cross-dressers, which is considered derogatory and offensive, thus the term is not commonly used.

▼ **Trans Woman or Transwoman**

TRANS WOMAN OR TRANSWOMAN

▼ noun

A transgender person who was assigned male at birth (AMAB) but whose gender identity is female and/or woman.

SEE ALSO

TRANSFEMININE

❝ *I am a transwoman and I am living my life*

*authentically, beautifully,
and expecting all great
things to come my way!"*

 **WANT MORE INFO?
THINK: LAVERNE COX,
RACHEL LEVINE, SARAH
MCBRIDE.**

TRIED IT

▼ *idiom*

Overstepped boundaries.

❝ *Ooh, you tried it by
eating my last chocolate
chip cookie!"*

 **WANT MORE INFO?
THINK: STAY IN YOUR
LANE.**

USAGE NOTE: This term originated in
ballroom culture and is
commonly used in the
larger queer and trans people of
color (QTPOC) community.

THIRD GENDER

▼ *adjective*

A person who identifies
as a gender not limited
to the gender binary, but
rather as neither, both, or a
combination of male, female,
and/or another gender
identity.

SEE ALSO
POLYGENDER, PANGENDER, GENDERFLUID, GENDERFLUX, BIGENDER, HIJRA, NONBINARY

❝ *More countries are now
recognizing a third gender
and providing the option
on legal forms to identify as
male, female, or other.*

 **WANT MORE INFO?
THINK: SOMEONE WHO
IS NEITHER MAN NOR
WOMAN.**

USAGE NOTE: This term is commonly
used in the intersex,
transgender, nonbinary,
and gender nonconforming
communities.

TUCK

▼ *verb*

To conceal the penis and testicles by tucking them between the legs and taping the area in a particular way. This is a practice utilized to help someone create a body that is more gender affirming or by transgender women or cisgender men who perform in drag.

SEE ALSO
GAFF, "Tucking & Binding 101," p. 163

❝ *Your first time tucking may feel odd, but over time you will get the hang of it.*"

 WANT MORE INFO? *THINK:* **HIDE THE CROTCH BULGE OF A PENIS.**

USAGE NOTE: This term is commonly used in the transgender, nonbinary, gender nonconforming, and drag communities.

TUH

▼ *exclamation*

SEE **CH**

TUNA

▼ *noun*

A word, often used in the gay male or drag scene, for a cisgender girl or woman. A feminine-presenting person.

❝ *Why is there so much tuna in here? This is the boy's locker room! I need some privacy!*"

 WANT MORE INFO? *THINK:* **FEMALE.**

USAGE NOTE: This term is commonly used in the drag community and larger gay male community. It may be considered derogatory.

TURNED OR TURNT

▼ *adjective*

Exciting or extremely

high-energy. The term "lit" is also used.

❝ *Last night's BET Awards show was turnt! All my favorite rappers performed.*"

 WANT MORE INFO? *THINK:* **HYPED.**

▼ *verb*
Surpassed.

❝ Black Panther *and* Wakanda Forever *were so turnt! They are more than just Marvel superhero movies; they celebrate cultures and histories from around the world! #wakandaforever!*"

 WANT MORE INFO? *THINK:* **SHATTERED, WAS SUPERIOR TO.**

 USAGE NOTE: This term originated in Black American culture and is commonly used in the Black gay and queer community. It has been appropriated by mainstream culture.

TWINK

▼ *noun*

A body label for a gay, bisexual, or queer young man who has a youthful appearance and a petite body frame. He also has very little to no facial hair.

> **SEE ALSO**
> **PUP, "Help! What Type of Gay Am I?," *p. 203***

❝ *Super-tight jeans, plaid shirt, and the face of a cherub? Yep, that's a twink.*"

 WANT MORE INFO? *THINK:* **BABY-FACED, SKINNY GAY GUY.**

 USAGE NOTE: This term originated in the white gay male community.

THE QUEENS' ENGLISH

TWIRL

▼ verb

To dance or move with great skill or urgency.

 Everyone twirled for their life in this season's finale of So You Think You Can Dance!"

 WANT MORE INFO? *THINK:* **WORK THE DANCE FLOOR.**

USAGE NOTE: This term is commonly used in ballroom culture and the drag community.

TWO-SPIRIT OR TWO SPIRIT

▼ noun

For Western world understanding, this umbrella term is used to identify the history of gender and sexuality diversity celebrated in indigenous Native American culture, and that a third gender role is identified and commonly expressed within that culture. Each indigenous tribe refers to third-gender people by different names, in their native spoken language. Lakota people use the word "winkte," the Zuni tribe "lhamana," and the Navajo tribe "nádleehi." The inclusion of two-spirited people is often seen in the queer community's acronym LGBTQ2.

RELATED
TWO-SPIRITED *adjective*

 Tobey and I spoke more about two-spirit identity. 'Life is sacred.' That keeps ringing in my head."

WANT MORE INFO? *THINK:* **THE DIVERSITY OF IDENTITY WITHIN NATIVE AMERICAN CULTURE.**

DID YOU KNOW The term "two-spirit" was coined at the Native American Gay and Lesbian Gathering in 1990 in an effort to solve what native scholars called "the problem of naming." The term gives Native people a unifying term to use for a variety of gender- and sexuality-based roles. Two-spirited people are often revered for fulfilling a unique role in their society—from spiritual protection to healing and guiding others. Native American Heritage Month is celebrated annually every November. It is a time to highlight the rich history, art, and traditions of Indigenous cultures and recognize trailblazing people who have made historical contributions. Two-spirited and Indigenous queer people like Osh-Tisch (Crow, Apsáalooke) We'wha (Zuni), DeLesslin "Roo" George-Warren (Catawba), Storme Webber (Alutiiq, Black, Choctaw), Qwo-Li Driskill (Cherokee, Lenape, Irish), Susan Allen (Lakota), Sharice Davids (Ho-Chunk), Chrystos (Menominee), and Jewelle Gomez (Ioway, Black) have paved the way for the Native American LGBTQIA+ community and beyond.

TWUNK

▼ *noun*

A body label for a gay, bisexual, or queer young man with a small but muscular body frame. A portmanteau of "twink" and "hunk."

SEE ALSO
**"Help! What Type of Gay Am I?," *p. 203*

66 *Samuel's been to the gym! He's graduated from twink to twunk!"*

 WANT MORE INFO?
THINK: **A TWINK WITH MUSCLE.**

 This term originated in the white gay male community.

USAGE NOTE:

Uu

U-HAUL

▼ *idiom*

A lesbian term referring to a girl's or woman's readiness to quickly commit and even move in with a new romantic interest.

"

DOMINIQUE: *Lela has been seeing Hope for a week. I call U-Haul in about five more days.*
IRIS: *No way. They'll be U-Hauling tomorrow!*

 WANT MORE INFO?
THINK: **THE ULTIMATE LESBIAN STEREOTYPE.**

USAGE NOTE: This term originated in the lesbian community.

UNAPOLOGETIC

▼ *noun*

To show extreme confidence and willingness to be authentic to one's full self— identity, choices, behavior, and speech.

RELATED
UNAPOLOGETICALLY
adverb

 Be yourself unapologetically. Understand that the world has not been set up for people as strong in their

truth and identity as LGBTQ people are. Trust what you feel to be right and not what others are telling you that you should be."

—GEORGE M. JOHNSON

 WANT MORE INFO? *THINK:* **PURE CONFIDENCE AND SELF-LOVE!**

URSULA

▼ *noun*

A butch lesbian who enjoys celebrating bear culture.

SEE ALSO
BEAR, GOLDILOCKS

 There goes Ursula and her best friend, Mr. Bear."

 WANT MORE INFO? *THINK:* **A FEMALE LUMBERJACK.**

U-Haul   ▲

USA Gayborhoods

GAYBORHOODS OR GAY villages have become the geographical center for LGBTQIA+ people. Our communities are usually identified by pride rainbow flags and signs hanging from windows and storefronts of bars, nightclubs, restaurants, residences, and shops. Gayborhoods cater to the safety and inclusiveness of all people who identify on the queer spectrum and have transformed cities into rainbow havens for LGBTQIA+ culture.

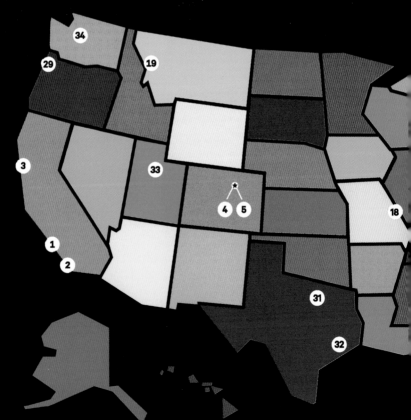

1   WEST HOLLYWOOD, LOS ANGELES, CA

2   HILLCREST, SAN DIEGO, CA

3   THE CASTRO, SAN FRANCISCO, CA

4   CAPITOL HILL, DENVER, CO

5   NORTH RIVER, DENVER, CO

6   DUPONT CIRCLE, WASHINGTON, DC

7   REHOBOTH BEACH, DE

8   WILTON MANORS, FL

9   WYNWOOD, MIAMI, FL

10 MIDTOWN, ATLANTA, GA

11 ANDERSONVILLE, CHICAGO, IL

12 BOYSTOWN, CHICAGO, IL

13 FRENCH QUARTER, NEW ORLEANS, LA

14 BYWATER, NEW ORLEANS, LA

15 MARIGNY, NEW ORLEANS, LA

16 THE SOUTH END, BOSTON, MA

17 PROVINCETOWN, MA

18 THE GROVE, ST. LOUIS, MO

19 MISSOULA, MT

20 ASHEVILLE, NC

21 ASBURY PARK, NJ

22 ALLENTOWN, BUFFALO, NY

23 HUDSON, NY

24 FIRE ISLAND, LONG ISLAND, NY

25 CHELSEA, NEW YORK CITY, NY

26 HELL'S KITCHEN, NEW YORK CITY, NY

27 WEST VILLAGE, NEW YORK CITY, NY

28 SHORT NORTH ARTS DISTRICT, COLUMBUS, OH

29 PORTLAND, OR

30 THE GAYBORHOOD, PHILADELPHIA, PA

31 OAK LAWN, DALLAS, TX

32 MONTROSE, HOUSTON, TX

33 THE MARMALADE, SALT LAKE CITY, UT

34 CAPITOL HILL, SEATTLE, WA

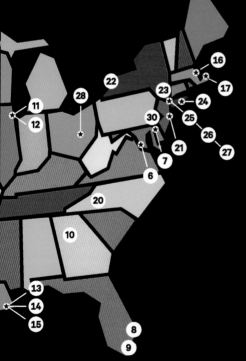

Hate Crime Epidemic

"When we allow violence against some, we enable violence against all." —DASHANNE STOKES

BY DEFINITION, A hate crime is an intimidating, aggressive, and/or violent crime, usually motivated by prejudice against a specific race, religion, sexual orientation, gender expression, or bias. Homophobia, biphobia, transphobia, queerphobia, xeno-phobia, racism, sexism, genderism, misogyny, transmisogyny, and ableism are forms of hate that plague our LGBTQIA+ community. Mainstream culture has labeled us as outcasts, deplorables, and sinners, subjecting our community to gener-ations of abuse.

Former President Barack Obama understood the prevalence of these crimes when he signed the Matthew Shepard and James Byrd Jr. Hate Crimes Prevention Act into law. This act expanded on the previous United States federal hate crime law to protect against crimes based on gender, sexual orientation, gender identity, or disability. Even still, the American Medical Association has tracked a disproportionate increase in violence toward members of the trans community, with particularly shocking statistics on the increased murders of Black trans women. The deadliest LGBTQIA+ hate crime took place on June 12, 2016, when a shooter entered Pulse Nightclub—a gay night club in Orlando, Florida—and opened fire, killing forty-nine people and injuring fifty-three more. In 2020, when yet another unarmed Black man was callously murdered by police officers, the Black Lives Matter (BLM) movement propelled the world to open their eyes to the hate and injustices experienced by all Black people—including Black LGBTQIA+ people. The mission of BLM is to dismantle the hate that is deeply rooted in our history and current society. In 2021, the Stop Asian Hate movement protested and rallied in response to the racial discrimination, anti-Asian violence, and xenophobia Asian Americans faced related to the COVID-19 pandemic. A lethal shooting spree occurred at three spas in Atlanta, Georgia, where a white man killed eight people and six were Asian. The organization Stop AAPI Hate formed to unite Asian Americans to stand together against hate crimes, racism, and erasure. In 2022, there was yet another LGBTQ nightclub shooting at Club Q in Colorado Springs, Colorado. The shooter killed five people and injured twenty-five more.

Despite the pain our community has endured, our tenacity was built upon hate. Our power, as a community, blazes to life in our fight, our persistence, our fire, our resilience, and our courage. Even though much work has been done to protect queer bodies, we still have a long way to go.

Hope is built upon resistance. We fight. We protest. We will not be erased.

Vv

VAGINOPLASTY

▼ *noun*

SEE **BOTTOM SURGERY**

VISIBILITY

▼ *noun*

In the LGBTQIA+ community, this is an act of raising awareness and providing support to marginalized identities and communities.

❝ *I remember seeing a trans/nonbinary person on TikTok and I said, 'That's me!' I was able to relate to them and I was so happy and felt not so alone. Visibility is important.*❞

 WANT MORE INFO?
THINK: **POSITIVE REPRESENTATION MATTERS!**

DID YOU KNOW The LGBTQIA+ community celebrates days of visibility throughout the year. Here are a few: Aromantic Spectrum Awareness Week—After February 14, International Transgender Day of Visibility—March 31, Lesbian Visibility Day—April 26, Pansexual and Panromantic Visibility Day—May 24, LGBTQ Equality Day—June 26, International Non-Binary People's Day—July 14, Bisexuality Day—September 23, National Coming Out Day—October 11, Intersex Awareness Day—October 26, International

Day of Persons with Disabilities—
December 3, and many others!

VITO RUSSO TEST, THE

▼ *noun*

A test inspired by the Bechdel Test used to examine how queer characters are represented in film. A film that passes the test has an LGBTQIA+ character who is not solely defined by their sexuality and is crucial to the plot of the film.

SEE ALSO

BECHDEL TEST, THE

❝ *I just read up on this year's Vito Russo Test results and the TV industry is at an all-time high with LGBTQIA+ representation, with projection to rise again in the next year! Television is queerer than it has ever been!"*

 WANT MORE INFO?
THINK: A BAROMETER FOR POSITIVE QUEER REPRESENTATION IN FILM AND TELEVISION.

DID YOU KNOW In 1985, LGBTQ activist, author, and film historian Vito Russo cofounded the Gay and Lesbian Alliance Against Defamation (presently known as GLAAD) to change the negative stereotypes and depictions of homosexuality in media. Russo's passion for fair representation for LGBTQIA+ people paved the way for filmmakers and journalists alike to write more inclusively, using guides like his book *The Celluloid Closet* and the Vito Russo Test as tools to analyze their work.

The Vito Russo Test ▼

Vogue ▼

VOGUE

▼ noun

A modern house dance that combines stylized movement and model-like poses with intricate angular arm and leg movements. Voguing is an evolving art form that originated in the late 1980s as an artistic form of "throwing shade." Styles include NEW WAY, OLD WAY, and VOGUE FEMME.

▼ verb

To dance in the style of vogue.

❝ *I saw Amina voguing down at the pier and she is ready to take the title.*❞

 WANT MORE INFO?
***THINK:* "STRIKE A POSE,**

THERE'S NOTHING TO IT. VOGUE!" —MADONNA

DID YOU KNOW By the late 1980s, voguing was a fully developed house dance technique that evolved from the work of Black and Latinx dancers in Harlem. Willi Ninja, known as the godfather of voguing, is widely credited for bringing the art form to mainstream culture. The technique was inspired by high fashion models' poses in *Vogue* magazine, Egyptian hieroglyphics, and African art. In the 1990s, Madonna's hit song "Vogue"—which was inspired by house culture vogue dance and featured dancers like Jose and Luis Xtravaganza from New York's underground ballroom culture—became an international chart-topper.

USAGE NOTE: This term originated in ballroom culture. It has been appropriated by mainstream culture.

VOGUE FEMME

▼ *verb*

The modern technique of vogue house dance that was established around 1995. This technique is noted for its rhythm, dramatics, and extreme femininity; it consists of five main elements: catwalk, hands performance, spins and dips, duckwalk, and floor performance.

SEE ALSO

BALL, BALLROOM SCENE, NEW WAY, OLD WAY, VOGUE

 The NYC Awards Ball was so fiyah this year! The butch queens ate it in Vogue Femme."

 WANT MORE INFO? *THINK*: **WALK THE RUNWAY OR BE CHOPPED, HI-YAH!**

USAGE NOTE: This term originated in ballroom culture.

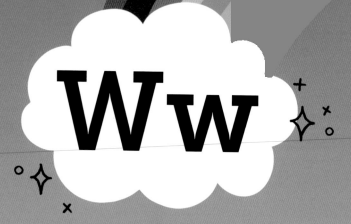

Ww

WALKING

▼ *verb*

In ballroom culture, this term means competing in a ball competition before a panel of judges.

RELATED
WALKER noun

66 *Are you walking Face tonight? It's going for fifteen hundred dollars.*"

 WANT MORE INFO?
THINK: **TO COMPETE IN A CATEGORY ON A RUNWAY OR DANCE FLOOR.**

WENDY

▼ *noun*

A Caucasian person (of any gender). The term BECKY can also be used.

66

DAQUAN: *When did Wendy and Becky get the memo to start coming to Black churches?*

TAMIA: *When they got tired of falling asleep at their churches.*

 WANT MORE INFO?
THINK: **WHITE PEOPLE.**

WENT IN

▼ *verb*

Went all out.

 "Leonardo went in on Mona Lisa! Smile, boo!"

 WANT MORE INFO?
THINK: **ACHIEVED EXCELLENCE.**

Was extremely engaged.

"Oh girl, last night was everything! We went in watching Pose. You missed it!"

 WANT MORE INFO?
THINK: **WAS COMPLETELY INVESTED.**

USAGE NOTE: This term originated in the Black American culture and is commonly used in the Black gay and queer community. It has been appropriated by mainstream culture.

WENT TO A PLACE

▼ *idiom*

To have an out-of-body experience or to daydream.

 "Baby, I went to a place when I got my Swedish massage! I saw rainbows, waterfalls, and felt all the body tingles."

 WANT MORE INFO?
THINK: **MENTALLY TRAVELED TO A WORLD OF SUGAR, SPICE, AND EVERYTHING NICE.**

USAGE NOTE: This term is commonly used in the Black gay and queer community.

▼   **Went to a Place**

▶

Went In

WHAT ARE YOU GIVING?

▼ *idiom*

Questioning someone's appearance or behavior. This can be lighthearted or antagonistic. The term can also be used to inquire about particular situations (e.g., her biology exam, this ugly throw pillow, someone's cooking ability, etc.). The phrases "what she gave" and "what it gave" can also be used.

❝ *What are you giving? No makeup, hair in a bun, and sweatpants, this isn't like you. Do you need a hug?"*

 WANT MORE INFO?
THINK: **"I DON'T UNDERSTAND WHAT'S GOING ON HERE."**

USAGE NOTE: This term is commonly used in the Black gay community and the larger queer and trans people of color (QTPOC) community.

WHAT'S THE GAGA

▼ *idiom*

A phrase used to ask someone about the latest gossip or news. This phrase is a variation on the idiom "What's the T?"

❝ *I know you know, Evan. Are we getting new cheerleading uniforms? What's the gaga?"*

 WANT MORE INFO?
THINK: **"WHAT'S THE LATEST?"**

SEE ALSO
WHAT'S THE T?

WHAT'S THE GOODIE

▼ *idiom*

SEE **WHAT'S THE T**

WHAT'S THE T

▼ *idiom*

A phrase used to ask someone about current events or the latest goings-on in one's life. "T" refers to the "Truth." The phrase WHAT'S THE GOODIE can also be used.

SEE ALSO

T, THE, SPILL THE T

 What's the T? You dating him now?"

 WANT MORE INFO? THINK: "WHAT'S THE DEAL? WHAT'S THE GOSSIP?"

USAGE NOTE: This term originated in ballroom culture. It has been appropriated by the larger LGBTQIA+ community and mainstream culture.

WHITE FEMINISM

▼ *noun*

Feminist thoughts and theories that are rooted in white privilege, lacking an intersectional look at oppressed girls and women of other races, classes, and abilities.

66 *The #MeToo movement has been an incredible initiative, calling out toxic masculinity in all areas of leadership. But let's not let white feminism take over what Tarana Burke started. This feminist fight is for every woman."*

 WANT MORE INFO? *THINK:* **BIASED FEMINISM THAT DOES NOT TAKE EVERYONE'S EXPERIENCE INTO ACCOUNT.**

WHITE PRIVILEGE

▼ *noun*

The inherent rights and immunities granted to white people.

SEE ALSO
PRIVILEGE, CISGENDER PRIVILEGE, MALE PRIVILEGE, STRAIGHT PRIVILEGE

66 *White privilege begins at birth. Your skin color gives you a sense of protection, access, entitlement, and means to move about your life without being a target."*
—MAISHA PINKARD

 WANT MORE INFO? *THINK:* **THE ENTITLEMENT OF WHITE PEOPLE.**

WIG

▼ noun

Someone's hair or hairstyle. Often used within the Black, drag, and transgender communities but can be used by anyone.

❝ *I was going to ask you who did your braids because that wig is done!"*

 WANT MORE INFO? *THINK:* **HAIR, WEAVE, EXTENSIONS, LOCS, BRAIDS, LACE FRONTS, FADES, UNITS, YOU NAME IT.**

▲ **Wig**

▼ **Will & Grace**

WILL & GRACE

▼ noun

A close and playful friendship between a gay man and a straight woman, derived from the popular sitcom *Will & Grace*.

SEE ALSO
GAY HUSBAND

❝ *They wish they were Jack and Karen, but we are totally Will and Grace."*

 WANT MORE INFO? *THINK:* **A TIGHT BOND BETWEEN A GAY MAN AND HIS BEST FEMME.**

WITCH

▼ noun

A person who practices witchcraft.

❝I met this cool witch at movie night in the park. She was reading a book called The Witch Boy. *We talked about shapeshifting, witchcraft, and everything!"*

 WANT MORE INFO? *THINK:* YOUR QUEER FRIEND WHO LOVES TAROT, CRYSTALS, AND ASTROLOGY.

DID YOU KNOW In the mid to late twentieth century, many feminists explored witchcraft, regarding the practice as an embodiment of the divine feminine and female power. In today's world, witchcraft has created a community for LGBTQIA+ people. Not only is it a form of spirituality rooted in a celebration of femininity and otherness, but it also acts as a form of self-care, healing, and protection against the negativity received from outside world.

Witch ▲

WOC

▼ noun

An abbreviation for woman/ women of color, referring to a person who identifies as such.

SEE ALSO
MOC, POC, QPOC, QWOC

❝When [WOC] speak out of the anger that laces so many of our contacts with white women, we are often told that we are 'creating a mood of hopelessness,'

'preventing white women from getting past guilt,' or 'standing in the way of trusting communication and action.'" —AUDRE LORDE

 WANT MORE INFO? *THINK:* **A NONWHITE FEMALE.**

WOLF

▼ *noun*

A body label for a gay, bisexual, or queer man who is lean and muscular, with an average amount of body hair.

SEE ALSO
"Help! What Type of Gay Am I?," *p. 203*

❝

CALEB: *These body labels are confusing. Am I a wolf or an otter? What's the difference? What are the hair requirements again?*
JACK: *I say wolf. You have a good muscular build and you are only semi-hairy.*

 WANT MORE INFO? *THINK:* **A MUSCULAR, HAIRY GUY.**

USAGE NOTE: This term originated in the white gay male community.

WOMAN LOVING WOMAN (WLW)

▼ *adjective*

SEE **SAPPHIC**

Woman Loving Woman (WLW) ▲

WOMXN

▼ *noun*

An alternate spelling of the word "woman," used to fuel the idea that women can exist without "man" or "men."

❝ *We are womxn. Strong, Black, brown, red, yellow, white, masc, femme, trans, fluid, queer, fat, skinny, shapely, and bold womxn.*"

 WANT MORE INFO? *THINK:* **A SYMBOL OF WOMAN'S LIBERATION FROM MAN.**

DID YOU KNOW

The term "womyn" became popular in the 1970s, with the rise of second-wave feminism. In 1975, the term first showed up in an issue of *Lesbian Connection*, describing a local womyn's festival occurring in July of that year. In 1976, it showed up in print again, advertising the Michigan Womyn's Music Festival. Many womyn's music festivals became notorious for discriminating against and excluding trans women—claiming they weren't "born womyn"—so many feminists and trans allies began to move away from the spelling of "womyn," replacing the *y* with a more inclusive *x*.

WORK

▼ *exclamation*

A complimentary exclamation of high praise. Can also be seen as "werk" or "werq."

❝ *WERK! You got all A's this quarter!*"

 WANT MORE INFO? *THINK:* **"GET IT! YOU DID THAT AND DID IT WELL!"**

 USAGE NOTE: This term originated in the Black gay community. It has been appropriated by the larger LGBTQIA+ community and mainstream culture.

Work

XE/XEM/XYRS

▼ *pronouns*

SEE **"Common Pronouns 101,"** *p. 101*

X-GENDER

▼ *noun*

A person who does not identify with the binary gender—male or female and boy or girl—but as a third gender. This label often includes people who identify as nonbinary, agender, pangender, or genderqueer.

SEE ALSO

GENDER NONCONFORMING, GENDERQUEER, NONBINARY

66 *Many government agencies and health organizations are now including more gender identity options on their official enrollment or application forms, like X-gender."*

 WANT MORE INFO? *THINK:* **NOT EXCLUSIVELY MALE OR FEMALE.**

USAGE NOTE: This term originated and was popularized by queer organizations in Japan. It is commonly used in the transgender, nonbinary, and gender nonconforming communities.

XTRA

▼ *adjective*

SEE **EXTRA**

(E)XTRAVAGANZA

▼ *noun*

A spectacular and elaborate show.

❝ *Tonight will be the biggest xtravaganza of all time!"*

 WANT MORE INFO?
***THINK*: A LAVISH EVENT.**

A prominent gay and transgender social house in ballroom culture that is famous for being the first social family structure for the Latinx community.

❝ *We honor our legendary father, Hector, and mother, Angie, for giving us the House of Xtravaganza! We will forever honor your name."*

 WANT MORE INFO?
***THINK*: ONE OF THE MOST WELL-KNOWN GAY BALLROOM HOUSES IN NEW YORK CITY.**

Yy

YAS

▼ **exclamation**

An affirmative exclamation. The number of *a*'s and *s*'s can vary depending on the tone and use. The gesture of quickly waving the index finger with approval is sometimes done to emphasize the expression. Often used in the phrases "yas, queen," "yas, girl," and "yas, gawd."

" *Yaaaassssss! She slayed that question. Miss Georgia is about to win the crown!*"

 WANT MORE INFO?
THINK: "I SUPPORT AND BELIEVE IN YOU."

USAGE NOTE: This term originated in ballroom culture. It has been appropriated by the larger LGBTQIA+ community and mainstream culture.

Yas ▼

YES, GAWD!

▼ *exclamation*

A phrase to proclaim extreme approval and/or support. Variations on the phrase include "yes, girl!" and "yes, queen!"

❝ *YES, GAWD! That's the winning look!"*

 WANT MORE INFO?
THINK: "YOU GO, GIRL!"

 USAGE NOTE: This term originated in ballroom culture. It has been appropriated by the larger LGBTQIA+ community and mainstream culture.

YES, GIRL!

▼ *idiom*

SEE **YES, GAWD!**

YES, QUEEN!

▼ *idiom*

SEE **YES, GAWD!**

YESTERGAY

▼ *noun*

A "former" gay or lesbian person who currently identifies as heterosexual.

SEE ALSO
EX-GAY

❝ *Sure, yestergay is a thing. Look, your sexuality can definitely change. Your attraction may be one way now and when you get older it just changes. Just be true to yourself and try not to let other people's idea of you change that."*

 USAGE NOTE: This term negates any notion that a person could be sexually fluid, bisexual, queer, or any number of fluid identifiers. It forces sexuality to exist within a binary and can therefore be construed as negative or harmful.

YOU BETTER WORK

▼ *idiom*

An exuberant affirmation. The phrase may also be

spelled "you betta werk."

SEE ALSO
WORK

❝ *You better work/ (Cover Girl)/Work it girl/ (Give a twirl)/Do your thing on the runway"* —RUPAUL, "SUPERMODEL (YOU BETTER WORK)"

 WANT MORE INFO? *THINK:* **THE BEST POSITIVE REINFORCEMENT ONE CAN GIVE/RECEIVE.**

USAGE NOTE: This term was coined by American drag queen RuPaul Charles. It has been appropriated by the larger LGBTQIA+ community and mainstream culture.

YOU COULD NEVER

▼ *idiom*

An expression of superiority.

❝ *Beat me?! You could never! I've been top player for two weeks on this video game. Call me the next Ninja!"*

 WANT MORE INFO? **THINK: "YOU'LL NEVER BE ON MY LEVEL."**

USAGE NOTE: This term is commonly used in the Black gay and queer community.

YOU DID THAT

▼ *idiom*

A compliment given for something exceptional.

❝ *The Queens' English is here for all you queers! To the LGBTQIA+ community: you did that! We created a language of our own, heck yeah!"*

 WANT MORE INFO? *THINK:* **HEAR YE, HEAR YE: THIS IS A JOB WELL DONE!**

USAGE NOTE: This term originated in the Black gay and queer community.

YOU TRIED IT

▼ *idiom*

SEE **TRIED IT**

Zz

ZADDY

▼ noun

A person—typically masc or male-identifying—who is extremely eye-catching and put together. A zaddy exudes a confident demeanor and oozes personality.

SEE ALSO
DADDY, MOMMI

❝

ISAAC: *Zaddy alert, zaddy alert!*

DRE: *That guy over there? Uh-uh, I don't see it.*

ISAAC: *Zaddy is in the eye of the beholder. Now, if you'll excuse me. I need to introduce myself!*

 WANT MORE INFO? *THINK:* **A FIIIIIINE PHYSICAL SPECIMEN WITH SWAGGER TO SPARE.**

USAGE NOTE: This term originated in Black American culture and is commonly used in the Black gay and queer community. It has been appropriated by mainstream culture.

ZE/HIR/HIRS

▼ pronouns

SEE **"Common Pronouns 101,"** p. 101

ZEDSEXUAL

▼ *adjective*

SEE **ALLOSEXUAL**

ZIE/ZIR/ZIRS

▼ *pronouns*

SEE **"Common Pronouns 101,"** *p. 101*

ZUCCHINI

▼ *noun*

A partner in a queer platonic relationship. The terms QUEER PLATONIC PARTNER or SQUISH can also be used.

> *SEE ALSO*
> **QUEER PLATONIC RELATIONSHIP**

❝

MALCOLM: *I have seen you two attached at the hip almost every day. Are you crushing on him?*

DONNIE: *Nah, he's my squish. My zucchini.*

 WANT MORE INFO?
THINK: **SOULMATE.**

 USAGE NOTE: This term originated in the asexual and aromantic community.

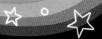

Resources

* ACT UP actupny.org

* Affinity affinity95.org

* African Ancestral Lesbians United for Societal Change (AALUSC) astraeafoundation.org

* All Out allout.org

* Asian Pride Project asianprideproject.org

* Advocates for Youth advocatesforyouth.org

* The Ali Forney Center aliforneycenter.org

* The Audre Lorde Project alp.org

* Bisexual Resource Center biresource.org

* bklyn boihood bklynboihood.com

* Black Lives Matter blacklivesmatter.com

* Broadway Cares/Equity Fights AIDS broadwaycares.org

* Brown Boi Project brownboiproject.org

* Center for Black Equity centerforblackequity.org

* Center for the Study of Social Policy cssp.org

* CenterLink lgbtcenters.org

* COLAGE colage.org

* Covenant House covenanthouse.org

* Desi LGBTQ+ Helpline for South Asians deqh.org

* Encircle encircletogether.org

* Equality Florida eqfl.org

* Familia TQLM familiatqlm.org

* Family Acceptance Project familyproject.sfsu.edu

* Family Equality familyequality.org

* FIERCE fierce.nyc

* Gender Spectrum genderspectrum.org

* GLAAD glaad.org

* GLBTQ Legal Advocates & Defenders glad.org

* GLMA glma.org

* GLSEN glsen.org

* GMHC gmhc.org

* GSA Network gsanetwork.org

* Harbor Camps harborcamps.org

* Hetrick-Martin Institute hmi.org

* Homeless Youth Alliance homelessyouthalliance.org

* Human Rights Campaign hrc.org

* Immigration Equality immigrationequality.org

* Institute for Judaism & Sexual Orientation ijso.huc.edu

RESOURCES

* interACT interactadvocates.org

* International Lesbian and Gay Association (ILGA) ilga.org

* Intersex Society of North America isna.org

* It Gets Better Project itgetsbetter.org

* Keshet keshetonline.org

* Kinsey Institute kinseyinstitute.org

* Lambda Legal lambdalegal.org

* Lambda Literary lambdaliterary.org

* Lesbian, Gay, Bisexual & Transgender Community Center gaycenter.org

* Lesbian Herstory Archives lesbianherstoryarchives.org

* LGBT National Help Center glnh.org

* Los Angeles LGBT Center lalgbtcenter.org

* Many Voices manyvoices.org

* Marsha P. Johnson Institute marshap.org

* Metropolitan Community Churches mccchurch.org

* Muslims for Progressive Values mpvusa.org

* NAACP naacp.org

* The Naming Project thenamingproject.org

* National Black Justice Coalition nbjc.org

* National Center for Lesbian Rights nclrights.org

* National Center for Transgender Equality transequality.org

* National Coalition for the Homeless nationalhomeless.org

* National Immigrant Justice Center immigrantjustice.org

* National LGBT Chamber of Commerce nglcc.org

* National LGBTQ Task Force thetaskforce.org

* National Queer Asian Pacific Islander Alliance nqapia.org

* National Youth Advocacy Coalition nyacyouth.org

* New Alternatives newalternativesnyc.org

* OutFront Minnesota outfront.org

* Out Right Vermont outrightvt.org

* Partners for Youth with Disabilities pyd.org

* PFLAG pflag.org

* Pride Liberation Project prideliberation.org

* Project Lotus theprojectlotus.org

* The Pipeline Project devex.com/organizations/the-pipeline
  -project-110204

* QLatinx qlatinx.org

* Q-WAVE q-wave.org

* The Queens' English thequeensenglishus.com

* Ramapo for Children ramapoforchildren.org

* Resource Center myresourcecenter.org

* Ruth Ellis Center ruthelliscenter.org

* Stop Ableism stopableism.org

RESOURCES

* SF LGBT Center sfcenter.org

* SMYAL smyal.org

* Sylvia Rivera Law Project srlp.org

* Thrive Youth Center thriveyouthcenter.com

* TransKids Purple Rainbow Foundation transkidspurplerainbow.org

* Transgender Law Center transgenderlawcenter.org

* Transgender Legal Defense and Education Fund transgenderlegal.org

* Trans Youth Equality transyouthequality.org

* The Trevor Project thetrevorproject.org

* Trikone trikone.org

* True Colors United truecolorsunited.org

* URJ Camp Harlam campharlam.org

* Victory Fund victoryfund.org

* Visibility Project visibilityproject.org

* We Are Family wearefamilycharleston.org

* Youth Celebrate Diversity (Disability Justice and Youth) ycdiversity.org

* Youth Pride Association ypapride.org

* Zuna Institute zunainstitute.org

Acknowledgments

THANK YOU TO all the voices who have contributed to the creation, design, and production of *The Queens' English*. I am awestruck! You not only helped make my dream come true, but also renewed my passion for it daily. I figured I would thank each person with a star, so look up at the sky tonight. There will be a star with your name on it.

Sincere thanks to the Philadelphia Dance Company—all my PHILADANCO! guys and dolls—and its fearless leaders, Joan Myers Brown, Kim Bears-Bailey, and the beautiful angel, Debora Chase-Hicks. The idea to write the dictionary started here, and I am so grateful for how you provided me with a creative space to discover all my talents.

Huge round of applause goes to my most supportive parents, John and Rose Davis. I love you! Thank you for believing in me and reminding me to stay creative, persistent, dedicated, and patient. Ebony Barrett—sis, you are my light and number-one fan. I love you, Pono, and Sir. Thank you to Eleven Burdine, LaMar Baylor, A. Maverick, Odara Jabali-Jeter, Tommie Waheed Evans, Priscilla Jackson, Maisha Pinkard, and Teneise and Hassan Ellis. I appreciate you for standing by me and for me in ways I never knew I needed, encouraging me on my journey into the beautiful life of free thinking and free being. Shout-out and all my love to my complete varsity cheering squad—all my family, all my friends, and all my supporters. You are awesome, selfless, and kind. I would like to thank Sara Neville, Mireille Harper, Troy Lambert, James Harris, Kyle Jones, Daniel Banks, and Persephone Valentine for being instrumental in my writing journey and moving me along with ease, strength, and comfort.

To all the extraordinary illustrators, your creative input and thoroughness truly brought this dictionary to life. The illustrations are FIERCE and celebrate LGBTQIA+ culture, identity, and PRIDE! I am most grateful to the many individuals who participated in interviews and group discussions. Your wisdom, input, words, and stories helped create this body of work!

Special thank-you to my amazing theater community; Jordan Budd; Ross Murray; Erica Corbin and Worokya Duncan; Pam Sandonato; Lisa David and Lori Zlotoff; Nancy Henry, Lauren Ricke, and Rebecca Fagin; Meghan Biron; and Jennifer, Lexie, and Oliver Kempinski, for your unwavering support!

Wow, what an incredibly talented production team I have! This book brings me tears of joy because I have always wanted a fun and engaging resource for youth to celebrate their identity and feel seen, heard, and appreciated. To my rock-star literary agent, Leila Campoli, the first person to believe that *The Queens' English* would be a resource for all people and who worked effortlessly to find the best home for it: thank you for representing me and my creation. To my editor, Krista Vitola, I cannot thank you enough for advocating for this book and bringing it to Simon & Schuster Books for Young Readers. Your passion is inspiring! You believe that our youth deserve to read books that celebrate who they are, giving them a sense of belonging, community, and empowerment. Our society continues to challenge the need for LGBTQIA+ books, but you are an incredible leader that dismantles this bias and marches forward for inclusivity, diversity, and equality. I thank you, Krista. Thank you to the team at Simon & Schuster Books for Young Readers, especially Laura Eckes, Alyza Liu, Morgan York, Jenica Nasworthy, Chava Wolin, Mitch Thorpe, Brian Murray, and Nicole Benevento, for transforming the vision of *The Queens' English* into a tangible, creative masterpiece. Look at what we have done, the lives we have touched, the understanding we are providing. So, I say thank you! You did that! You slayed, pushed through, snatched wigs, and showed up! My heart is warm with gratitude.

Illustration Credits

* Image on p. 14 by Alexey Yaremenko/iStock

* Image on p. 18 by Red Diamond/iStock

* Images on p. 21 by Paper Trident/iStock (person); by LSOphoto/iStock (dog photo)

* Image on p. 22 © 2021 by Chloe O. Davis

* Image on p. 25 © 2024 by Siobhán Gallagher. All rights reserved.

* Image on p. 27 © 2017 by Eleonora Arosio. Nonexclusive rights.

* Image on p. 28 © 2021 by Caitlin Blunnie. Nonexclusive rights.

* Image on p. 32 © 2022 by Ana Jaks. Nonexclusive rights.

* Image on p. 33 by Devita ayu Silvianingtyas/iStock

* Image on p. 34 © 2021 by Kat Flores. Nonexclusive rights.

* Image on p. 35 by Ekaterina Popova/iStock

* Image on p. 46 by Nopparat Promtha/iStock

* Image on p. 47 by Igor Zakowski/iStock

* Image on p. 50 by Sashica/iStock

* Image on p. 51 by briang77/iStock

* Image on p. 52 © 2024 by Siobhán Gallagher. All rights reserved.

* Image on p. 54 by Nazarii/iStock

* Image on p. 57 by Troy Lambert with contributions from Cassandra Fountaine, Mark Uhre, and Shanée Benjamin

* Image on p. 59 by Ekaterina Popova/iStock

* Image on p. 61 by Ahmed Benzerguine/iStock

* Image on p. 64 by Denis Pesterev/iStock

* Image on p. 67 by simplehappyart/iStock

* Image on p. 69 by vector illustration/iStock

* Image on p. 70 by lemono/iStock

* Image on p. 71 by Elizaveta Bochkova/iStock

* Image on p. 74 by Troy Lambert with contributions from Cassandra Fountaine, Mark Uhre, and Shanée Benjamin

* Image on p. 81 by Troy Lambert with contributions from Cassandra Fountaine, Mark Uhre, and Shanée Benjamin

* Image on p. 82 by Troy Lambert with contributions from Cassandra Fountaine, Mark Uhre, and Shanée Benjamin

* Image on p. 84 © 2020 by Jessica Vosseteig. Nonexclusive rights.

* Image on p. 85 © 2023 by Milo Wren. Nonexclusive rights.

* Image on p. 91 © by Rahana Dariah/agoodson.com. Nonexclusive rights.

* Image on p. 93 by Tedi sutardi/iStock

* Image on p. 94 by nadia_bormotova/iStock

* Image on p. 97 by Aratehortua/iStock

* Image on p. 99 by Flashvector/iStock

* Image on p. 107 © 2023 by Jules Scheele. Nonexclusive rights.

* Image on p. 109 by Troy Lambert with contributions from Cassandra Fountaine, Mark Uhre, and Shanée Benjamin

* Image on p. 111 by Troy Lambert with contributions from Cassandra Fountaine, Mark Uhre, and Shanée Benjamin

ILLUSTRATION CREDITS

* Image on p. 113 © 2022 by Caitlin Blunnie. Nonexclusive rights.

* Image on p. 114 by Alona Savchuk/iStock

* Image on p. 119 © 2023 by Sirima De Rességuier. Nonexclusive rights.

* Image on p. 121 by hisa nishiya/iStock

* Image on p. 123 by Uniyok/iStock

* Image on p. 125 by nadia_bormotova/iStock

* Image on p. 127 © by Rahana Dariah/agoodson.com. Nonexclusive rights.

* Image on p. 128 © 2020 by Lucia Picerno. Nonexclusive rights.

* Image on p. 130 by Alexey Yaremenko/iStock

* Image on p. 135 by Jcomp/iStock

* Image on p. 140 by Daniela Chirpac/iStock

* Image on p. 143 © 2021 by Jessica Vosseteig. Nonexclusive rights.

* Image on p. 145 © by Rahana Dariah/agoodson.com. Nonexclusive rights.

* Image on p. 150 © 2020 by Lucia Picerno. Nonexclusive rights.

* Image on p. 155 by onetime/iStock

* Image on p. 156 by klyaksun/iStock

* Image on p. 157 by klyaksun/iStock

* Image on p. 159 by woocat/iStock

* Image on p. 161 by Betka82/iStock

* Image on p. 162 by Troy Lambert with contributions from Cassandra Fountaine, Mark Uhre, and Shanée Benjamin

* Image on p. 166 by jemastock/iStock

* Image on p. 169 by klyaksun/iStock

* Image on p. 170 by Kudryavtsev Pavel/iStock

* Image on p. 173 by lemono/iStock

* Image on p. 175 by Troy Lambert with contributions from Cassandra Fountaine, Mark Uhre, and Shanée Benjamin

* Image on p. 182 © 2021 by Caitlin Blunnie. Nonexclusive rights.

* Image on p. 184 by Nadzeya_Dzivakova/iStock

* Image on p. 185 by Lukman Hakim/iStock

* Image on p. 189 by Annaspoka/iStock

* Image on p. 192 by Valerie Gamolina/iStock

* Image on p. 198 by VectorMoon/iStock

* Image on p. 200 by Nadezhda Kurbatova/iStock

* Image on p. 203 by Alexey Yaremenko/iStock

* Image on p. 207 by lemono/iStock

* Image on p. 208 by Vladimir Ivankin/iStock

* Image on p. 212 by barkarola/iStock

* Image on p. 217 by Sirintra_Pumsopa/iStock

* Image on p. 220 by Troy Lambert with contributions from Cassandra Fountaine, Mark Uhre, and Shanée Benjamin

* Image on p. 226 by Anna Semenchenko/iStock

* Images on p. 229 by Alexey Yaremenko/iStock (person); by Aratehortua/iStock (ice cream)

* Image on p. 231 by Troy Lambert with contributions from Cassandra Fountaine, Mark Uhre, and Shanée Benjamin

* Image on p. 235 © 2022 by Jessica Vosseteig. Nonexclusive rights.

* Image on p. 237 by Aratehortua/iStock

ILLUSTRATION CREDITS

* Image on p. 315 by Uniyok/iStock

* Image on p. 316 by TopVectors/iStock

* Image on p. 317 by Maria Shapilova/iStock

* Image on p. 319 by Troy Lambert with contributions from Cassandra Fountaine, Mark Uhre, and Shanée Benjamin

* Image on p. 324, 325 by ma_rish/iStock

* Image on p. 327 by Katarina Halko/iStock

* Image on p. 337 by Troy Lambert with contributions from Cassandra Fountaine, Mark Uhre, and Shanée Benjamin

* Image on p. 338 by Daria Zagrebova/iStock

* Image on p. 339 by TopVectors/iStock

* Image on p. 341 by Daria Sokolova/iStock

* Image on p. 342 by Troy Lambert with contributions from Cassandra Fountaine, Mark Uhre, and Shanée Benjamin

* Image on p. 344 by Troy Lambert with contributions from Cassandra Fountaine, Mark Uhre, and Shanée Benjamin

* Image on p. 350 by Alona Savchuk/iStock

* Image on p. 353 by Alisa Zahoruiko/iStock

* Image on p. 357 by Troy Lambert with contributions from Cassandra Fountaine, Mark Uhre, and Shanée Benjamin

* Image on p. 358 by Inna Polekhina/iStock

* Image on p. 359 by Nadezhda Kurbatova/iStock

* Image on p. 365 by Marina Dekhnik/iStock

* Image on p. 371 by angelha/iStock

* Image on p. 374 by Troy Lambert with contributions from Cassandra Fountaine, Mark Uhre, and Shanée Benjamin

ILLUSTRATION CREDITS